Medieval Academy Reprints for Teaching
13

Medieval Academy Reprints for Teaching

SIDNEY PAINTER

William Marshal
Knight-Errant,
Baron, and Regent
of England

Published by University of Toronto Press
Toronto Buffalo London
in association with the Medieval Academy of America

First published by the Johns Hopkins Press in 1933
This edition reprinted from the 1971 printing by arrangement with
Professor Sidney Painter

TO

H. McM. PAINTER

PREFACE

The various phases of the history of the late twelfth and early thirteenth centuries have been dealt with by many competent scholars, but few of them have essayed the field of biography. The reason for this omission is evident. The paucity of the available evidence makes it practically impossible to unearth enough information about any non-royal figure of this period to justify a biographical study. Yet biography is an essential part of historical literature. It cuts across the fields of history, political, social, and economic, and shows how an individual lived in his world. Without the aid of biographies one cannot fully comprehend the life of any age.

As mediaeval society was dominated by the feudal caste, a biography that depicts the position, activities, manners, and thoughts of a member of that class might do much to elucidate the history of the period. With this in view I have undertaken to write the life of William Marshal. The subject has proved a peculiarly fortunate one. The fourth son of John fitz Gilbert, marshal of the king's court, William for the first forty years of his life was a landless knight who devoted most of his time and energy to tournaments. Here one can see chivalry as a living institution rather than as a mere inspiration for chivalric romances. In the year 1189 by his marriage to the daughter and heiress of Earl Richard of Pembroke William became a great feudal lord with fiefs in Normandy, England, Wales, and Ireland. Thus his biography will depict the two extremes of feudal society—the landless knight and the rich baron. Finally in 1216 he was chosen regent of England for the young king, Henry III, and his biography becomes for three years the history of England.

I hope that this work will contribute to our knowledge of the history of the period it embraces in two ways. Here and there it may contain pieces of information which are definite additions to the sum total of historical knowledge. Perhaps, however, this is a secondary function. If the reader obtains from these pages an understanding of William Marshal and the society in which he lived, my principal purpose will have been fulfilled. To know a typical feudal baron is to have a fuller comprehension of feudal society as a whole.

Historians owe the possibility of knowing William Marshal to a nameless trouvère who, at the request of William's son, composed a rhymed chronicle of his life. This has been edited by M. Paul Meyer for the Société de l'Histoire de France. Without M. Meyer's critical edition of the chronicle this biography could not have been written.

In addition to the editing of the text M. Meyer has written an introduction which includes a discussion of the historical and literary importance of the poem and an abbreviated translation into modern French. The latter is of inestimable importance to the historian who is not an expert in Norman French. Many difficult passages, especially a number of conversations, would have been almost impossible to interpret were it not for M. Meyer's translation. While he has abbreviated the text to some extent, he has, with some few exceptions, fulfilled his promise that he would omit no material of historical value. In addition M. Meyer's historical notes have been of considerable use to me especially by indicating possible sources of information. In short, this biography owes a great deal to M. Meyer's edition of *L'Histoire de Guillaume le Maréchal*.

Finally I wish to express my gratitude to my friends, colleagues, and masters who have assisted me with advice and encouragement. No student could have a more discerning and kindly critic than Professor Sydney K. Mitchell of Yale University under whose supervision this biography was originally written as a dissertation for the degree of Doctor of Philosophy in Yale University. Professors John M. S. Allison and Erwin R. Goodenough of Yale University and Professor Kent Roberts Greenfield of The Johns Hopkins University devoted much time and patience to reading the manuscript and making many valuable suggestions.

To the staffs of the Public Record Office, the Department of Manuscripts of the British Museum, and the libraries of Yale and The Johns Hopkins Universities I owe deep appreciation of their unfailing kindliness and courtesy.

S. P.

THE JOHNS HOPKINS UNIVERSITY

TABLE OF CONTENTS

CHAPTER I

JOHN FITZ GILBERT

William Marshal was of knightly birth. Two vigorous generations had raised his family to a place within the pale of the nobility. The feudal aristocracy never really accepted anyone who had been born outside its ranks. No matter how capable or how successful an upstart might be he was always hampered by the contempt, dislike, and distrust of the dominant class. But within this charmed circle the distinctions, great as they were, were economic rather than social. While the heir of an earl who was lord of two hundred knightly vassals inherited a position which one less fortunate could scarcely hope to attain, he was perfectly willing to accept as a peer any man of knightly birth who might acquire equal feudal power. One well-worn path—the service of the crown—had led many a landless English noble into the ranks of the baronage. If a member of the feudal aristocracy could not assure his son of a position in society by leaving him a fief, he could lay open before him the road to ultimate success by endowing him with the royal favor and the abilities required to turn it to account. In this latter respect the father of William Marshal was eminently successful.

The Marshal family first rose to prominence in one of the most tumultuous eras of England's history. Toward the end of November, 1135, Henry, king of England and duke of Normandy, the youngest son of William the Conqueror, after a strenuous day's hunting in the forest of Lyons regaled himself too generously with lampreys, a dish forbidden by his physician.[1] He died a week later. His death delivered his broad domains to the anarchy, inherent in the feudal system, which had lain dormant during the latter years of his vigorous

[1] Henry of Huntingdon, *Historia Anglorum* (ed. Thomas Arnold, *Rolls Series*), p. 254.

1

reign. The spontaneous outburst of feudal disorder following the death of the master who had known how to control it was aggravated by a disputed succession. After the death of his sole legitimate son, Henry had compelled his prelates and barons to do homage to his daugher, Matilda, as his rightful heir. The widow of Henry V, Holy Roman Emperor, Matilda was the wife of Geoffrey Plantagenet, count of Anjou, a man who could well supply the masculine arm so sorely needed until his young son, the future Henry II, should come of age. But Theobald, count of Blois, and his brother Stephen, count of Boulogne and Mortain, sons of Stephen, count of Blois and Adela, daughter of William the Conqueror, laid claim to the throne on the ground that they were the only surviving male descendants of the Conqueror old enough to rule. According to feudal custom their right as heirs male was superior to that of Matilda herself, but inferior to that of her infant son, Henry Plantagenet. But there were other considerations. On the one hand the great men of England had sworn allegiance to Matilda as her father's heir—on the other many claimed that the English crown was elective and that the oaths forced from them by Henry were not binding. The country needed the hand of a man, and few wanted the hand to be that of Geoffrey Plantagenet. Confusion reigned. While the barons of Normandy were acclaiming as their duke Count Theobald of Blois, Geoffrey of Anjou was advancing on the duchy.[2]

The question was decided, at least temporarily, by the energetic action of Count Theobald's brother, Stephen. From the vantage point of his county of Boulogne, he promptly crossed to England where he was accepted as king by a part of the baronage and duly crowned by the archbishop of Canterbury. His brotherTheobald immediately resigned his claim in his favor and, after concluding a truce with the count of Anjou, retired from Normandy. Stephen was in possession of the throne, but his position was still far from secure. While he had a number

[2] For a thorough study of the dispute concerning the succession see J. H. Round, *Geoffrey de Mandeville*, Chapter I.

of staunch adherents, most of the barons remained aloof with the obvious intention of selling him their support at a high price in lands and privileges. For a time his cause prospered. Most of the important men of England assembled at his Easter court in 1136, and shortly thereafter the most powerful baron of the realm, Robert, earl of Gloucester, an illegitimate son of Henry I, made his submission. The apparent unanimity of the barons' acceptance of Stephen was, however, a mirage that was soon to fade from view. Within a year Robert of Gloucester was in Normandy plotting with Matilda. Here and there throughout England and Normandy individual barons rose in revolt. Stephen's efforts to restore order were of no avail— when one rebel was crushed several more appeared. The arrival in England in September 1139 of Matilda and Robert of Gloucester was the signal for the outbreak of civil war. From his bases at Bristol and Gloucester Earl Robert ravaged the lands of those who remained loyal to the king—a policy that was followed by the other partisans of Matilda operating from their various castles. Stephen occupied himself with retaliations on the lands of his enemies and attempts, usually fruitless, to reduce their castles.[3] On February 2, 1141 he was defeated under the walls of Lincoln and fell into the hands of Robert of Gloucester who imprisoned him in Bristol castle.[4] For the time being Matilda was mistress of England. Discouraged by the king's capture, most of Stephen's partisans hastened to submit to the countess of Anjou. Among these was John fitz Gilbert, the marshal of the court.

The origins of the Marshal family are veiled in obscurity. John's father, Gilbert, was marshal of the court to King Henry I and held some land in Wiltshire. On one occasion father and son successfully maintained before the king's court, probably in a trial by battle, their right to the family office which was

[3] *Gesta Stephani regis Anglorum* in *Chronicles of the Reigns of Stephen, Henry II, and Richard I* (ed. Richard Howlett, *Rolls Series*), pp. 1-69.
[4] *Ibid.*, pp. 70-71.

contested by two other claimants.[5] Before his elevation to the marshalship Gilbert may have been a royal serjeant in Wiltshire, but the family cannot be identified with that of any Domesday tenant in that county. When Gilbert died about 1130, John paid a relief of £22 13s 4d for his land and *ministerium* and an additional forty marks for the office of marshal of the court.[6] At about the same time he married the daughter and heiress of Walter Pipard, a minor Wiltshire landholder.[7] John Marshal, as he was usually styled, attested at least eight acts of Henry I—three in England and five in Normandy.[8] While he was serving his master and acquiring a reputation as an energetic and capable soldier, his wife bore him two sons, Gilbert and Walter.[9] He was not a man of wealth or position, but simply a trusted royal official.

John Marshal recognized Stephen as cheerfully as the majority of his fellow barons, and in 1137 he accompanied his new master on his expedition to Normandy. Five of the acts issued by the king during the first four years of his reign were attested by his marshal.[10] John, however, was fully aware of the opportunities offered by the turbulent state of the country for improving his own fortunes by indulging in his favorite pastime—war. In 1138 he took possession of the castles of Marlborough and Ludgershall in Wiltshire and strengthened their fortifications.[11] Acting in the king's name, possibly at his express command, he was far more intent on consolidating his own position than on

---

[5] *Rotuli Chartarum* (ed. T. D. Hardy, *Record Commission*), p. 46 b.

[6] *Magnum rotulum scaccarii, 31 Henry I* (ed. Joseph Hunter, *Record Commission*), p. 18.   [7] *Ibid.*

[8] William Farrer, *An Outline Itinerary of King Henry the First*, pp. 128, 129, 135, 136, 138.

[9] *Histoire de Guillaume le Maréchal* (ed. Paul Meyer, *Société de l'histoire de France*), lines 67-79.

[10] Round, *Calendar of documents preserved in France* (*Rolls Series*), no. 570. *Calendar of Charter Rolls 1257-1300* (*Rolls Series*), p. 308; *ibid.* (*1300-26*), p. 375. *Calendar of Patent Rolls 1354-8* (*Rolls Series*), pp. 194, 195.

[11] *Annales monasterii de Wintonia* in *Annales Monastici* (ed. H. R. Luard, *Rolls Series*), II, 51.

furthering the cause of his master. His skill as a captain, his liberality to his followers, and his strong personality attracted to him a large number of knights. With a private army and two strongholds, John fitz Gilbert was in a position to dominate northern Wiltshire while he watched the course of events.

In 1140, the year after Matilda's arrival in England, a Flemish mercenary named Robert fitz Hulburt, who had at one time or another been in the service of both Stephen and Robert of Gloucester, collected a party of kindred spirits and surprised the royal castle of Devizes which lay to the southwest of Marlborough. He suggested to John that adhering neither to Stephen nor Matilda, they form a partnership for plundering the region. As this was just about what John was doing, the idea cannot have shocked him greatly, but he neither trusted Robert nor saw any reason for sharing his spoils with him. He followed a far more profitable course. Enticing Robert into his castle with fair words, he threw him into prison and later sold him to Robert of Gloucester for five hundred marks.[12] John's position at this time was decidedly equivocal. Holding his castles for his own profit, he was willing to negotiate with Robert of Gloucester but hesitated to espouse openly Matilda's cause. Too loyal or too wise to change his allegiance as frequently as did many of his fellow barons, he was far too canny to precipitate himself into the wrong camp.

The capture of King Stephen at Lincoln in February 1141 convinced John, as it did many more powerful barons, of the justice of Matilda's cause. The king's brother, Henry of Blois, bishop of Winchester, received the countess of Anjou in his city, and most of the great men of the land hastened to her court. There in the royal city of Winchester on April 8, 1141, Matilda was elected queen of England by the assembled magnates of the realm. But the citizens of London still hesitated to renounce their allegiance to Stephen, and it was not until about

[12] Florence of Worcester, *Chronicon* (ed. Benjamin Thorpe, *English Historical Society*), II, 126-7. William of Malmesbury, *Historiae novellae* (ed. William Stubbs, *Rolls Series*), II, 563-4. *Gesta Stephani*, pp. 65-67.

June 20th that she was able to proceed to that city for her coronation in Westminster Abbey. On June 24th, before the coronation had taken place, the citizens, stirred up by Stephen's wife, rose against Matilda and drove her from the city. While the countess retired to Oxford to muster her forces, the bishop of Winchester joined his sister-in-law in plotting Stephen's release from captivity.[13]

Toward the first of August Matilda left Oxford and marched on Winchester at the head of her partisans to the great surprise of the bishop who barely escaped through one gate while the countess rode in at the other. Making her headquarters in the royal castle, Matilda laid siege to the bishop's castle on the other side of the town. Meanwhile Henry of Blois summoned to its relief all those who were still loyal to King Stephen. His appeal was successful, and a formidable army was soon assembled under the command of Stephen's queen, also named Matilda. With Queen Matilda were a large force of Flemish mercenaries under their captain William des Ypres, the Londoners, and three powerful earls, Simon de St. Lis, earl of Northampton, Geoffrey de Mandeville, earl of Essex, and William de Warren, earl of Surrey. The queen then advanced to Winchester and proceeded to lay siege to the besieging force with such success that the countess and her army were soon in desperate straits for provisions.[14]

On September 14th, the leaders of the countess' party decided to send a strong force in the direction of Ludgershall. The authorities differ as to the object of this expedition. While John of Hexham states that its purpose was simply to bring in a convoy of supplies, the *Gesta Stephani* asserts that the partisans of the countess intended to fortify the passage of the river Test at Wherwell in the hope of breaking the blockade of Winchester.[15] The *History* furnishes what is probably the true

---

[13] See Round, *Geoffrey de Mandeville*, pp. 55-122.

[14] Florence of Worcester, II, 133-135. *Gesta Stephani*, pp. 79-81.

[15] John of Hexham, *Historia in Symeonis Monachi Opera* (ed. Thomas Arnold, *Rolls Series*), II, 310. *Gesta Stephani*, p. 81.

explanation of this manoeuvre. Finding themselves hemmed in by superior numbers, the first care of Matilda's partisans was to secure her person from capture. John Marshal suggested that she take refuge in his fortress of Ludgershall.[16] While the main body of the army under Robert of Gloucester occupied the attention of the royalists by continuing their siege of the bishop's castle, John with a force of some three hundred knights would escort Matilda to Ludgershall. Once their mistress was in safety, earl Robert and his followers would retire as best they could from their uncomfortable position.

The plan was almost frustrated by the alertness of the enemy. John and his party had barely commenced their journey when William des Ypres, the ablest of Queen Matilda's captains, started in pursuit with an overwhelmingly superior force. The countess, who was sitting sideways in her saddle, so greatly impeded the speed of her followers that the enemy gained on them rapidly. When they reached the village of Wherwell, John decided that the time had come for desperate measures. Persuading the countess to ride astride, he sent her on toward Ludgershall under the escort of her faithful retainer, Brian fitz Count, lord of Wallingford, while he and his knights prepared to dispute the passage of the river Test to cover her retreat. John and his men managed to hold their position long enough to allow Matilda to escape before they were crushed by the superior numbers of their adversaries. While some of his followers were killed and others captured, John himself with one knight took refuge in the church of Wherwell Abbey. Unwilling to face so redoubtable a warrior in his improvised stronghold, the enemy set fire to the church to drive him out. As the flames engulfed the building, John and his companion retired to the tower. The latter then suggested that the time had come to surrender, but John cheerfully offered to kill him with his own hands if he made any move in that direction. Finally the heat grew so intense that it melted the lead roof of the tower, and one of the drops of fluid metal fell on John putting out

[16] *Hist.*, 187-199.

one of his eyes. By that time the knights of William des Ypres were convinced that their enemy had perished in the burning church. While they rode back to Winchester rejoicing at the success of their expedition, John, wounded but still alive, made his way to his castle of Marlborough.[17] Within a few days he was once more harassing the royalists. But in spite of John's good fortune and the escape of Matilda, the day had been a sad one for the countess' cause. In an attempt to retire from Winchester, the main body of the army was routed, and Robert of Gloucester was captured by Earl William de Warren. When a month or so later he was exchanged for King Stephen, both parties were just where they had been before the battle of Lincoln, and England was doomed to continued civil war.

The varying fortunes of his mistress had little effect on the prosperity of John fitz Gilbert. From his bases in the castles of Marlborough and Ludgershall he ravaged and plundered the lands of the royalist lords of the neighborhood. A perennial menace to the peace of the region, he was a most annoying thorn in the side of Stephen's party, and the loyal barons were determined to remove him. One in particular, Patrick, constable of Salisbury, a great landholder in Wiltshire, was most anxious to free the countryside from the ravages of the castellan of Marlborough. One day some time after the affair at Wherwell, John was at his castle of Ludgershall when Patrick and other royalist leaders sent word from Winchester that if he would await them, they would attack him next day. Encouraged by John's reply that he certainly would not wait for them, they prepared to move against him in force. At dawn the next day the royalist barons started the long ride from Winchester to Ludgershall. Confident that their enemy was retiring before their advance and unwilling to burden themselves on the journey, they did not put on their helmets or hauberks. But they had underestimated the daring of their opponent. Before

---

[17] For an attempt to reconcile the conflicting accounts of the events of this day see Sidney Painter, " The Rout of Winchester ", *Speculum*, VII (1932), 70-75.

they had gone very far, John and his knights, fully armed, sprang on them from ambush. Unarmed and confounded by the sudden apparition of an enemy whom they had believed to be miles away, the royalists were an easy prey. Killing, wounding, or capturing many of the knights, John and his men took a rich booty in the form of horses and arms. In that fierce combat Patrick of Salisbury lost many of his best men.[18]

This affray merely increased Patrick's anxiety to put an end to John Marshal's activities. So energetically did he press his attacks on John's men and lands that the castellan of Marlborough longed for peace with his too powerful neighbor. Patrick on his side was far more interested in the peace and safety of his Wiltshire lands than in the cause of Stephen. Thus a compromise was reached. John Marshal put aside his wife and married the lady Sibile, a sister of Patrick, while the constable himself went over to Matilda and was, in due time, rewarded with the dignity of earl of Salisbury.[19] This arrangement was eminently satisfactory from John's point of view. Not only had he removed his most dangerous enemy, but he had decidedly increased his social position by a marriage alliance with one of the great feudal families of England. Such advantages were well worth the trouble of changing wives.

The civil war was fulfilling John's fondest hopes. With Patrick of Salisbury as his ally he could plunder and oppress at will the people of Wiltshire, Berkshire, and Hampshire. The *Gesta Stephani* kindly describes him as " a limb of hell and the root of all evil." It charges him with building adulterine castles, seizing the lands of both clergy and laity, and exacting contributions from the church.[20] While the author of the *Gesta* was a partisan of Stephen and hence prejudiced against John, there was undoubtedly much truth in his accusations. John needed money to pay and support his followers, and he doubtlessly levied it from the countryside. The castle at Newbury in

[18] *Hist.*, 283-354.
[19] *Ibid.*, 360-375. Patrick was an earl by 1149 (*Sarum Charters, Rolls Series*, p. 16). [20] *Gesta Stephani*, pp. 107-8.

Berkshire which was in his possession in 1152 may have been one of the adulterine castles referred to in the *Gesta*. All in all, John's position was excellent. From his castles of Marlborough, Ludgershall, and Newbury he could dominate the entire region. He was high in the favor of Matilda who demonstrated her regard for him by making his brother, William, her chancellor.[21] Meanwhile in the security of one of his strongholds his new wife had faithfully performed her task of bearing him children —four sons and two daughters of which the two elder sons at least were born before 1152.[22] As he already had two sons by his first wife, the doughty John was well supplied with progeny to enjoy the fruits of his labor.

The time was approaching when the partisans of Matilda were to be rewarded for their fidelity to her cause. In 1153 the civil war was brought to an end by a treaty between King Stephen and Henry Plantagenet, duke of Normandy, the eldest son of Matilda and Geoffrey of Anjou. By its terms Stephen was to rule in peace for the rest of his life, but Henry was to succeed him on the throne. Stephen died on October 25, 1154, and on December 19th Henry Plantagenet was crowned king of England. John Marshal had chosen the right party—the son of his patroness Matilda was master of England. The castellan of Marlborough did not fail to reap the reward of his faithful service to the house of Anjou. Henry gave him the manors of Marlborough, Wexcombe, and Cherhill in Wiltshire yielding a total annual revenue of eighty-two pounds.[23] In 1158 the king gave Marlborough to Alan de Neville, but John retained Wexcombe and Cherhill until his death.[24] In addition to these manors and the lands in Wiltshire which he had inherited from his father, he possessed some seven scattered knights fees. Thus he held land of the bishops of Winchester, Exeter, and Worces-

---

[21] See Matilda's charter to Aubrey de Vere (Round, *Geoffrey de Mandeville*, p. 182).   [22] *Hist.*, 381-398; 480-492.

[23] *Pipe Roll 2 Henry II* (ed. Joseph Hunter, *Record Commission*), p. 57.

[24] *Pipe Roll 4 Henry II* (ed. Hunter), p. 116. Pipe Roll 10 Henry II, *Pipe Roll Society*, VII, 14.

ter, of the abbot of Abingdon, and of three lay lords, Richard de Candos, Manasser Arsic, and Geoffrey de Mandeville.[25] While in point of wealth he was still a very minor baron, he had materially increased the inheritance left him by Gilbert Marshal. Unfortunately the most valuable of his acquisitions, Wexcombe and Cherhill, were not hereditary grants and reverted to the crown at his death. Despite his energetic and faithful service to Henry I, Matilda, and Henry II he lacked enough lands to endow his sons. The eldest would be the king's marshal and a minor baron—the younger ones would have to shift for themselves.

If the sons of John Marshal inherited his qualities of mind and body, they would be well able to make their own way in the world. Little as is known of John's life, one can get a fairly clear impression of his character. He was known primarily for his ability as a soldier—one chronicler describes him as " a man illustrious as a knight." [26] The *History* praises his liberality to his followers, a quality very necessary for a successful captain.[27] William of Malmesbury states that he was "a man of great cunning" while the *Gesta Stephani* mentions his fondness for stratagems.[28] Almost completely heartless, he was ruthless in his oppression of the countryside and cared but little for his own family. To make peace with Patrick of Salisbury he cheerfully gave up his wife and as we shall see, he valued a son far less than a castle. A skilful captain who knew how to attract men and hold their loyalty, a clever, unscrupulous, ruthless baron with tremendous daring, energy, and ambition—such is the picture of John Marshall.

Of far greater value to John's sons than the property or the personal qualities which they might inherit from him were the confidence and favor of Henry Plantagenet. From the point of view of a feudal sovereign fidelity was the supreme virtue—

[25] *The Red Book of the Exchequer* (ed. Hubert Hall, *Rolls Series*), pp. 207, 250, 284, 300, 304, 306, 347.
[26] Florence of Worcester, II, 126.   [27] *Hist.*, 32-35.
[28] William of Malmesbury, II, 564. *Gesta Stephani*, pp. 66, 107.

an unreliable vassal was only more dangerous if he were a man of ability. While John Marshal had failed in loyalty to King Stephen, once he had given his allegiance to Matilda he had served her faithfully both in prosperity and in adversity. Considering the frequency with which such barons as Hugh Bigod and Geoffrey de Mandeville changed sides during the course of the civil war, John with his one change of allegiance was a model of fidelity. But his service to Matilda was more than passive loyalty to her cause. In the retreat from Winchester he risked his life to hold back the enemy while she made good her escape. To him the countess owed her control of northern Wiltshire and the adherence to her party of Patrick of Salisbury. When Henry Plantagenet came to the throne, he recognized and paid the debt which the house of Anjou owed to its marshal. If fate were kind enough to give John Marshal's sons his abilities, they were sure of an opportunity to use them in the king's service. Prowess and loyalty, the two knightly virtues through which John obtained the favor of Henry Plantagenet, were to be the most salient qualities of his son, William Marshal.

CHAPTER II

SQUIRE AND BACHELOR

William Marshal was the fourth son of John fitz Gilbert and the second of those born to the castellan of Marlborough by the sister of Earl Patrick of Salisbury. Our knowledge of William's youth is confined to a few brief glimpses through the fog of time—scenes which made so vivid an impression on his mind that he could recount them years later to his squire and biographer, John d'Erley. The earliest of these recollections concerned a comparatively unimportant incident in the contest between Stephen and Matilda. In the year 1152 King Stephen at the head of a strong force suddenly swooped down on John Marshal's castle of Newbury at a time when it was inadequately garrisoned and poorly stocked with provisions.[1] The constable, a man both brave and loyal, indignantly refused the king's demand for the immediate surrender of the fortress. When the garrison successfully repulsed an attempt to take the place by storm, Stephen prepared for a regular siege and swore that he would not leave until he had captured the castle and hanged its defenders.[2] The constable, realizing that his lack of provisions made an extended resistance impossible, asked for and obtained a day's truce so that he might make known his plight to his lord, John Marshal. This was the customary procedure for a castellan who found himself in a hopeless position. Once granted a truce, he would inform his master that unless he were relieved by a certain day, he would be forced to surrender. If no assistance appeared within the specified time, the commander could surrender the castle without failing in his duty to his lord. The besieging force was usually willing to grant a truce in the hope of obtaining the castle without long, wearisome, and expensive siege operations. When John Mar-

[1] Henry of Huntingdon, p. 284. *Hist.*, 400-1.   [2] *Ibid.*, 401-460.

13

shal learned of the predicament of his garrison of Newbury, he was sadly perplexed. As he could not muster enough men to drive off Stephen's army, his only hope of saving his fortress lay in a resort to strategy. John asked Stephen to extend the truce while he sought aid from the Countess Matilda in whose name he held the castle. The king did not trust his turbulent marshal, but he finally agreed to give the garrison of Newbury a further respite if John would surrender one of his sons as a guarantee that he would observe the terms of the truce. John was to use the days of grace to communicate with Matilda— the hostage would be his pledge that he would not reinforce or provision the castle. Acceding to Stephen's demand, John gave the king his son William as a hostage. Then he promptly sent into Newbury a strong force of knights, serjeants, and archers with a plentiful supply of provisions. Newbury was prepared to withstand a siege—the cunning of John Marshal had saved his castle.[3]

His father's clever strategem left William in an extremely precarious position. By the customs of the time his life was forfeited by his father's breach of faith. Stephen's entourage urged him to hang William at once, but the king was unwilling to execute the child without giving his father a chance to save him by surrendering Newbury. But John Marshal, having four sons and a fruitful wife, considered the youngest of his sons of far less value than a strong castle. He cheerfully told the king's messenger that he cared little if William were hanged, for he had the anvils and hammers with which to forge still better sons. When he received this brutal reply, Stephen ordered his men to lead William to a convenient tree. Fearing that John planned a rescue, the king himself escorted the executioners with a strong force. William, who was only five or six years old, had no idea what this solemn parade portended. When he saw William, earl of Arundel, twirling a most enticing javelin, he asked him for the weapon. This reminder of Wil-

[3] *Ibid.*, 461-508.

liam's youth and innocence was too much for King Stephen's resolution, and, taking the boy in his arms, he carried him back to the camp. A little later some of the royalists had the ingenious idea of throwing William over the castle walls from a siege engine, but Stephen vetoed that scheme as well. He had decided to spare his young prisoner.

For some two months William was the guest of King Stephen while the royal army lay before Newbury. One day as the king sat in a tent strewn with varicolored flowers William wandered about picking plantains. When the boy had gathered a fair number, he asked the king to play " knights " with him. Each of them would take a " knight " or plantain, and strike it against the one held by the other. The victory would go to the player who with his knight struck off the clump of leaves that represented the head of his opponent's champion. When Stephen readily agreed to play, William gave him a bunch of plantains and asked him to decide who should strike first. The amiable king gave William the first blow with the result that the royal champion lost his head. The boy was vastly pleased with his victory. While Stephen, king of England, was playing at knights with the young son of his rebellious marshal, a servitor whom Lady Sibile had sent to see how her son fared glanced into the tent. As war and enemies meant nothing to William, he loudly welcomed the familiar face. The man, utterly terrified, fled so hastily that the pursuit ordered by the king was fruitless.[4]

This story of William and King Stephen is, no doubt, merely, reminiscence recounted years later with the embellishments usual in such tales, but it bears all the ear-marks of veracity. It serves to confirm the statements of the chroniclers as to Stephen's character—that he was a man of gentle nature, far too mild to rule the barons of England.[5] Furthermore the incidents of the tale are essentially probable. It was quite custom-

[4] *Ibid.*, 509-650.

[5] *Gesta Stephani*, p. 5; *Histoire des Ducs de Normandie et des rois d'Angleterre* (ed. F. Michel, *Société de l'Histoire de France*), p. 80.

ary to give young children as hostages to guarantee an agreement and equally so to make them suffer for their parents' bad faith. When Eustace de Breteuil, the husband of a natural daughter of Henry I, put out the eyes of the son of one of his vassals, the king allowed the enraged father to mutilate in the same way Eustace's daughter whom Henry held as a hostage for his son-in-law's good behavior.[6] Again in the year 1211 when Maelgwyn ap Rees, prince of South Wales, raided the marches, Robert de Vieuxpont hanged the prince's seven-year-old son who was in his hands as a pledge that Maelgwyn would keep the peace.[7] The fact that Earl William of Arundel is known to have taken part in the siege of Newbury and might well have twirled his javelin before the fascinated William tends to confirm this story still further.[8] Hence one can accept as essentially true this pleasant and very human picture of a dark age and an unfortunate king.

When peace was finally concluded between Stephen and Henry Plantagenet, William was returned to his parents who, according to the *History,* had been very unquiet about him. While John Marshal had probably counted to some extent on Stephen's notorious mildness, he had had plenty of justification for any fears he may have felt for his son's safety. Meanwhile the boy was growing rapidly. Within a few years the Marshal family would be forced to consider his future. If the romances of the time are to be believed, it was customary for a baron of any importance to entrust his sons' education to some friendly lord. John Marshal decided to send William to his cousin, William, lord of Tancarville and hereditary chamberlain of Normandy.[9] The chamberlain was a powerful baron with a great castle on the lower Seine and ninety-four knights to follow his banner.[10] Being himself a well known knight and a

---

[6] Ordericus Vitalis, *Historia ecclesiastica* (ed. Auguste le Prévost, *Société de l'Histoire de France*), IV, 336-7.

[7] *Brut y Tywysogion* (ed. John Williams ab Ithel, *Rolls Series*), p. 272.

[8] Charter of Stephen quoted by Meyer, *Hist.,* III, 9, note 1.

[9] *Hist.,* 703-749.   [10] *Red Book of the Exchequer,* p. 629.

frequenter of tourneys, he was well fitted to supervise the military education of his young kinsman and to give him a good start on his chivalric career. When he was about thirteen years old, William started for Tancarville attended by a *valet,* or companion of gentle birth, and a servant. The fourth son of a minor English baron was setting forth to seek his fortune.[11]

For eight years William served as a squire to the chamberlain of Tancarville.[12] During this time his principal duty was to learn the trade of arms. The squire's body was hardened and his skill in the use of weapons developed by frequent and strenuous military exercises. While the chain mail of the twelfth century was far lighter and less cumbersome than the plate armor of later times, the mere wearing of it required considerable physical strength. To be able, as every squire must, to leap fully armed into the saddle without touching the stirrup, was a feat which must have required long and rigorous training. The effective use of the weapons of a knight—the spear, sword, and shield—was a highly intricate science which a squire was forced to master if he wished to excel in his chosen profession. In addition a knight should know how to care for his equipment. A squire spent long hours tending his master's horses and cleaning, polishing, and testing his arms and armor. William's success in battle and tourney will show how thoroughly he mastered these fundamentals of his profession. But while it was essential that a knight be brave and skilful in the use of his weapons, other quite different qualities were also expected of him. God and Woman, the church and the troubadour cult of Courtly Love, were beginning to soften and polish the manners of the feudal aristocracy. For a long time the church had demanded that a knight be pious, now ladies were

---

[11] *Hist.,* 750-759.

[12] The *History* states that William was a squire for twenty years (*Hist.,* 772-3). Meyer suggests *uit* for the impossible *vint* in the text (*ibid.,* III, 14, note 3). This agrees with the testimony of the romances as to the usual length of service as a squire. Leon Gautier, *La Chevalerie* (Victor Palme, Paris, 1884), Chapter VI.

insisting that he be courteous. If a squire hoped to be acceptable to such devotees of the new movement as Eleanor of Aquitaine and her daughter, Marie of Champagne, he must learn some more gentle art than that of smiting mighty blows. If he could not write songs, he could at least learn to sing them. Finally the professional creators and distributors of the literature which embodied these new ideas, the trouvères and the jongleurs, were formulating another knightly virtue—generosity. Their existence depended on the liberality of their patrons, and they did not fail to extol the generous and heap scorn on the penurious. Every time the squire confessed to a priest, he was instructed in the church's conception of the perfect knight. As he sat in the great hall of the castle while some trouvère or jongleur told of Tristan and Iseut or of Lancelot and Guenevere, he was imbued with the doctrines of romantic chivalry. The squire himself might be expected to while away the leisure hours of his lady and her damsels with one of the gentle songs of the troubadours. Possibly William owed his love for singing which remained with him to his death to the advanced taste of the lady of Tancarville.

By the spring of 1167 William was approaching his twenty-first year. As a squire he seems to have given little promise of future greatness. He gained a reputation for drinking, eating, and sleeping, but for little else. His companions, who were jealous of the favor shown him by the chamberlain, made fun of his appetite, but he was so gentle and debonnaire that he always kept silent and pretended not to hear the remarks. A hearty, healthy, good natured, and rather stupid youth was young William.[13] The author of the *History* furnishes a personal description which probably belongs to this period of William's life. "His body was so well formed that if it had been fashioned by a sculptor, it would not have had such beautiful limbs. I saw them and remember them well. He had very beautiful feet and hands, but all these were minor details in the

[13] *Hist.*, 774-804.

ensemble of his body. If anyone looked at him carefully, he seemed so well and straightly made that if one judged honestly, one would be forced to say that he had the best formed body in the world. He had brown hair. His face even more than his body resembled that of a man of high enough rank to be the Emperor of Rome. He had as long legs and as good a stature as a gentleman could. Whoever fashioned him was a master." [14] Is this a purely conventional portrait or a true one of William Marshal as he reached man's estate?

In a military society, be it that of the early Germans or the feudal aristocracy, the youth comes of age when he is accepted as a full-fledged warrior. Every squire burned to end his apprenticeship by receiving the insignia of knighthood. The squire followed his master to battles and tournaments, cared for his horse and armor, nursed him if he were wounded, and often guarded his prisoners, but he himself could not take an active part in the combat. Being simply an attendant, the squire had no opportunity to win renown. As eight years was, at least according to the testimony of contemporary romances, a rather long time to remain a squire, William must have been extremely impatient for the day when he would be admitted into the chivalric order. [15] He longed for the time when the approach of a promising war or a great tourney would move the chamberlain to dub him a knight and give him a chance to show his worth.

The occasion for which William had hoped came in the summer of 1167. King Henry II was at war with his suzerain, Louis VII of France. [16] While Louis himself occupied Henry's attention by ravaging the Norman Vexin, the French king's allies, the counts of Flanders, Boulogne, and Ponthieu, invaded

[14] Ibid., 717-736.

[15] Gautier, La Chevalerie, Chapter VI.

[16] Robert de Torigni in Chronicles of the Reigns of Stephen, Henry II, and Richard I (ed. Richard Howlett, Rolls Series), pp. 231-2. Etienne de Rouen in Chronicles of the Reigns of Stephen, Henry II, and Richard I, book II, lines 455-595. Hist., 805-814.

the county of Eu.[17] Count John of Eu, unable to hold his own
against the invaders, was forced to retire to Neufchatel-en-Bray,
then called Drincourt. There he encountered a force of knights
which Henry had sent to his assistance under the command of
the constable of Normandy and the lord of Tancarville. The
chamberlain decided that this was an auspicious time for knighting William. A goodly array of Norman barons was at hand
to lend dignity to the occasion, and the future seemed to promise an opportunity for the young knight to prove his valor.
William's induction into the order of chivalry was attended by
little of the ceremony usually associated with the dubbing of a
knight. Dressed in a new mantle, the young man stood before
the chamberlain, who girt him with a sword, the principal emblem of knighthood, and gave him the ceremonial blow.[18]

William had not long to wait for an opportunity to prove
himself worthy of his new dignity. As Drincourt lay on the
northern bank of the river Bethune at the southern extremity
of the county of Eu, it was directly in the path of the army
which had been ravaging that district. Count John of Eu and
the constable of Normandy had no desire to await the advance
of the enemy. On the morning following William's knighting
they left Drincourt by the road which led south toward Rouen.[19]
Before they had gone very far, they were overtaken by a messenger with the news that the counts of Flanders, Boulogne,
and Ponthieu, and the lord of St. Valery were marching on
Drincourt at the head of a strong force of knights and serjeants.
As the two barons halted their party to consider what they
should do, they saw the chamberlain followed by twenty-eight
knights of his household riding toward them from the direction

[17] Gervase of Canterbury (ed. William Stubbs, Rolls Series), I, 203.

[18] Hist., 815-822; 1190-1.

[19] This account of the campaign of which the battle of Drincourt was an
incident is based largely on supposition. Gervase of Canterbury (I, 203) speaks
of the invasion of the county of Eu. The History describes the attack on
Drincourt. On Meyer's theory that this passage is simply a ridiculously inaccu-
rate account of the siege of Drincourt in 1173 see Kate Norgate, Minority of
Henry III, p. 64, note 2.

of Drincourt. As soon as he was within speaking distance, the
chamberlain addressed the constable, " Sire, it will be a great
disgrace if we permit them to burn this town." " You speak
truly, chamberlain," replied the constable, " and since it is your
idea, do you go to its defence." When they saw that they could
hope for no assistance from either the count of Eu or the constable, the chamberlain and his knights rode back toward Drincourt. Between them and the town ran the river Bethune.
When they reached the bridge which spanned this stream, they
found it occupied by a party of knights under the command of
William de Mandeville, earl of Essex, who, lacking sufficient
men to dispute the enemy's entrance into the town, had retired
to hold the passage of the Bethune. The chamberlain hurried
to join Earl William, and William Marshal, anxious to show
his mettle, spurred forward at his leader's side. The chamberlain turned to the enthusiastic novice, " William, drop back;
be not so impatient; let these knights pass." William, who considered himself most decidedly a knight, fell back, abashed.
He let three others go ahead of him and then dashed forward
again until he was in the front rank.

The combined forces of the chamberlain and the earl of
Essex rode into Drincourt to meet the enemy who were entering
the town from the north-east. The two parties met at full
gallop with a thunderous shock. William's lance was broken,
but, drawing his sword, he rushed into the midst of the enemy.
So fiercely did the Normans fight that they drove the French
out of the town as far as the bridge over the moat on the road
to Eu. There the enemy was reinforced, and the Normans were
pressed back through Drincourt to the bridge over the Bethune.
Once more the Normans charged, and once more they drove
the French before them. Just as their victory seemed certain,
Count Mathew of Boulogne came up with a fresh division.
Four times the enemy beat their way into the town, and each
time the Normans drove them out again. Once as William
turned back from a charge, a Flemish serjeant caught him by
the shoulder with an iron hook. Although he was dragged

from his horse in the midst of hostile foot-soldiers, he managed to disengage the hook and cut his way out, but his horse was killed. Meanwhile the good people of Drincourt had been watching from their windows the fierce battle being waged up and down the streets of the town. Hastily arming themselves, the burghers rushed to the aid of the Norman knights, and the enemy was completely routed.

That night the lord of Tancarville held a great feast to celebrate the victory. The burghers of Drincourt were loud in their praises of the chamberlain and his knights. While the constable and the count of Eu had deserted the town, the chamberlain and his household had saved it from burning and pillage. As the revelers discussed the incidents of the battle, someone remarked that William had fought to save the town rather than to take prisoners who could pay him rich ransoms. With this in mind the earl of Essex addressed the young knight—"Marshal, give me a gift, a crupper or an old horse collar." "But I have never possessed one in all my life." "Marshal, what are you saying? Assuredly you had forty or sixty today." The hardened warrior was gently reminding the novice that war was a business as well as a path to fame.[20]

The war was soon brought to an end by a truce between King Henry and Louis of France. As their services were no longer needed, the chamberlain and his entourage returned to Tancarville. Since no true knight would willingly rest peacefully in a castle, the lord of Tancarville gave his followers leave to seek adventure where they pleased. William now found himself in a most embarrassing position, for he had lost his war horse at Drincourt, and the cost of a new one was far beyond his resources. While he still had his palfrey, this light animal could not be expected to carry him in full armor through the shocks of a battle or tourney. The chamberlain, who normally would have seen to it that William as a member of his household was properly equipped, felt that the young man should be taught to take advantage of his opportunities to cap-

[20] *Hist.*, 827-1162.

ture horses in battle and hence showed little sympathy for his predicament. By selling the rich mantle which he had worn when he was dubbed a knight, William obtained twenty-two sous Angevin with which he purchased a baggage horse to carry his armor, but while this arrangement allowed him to travel in comfort, it would not enable him to take part in a tourney. One day word came to Tancarville that a great tournament was to be held near Le Mans in which the knights of Anjou, Maine, Poitou, and Brittany would oppose those of France, England, and Normandy. The chamberlain and his court received the news with joy and prepared to take part in the sport, but William, who could not go without a horse, was very sorrowful. The chamberlain, however, decided that his young cousin had had enough of a lesson in knightly economy and promised to furnish him with a mount. After a night spent in making ready their arms and armor, the knights gathered in the castle court while their lord distributed the war horses. William received a splendid one, strong and fast.[21] He never forgot the lesson taught him by the chamberlain and William de Mandeville. Never again did he neglect to capture good horses when he had the opportunity.

On the appointed day a fair sized company assembled to take part in the tournament. King William of Scotland was present with a numerous suite while the chamberlain himself took the field at the head of forty knights. This tourney was not to be one of those mild affairs in which everything was arranged beforehand even to the price of the ransoms, but a contest in which the vanquished would lose all they possessed. After the knights had armed in the refuges provided at each end of the field, the two parties advanced toward one another in serried, orderly ranks. William wasted no time in getting about the business of the day. Attacking Philip de Valognes, a knight of King William's household, he seized his horse by the rein and forced him out of the mêlée. Then after taking Philip's pledge that he would pay his ransom, William returned

[21] *Ibid.*, 1163-1302.

to the combat and captured two more knights. By his success in this tourney William not only demonstrated his prowess, but rehabilitated his finances as well. Each of the captured knights was forced to surrender all his equipment. William gained war horses, palfreys, arms, and armor for his own use, roncins for his servants, and sumpter horses for his baggage. His first tournament had been highly profitable.[22]

This success sharpened William's appetite for knightly sports. When word came to Tancarville of another tourney to be held in Maine, he asked the chamberlain, who had decided to stay at home, to allow him to attend. He arrived at the appointed place just as the last of the contestants were arming in their refuges, and leaping from his palfrey hastened to put on his armor and mount his charger. In the first onslaught the young knight handled his lance so skilfully that he was able to unhorse one of his opponents, but before he could complete the capture of the fallen knight he was attacked by five others. Although by drawing his sword and smiting lusty blows on every side William managed to beat off his enemies, he received a stroke on his helmet which turned it around on his head so that he could no longer breathe through the holes provided for that purpose. While he was standing in the refuge repairing this damage, two well known knights rode past, Bon Abbé le Rouge and John de Subligni. "Sir John," said the first, "who is that knight who is so capable with his weapons?" "That is William Marshal" replied the other. "There is no man more true. The device on his shield shows that he hails from Tancarville." "Surely," said Bon Abbé, "the band which he leads should be the gainer in valor and hardiness." [23] Much pleased by these words of praise, William put on his helmet again and reentered the contest. So well did he bear himself that he was awarded the prize of the tourney—a splendid war horse from Lombardy.

William now felt that he was well started on his chivalric career. He had achieved the dignity of knighthood and had

[22] *Ibid.*, 1303-1380. [23] *Ibid.*, 1381-1512.

shown his prowess in the combat at Drincourt and in two
tournaments. It was high time that he visited England to
parade his accomplishments before his admiring family. John
fitz Gilbert had died in 1165 while William was still a squire
at Tancarville.[24] Of his two sons by his first wife the elder
had outlived him but a year, the younger had predeceased
him.[25] Hence John, the eldest son by Sibile of Salisbury, had
inherited the family lands and the office of marshal.[26] When
William sought the chamberlain's permission to go to England,
the lord of Tancarville feared that his young cousin, being the
heir presumptive to the family lands, might be tempted to
settle down at home. He gave him leave to go, but urged him
to return as soon as possible. While England was a good
enough country for a man of mean spirit who had no desire
to seek adventure, those who loved the life of a knight-errant
and the excitement of the tourney should stay in Normandy
and Brittany where such pastimes were appreciated. If one
were to acquire the prizes of battle, one must live in a land of
tourneys. England seemed to the chamberlain to be an orderly,
dull, spiritless country. Carried across the channel by a fair
wind, William traversed Sussex and Hampshire on his way to
his Wiltshire home. At Salisbury he found his uncle, Earl
Patrick, who received him joyfully as a gallant young knight
and his own sister's son.[27]

William's vacation in England was destined to be a short
one. In December 1167 Earl Patrick was summoned to the
continent to aid the king in suppressing a revolt of the nobles
of Poitou led by the counts of La Marche and Angouleme and
the house of Lusignan. Being in all probability heartily tired
of his quiet life in England, William was only too willing to
follow his uncle to Poitou. King Henry captured the castle of
Lusignan, garrisoned it, and then turned north to keep an
appointment with Louis VII in the Norman marches near

[24] Pipe Roll 11 Henry II, *Pipe Roll Society*, VIII, 56.
[25] *Ibid.*, 12 Henry II, *Pipe Roll Society*, IX, 95.
[26] *Ibid.*, 13 Henry II, *Pipe Roll Society*, XI, 128.   [27] *Hist.*, 1526-1564.

Mantes. His wife, Eleanor, who was by right of her birth duchess of Aquitaine and countess of Poitou, stayed at Lusignan with Earl Patrick.[28] Their position was far from comfortable. Of all the restless nobility of Poitou none were more turbulent than the five de Lusignan brothers, and none played so great a part in the history of their day. Two of the brothers, Hugh and Ralph, became respectively counts of La Marche and Eu, while Guy and Aimery, expelled from Poitou for their perpetual rebellions, both attained the throne of Jerusalem. Such a family was unlikely to stand by quietly while an enemy held their ancestral castle, even if that enemy was their liege lord. One day near Eastertide as the queen and Earl Patrick were riding outside the castle, they were suddenly confronted by a strong force under the command of Geoffrey and Guy de Lusignan.[29] Although Patrick and his men were unarmed, the earl was unwilling to flee. Sending Eleanor to shelter in the castle, he called for his war horse and ordered his followers to prepare for battle. Unfortunately the de Lusignans were not sufficiently chivalrous to wait while their foes armed. Just as Earl Patrick was mounting his charger, a Poitevin knight killed him with a single blow at his unprotected back. Meanwhile William had donned his hauberk, but had not had time to put on his helmet. When he saw his uncle fall, he jumped on his horse and charged the enemy, sword in hand. The first man he met was cut down at a single stroke, but before he could satisfy his thirst for vengeance on the slayers of his uncle, a well directed thrust killed his horse. When he had freed himself from the saddle, William placed his back against a hedge to fight it out on foot as the loss of his horse made flight impossible. For some time he managed to hold his own by cutting down the chargers of his opponents, but at last a knight crossed the hedge, came up behind, and leaning over the barrier, thrust

[28] Robert de Torigni, pp. 235-6.
[29] The sources do not state where this ambush took place. The *History* mentions a castle but does not name it (*Hist.*, 1634). Robert de Torigni (p. 236) suggests that Henry left Eleanor and Patrick at Lusignan.

his sword into the young man's thigh. Disabled, William was easily made prisoner.

His captors mounted him on a mare and set off. No one paid any attention to William's wound, for, according to the *History*, they wanted him to suffer as much as possible so that he might be the more anxious to ransom himself. William took the cords which bound his braies and tied up his wound as best he could. Dreading the king's vengeance, the rebel band kept to the wooded country and made its halts in secluded spots. Henry Plantagenet was not a monarch who would permit the slayers of his lieutenant to go unpunished. One night while they were resting at the castle of one of their partisans, a lady noticed the wounded prisoner. She cut the center out of a loaf of bread, filled the hole with flaxen bandages, and sent the loaf to William. Her kindness enabled him to dress his wound properly. Another evening William's captors amused themselves by casting a great stone. William joined in the game and defeated all the others, but the exertion reopened his wound, and as he was forced to ride night and day with little rest, he grew better very slowly. Finally Queen Eleanor came to his aid. She gave hostages to his captors to guarantee that his ransom would be paid, and he was delivered to her. To recompense him for his sufferings, she gave him money, horses, arms, and rich vestments.[30]

The Poitevin campaign had a far-reaching effect on William's life. In it lay the origins of his intense hatred for the house of Lusignan and his close personal relationship with the Plantagenet family. To understand his bitter feud with the Lusignans one must realize that the killing of Earl Patrick, which seems to us a normal act of war, was in William's sight a dastardly crime. The author of the *History* calls the earl's slayer felon and assassin.[31] Not only did he strike down an unarmed man, an unknightly act in itself, but he slew the lieutenant of his feudal suzerain. The first of these offences probably did not trouble William greatly. Some years later when Richard Planta-

---

[30] *Hist.*, 1623-1881.   [31] *Ibid.*, 1648.

genet was in rebellion against his father, William came on that prince when he was unarmed and slew his horse.[32] William afterward insisted that it would have been no crime had he slain Richard himself.[33] To attack an unarmed man was at worst merely a breach of knightly courtesy. But for a rebel to kill the representative of his suzerain was the most serious of feudal crimes—treason. William held Geoffrey de Lusignan responsible for his uncle's death. Whether he simply blamed Geoffrey as the leader of the party and responsible for his men or whether he believed him the actual slayer is not clear. Geoffrey himself denied his guilt, and one chronicler places the blame on his brother, Guy.[34] One is inclined to believe that the two de Lusignan brothers were in command of the party, but had no intention of killing Earl Patrick. Some careless or over-enthusiastic subordinate struck down the earl whom the leaders were simply hoping to capture. This view is confirmed by the care exercised by the rebels to take William alive when, as he was fighting without his helmet, he could have been killed easily. But, rightly or wrongly, William never forgave the house of Lusignan.

The same brief combat which made William the mortal enemy of the de Lusignans brought him to the attention of Queen Eleanor, the ideal patroness for a young knight. The richest heiress of Europe by reason of the great duchy of Aquitaine which she had inherited from her father, Eleanor had at an early age married Louis VII of France. Divorced from him, she had promptly given her hând to Henry Plantagenet. As ruler of more than half of the homeland of the troubadours, as patroness of such artists as Bernard de Ventadour, and as the mother of the countesses of Champagne and Blois whose courts were centers of romantic literature, Eleanor was the high priestess of the cult of courtly love. Unfortunately little is known of William's relations with this great lady. One cannot say

---

[32] *Ibid.*, 8835-8849.   [33] *Ibid.*, 9336-7.

[34] *Ibid.*, 6455-6458. Benedict of Peterborough, *Gesta regis Henrici Secundi* (ed. William Stubbs, *Rolls Series*), I, 343.

whether she became interested in him because of his fondness for singing and his knightly courtesy, or simply because he had undergone hardships in her service. But whatever its origin, her favor was an invaluable asset. Normandy and England were full of brave young knights, but there were few who could say that they had suffered wounds and imprisonment in the service of Queen Eleanor and had been ransomed and reequipped by her.

When William Marshal left Poitou in the autumn of 1168, he may well have considered with satisfaction the accomplishments of his twenty-two years. While he had followed what the contemporary romances tell us was the usual course of a young man's education, he had done so with rare success. At the age of thirteen he had left home to seek his fortune in the service of William of Tancarville. At the chamberlain's court he had served his apprenticeship in the trade of arms and from his hand he had received the boon of knighthood. In the combat at Drincourt and in at least two tourneys he had shown himself a brave and capable warrior. The campaign in Poitou had not only given him a taste of the hardships of a soldier's life, but had gained him the favor of Eleanor of Aquitaine. William could with justice believe that he was on the high road to fame and fortune.

CHAPTER III

KNIGHT-ERRANT

In his youth a man should use without laziness or delay, his prowess, his valor, and the vigor of his body for the honor and profit of himself and his dependents; for he who passes his youth without exploit may have cause for great shame and grief. The young nobleman, knight, or man-at-arms should work to acquire honor, to be renowned for valor, and to have temporal possessions, riches, and heritages on which he can live honorably. . . .[1]

There could be no more suitable introduction to the next fifteen years of William's life than this sage counsel of Philip de Navarre. It was sound advice for any young man of the feudal class, but it was particularly applicable to a landless knight who hoped to make his fortune with his sword. During the period between his twenty-fifth and fortieth years William devoted himself to chivalry—not the chivalry of Launcelot or Galahad, but one which was purely military and feudal. He sought fame and fortune through knightly exploits. The romantic service of God and fair ladies was as unimportant in his mind as in that of the good Philip. For this decade and a half William's biography seldom touches the course of history. It follows the adventurous career of a knight-errant whose only connection with the political events of the day arose from the fact that the lord whom he served happened to be Henry Plantagenet, eldest son of Henry II and heir to the Angevin domains. Despite its apparent aimlessness this chivalric phase of William's life was of great importance for his future. In those merry days of his youth he acquired his close personal relationship with the house of Anjou, his renown as a knight, and his wide acquaintance among the prominent men of his day.

[1] Philippe de Navarre, *Les Quatre Ages de l'Homme* (ed. Marcel de Fréville, *Société des Anciens Textes Français*), pp. 38-9.

During the year 1169 William was probably once more in the service of William of Tancarville who had succeeded Earl Patrick as the king's lieutenant in Poitou, but he was soon to find a more exalted patron.[2] In the spring of 1170 Henry II decided to elevate to the dignity of king his eldest son, Henry, who was then fifteen years old. After the young prince had been consecrated at Westminster by Roger, archbishop of York, the earls, barons, and free tenants of England did him liege homage. This exaction from the king's vassals of an oath of homage to the heir to the throne was a customary precaution to insure a peaceful succession. Henry I had compelled his men to swear fidelity to his son, William, and later to his daughter, Matilda.[3] The actual crowning of the heir during his father's lifetime was a regular practice of the Capetian kings.[4] The ceremony did not alter the English vassals' obligations to Henry himself, but simply bound them to serve the new king against anyone except his father.[5]

While the coronation of young Henry impelled his father to furnish him with a household in keeping with his royal rank, the prince's youth made it desirable that his entourage should be composed of men who were well fitted to guide and counsel him. King Henry entrusted his son's political education to such tried royal officials as Richard of Ilchester and William de St. John.[6] But a mediaeval monarch had to be a warrior as well as an administrator. With this end in view Henry appointed William Marshal the young king's tutor in chivalry.[7] His task was to instruct his master in the handling of weapons, to instill in him the knightly virtues, and to guard his person in battle and tourney. William undoubtedly owed his selec-

[2] Walter Map, De nugis curialium (ed. Thomas Wright, Camden Society), p. 234.

[3] William of Malmesbury, II, 495, 529, 534.

[4] Achille Luchaire, Histoire des Institutions Monarchiques de la France (second edition, Paris, 1891), I, 60 et seq.

[5] Benedict of Peterborough, I, 5-6.

[6] R. W. Eyton, Court, household, and itinerary of Henry II, p. 151.

[7] Hist., 1939-1948.

tion in part to the services which his family had rendered to
the house of Anjou and in part to the influence of Queen
Eleanor, but he must have had a considerable reputation in his
own right to have been given so exalted a charge. His exact
position in the prince's household is rather hard to define. The
History shows him teaching his master the art of war and pro-
tecting his person—a tutor, guardian, friend, and companion.
He was the chief of the household knights who composed the
prince's mesnie.[8] Fortunately the young king's charters enable
one to verify the statements of the *History* which might well
exaggerate the rôle of its hero. William appears among the
witnesses to seven of the fourteen known acts of young Henry.[9]
In each case his name immediately follows those of the barons
who were present and precedes those of the other simple
knights. As the usage of the time required the witnesses to a
charter to be listed in accordance with a fixed order of prece-
dence, this confirms the *History's* estimate of William's position in the young king's court.[10] As chief of the knights of the
household, he might be likened to a particularly influential
captain of the Guard.

Prince Henry's military entourage was by no means fixed
either in size or in composition. Its members may be identified
by comparing the witnesses to his charters with the list of his
partisans in the rebellion of 1173 and the roll of the knights
who fought under his banner in a tournament in 1180.[11] Five
knights, William Marshal, Gerard Talbot, Robert de Tresgoz,
Simon Marsh, and Adam de Iquebeuf, witnessed three or more

---

[8] *Mesnie*—as used here and subsequently this term means military household.

[9] Leopold Delisle, *Récueil des actes de Henri II,* Introduction, pp. 257, 258,
260, 261, 268, 269. F. M. Stenton, *Facsimiles of Early Charters* (*Northants
Record Society,* vol. IV).

[10] The only actual proof of this usage was made for a later period. See J. C.
Russell, *The Significance of Charter Witness Lists in Thirteenth Century England* (New Mexico Normal University, *Bulletin,* August, 1930). I believe that
a study of 12th century Charters would yield the same result.

[11] For his partisans in 1173 see Benedict of Peterborough, I, 45-47. For the
roll of the mesnie at Lagni see *Hist.,* 4481-4749.

of the charters and were on both these lists. They may be considered as the permanent nucleus of the mesnie. Some thirteen other knights including such well known figures as John and Peter des Preaux, Saher de Quency the younger, and Baldwin de Bethune were frequently attached to it. On the occasion of the great tournament held at Lagni in 1180 knights from all over northern France to the number of two hundred followed the young king's standard. Apparently the knights of the household were divided into two groups—ordinary knights and bannerets. Each of the latter had some half dozen personal followers of knightly rank and received twenty-five sous a day for their maintenance. William was a banneret by 1180.[12] The household knights were an expensive but necessary part of the prince's establishment, and William, as their chief, was one of his most important servants.

During the years 1170 to 1173 William's principal duty was to instruct his master in the ways of chivalry. Although his coronation entitled young Henry Plantagenet to style himself king of England, duke of Normandy, and count of Anjou, he had not yet attained the dignity of knighthood. Until he received this final emblem of military maturity, he could take an active part neither in war nor in knightly sports. William's task was to prepare the young prince for his induction into the chivalric order. King Henry intended that in due time his son should be dubbed a knight by his father-in-law and suzerain, Louis VII of France.[13] But the elder king was in no haste to have this ceremony performed, for he realized that while his heir was an apprentice in arms he was unlikely to be troublesome politically.[14] Meanwhile the young prince, due partly to his natural aptitude and partly to William's teaching, became a model of all the knightly virtues and aspired to be known as a patron of chivalry and brave knights. Unfortunately he

[12] *Ibid.*, 4750-4776; 4609-4612.
[13] *Ibid.*, 2117-2122.
[14] Knighthood was in the 12th century a prerequisite for full majority. See P. Guilhiermoz, *L'Origine de la Noblesse en France*, pp. 393-400.

learned the knightly virtue of generosity too well to suit his
careful father who was extremely annoyed at his extravagance.
On his side Prince Henry chafed under the restraints imposed
upon him. He wished to become a knight and to rule, or at
least to enjoy the revenues of, a part of the Angevin domains.
Although the wiser members of his household counselled patience, others urged him to rebellion.[15] The latter were ably
assisted by King Louis who hoped to weaken Henry II by
encouraging his son's discontent.[16]

The relations between father and son were brought to a crisis
in the spring of 1173 by the former's negotiations with Hubert,
count of Maurrienne in Savoy, for the marriage of the count's
daughter with the king's youngest son, John. At a meeting held
at Limoges in February, King Henry wished to grant John the
castles of Chinon, Loudon, and Mirabeau in order to satisfy
the count of Maurrienne as to his prospective son-in-law's position. Young Henry, following the advice of his father-in-law
whom he had recently visited, refused to consent to this arrangement unless he himself were given actual sovereignty in England, Normandy, or Anjou. The elder king refused to accede
to his son's demand, and they started north together.[17] While
his father slept peacefully in Chinon castle, Prince Henry left
secretly and hastened with his household to the neighborhood
of Vendôme.[18] Realizing that his son's flight from Chinon was
virtually a declaration of war, King Henry prepared to march
against him with all the force at his command.[19] Prince Henry
on his side was in a most embarrassing predicament. If he was
to lead a rebellion against his father, it was essential that he
should be knighted immediately, but he dared not offend King
Louis by having another perform the ceremony which had been
reserved for the royal sword. As soon as the prince had crossed
the Rubicon by deserting his father at Chinon, he had sent
messengers to explain the situation to his father-in-law. King

[15] *Hist.*, 1959-2006.
[16] Benedict of Peterborough, I, 34.   [18] *Ibid.*, *Hist.*, 2035-2036.
[17] *Ibid.*, pp. 36-41.   [19] *Ibid.*, 2020-2036.

Louis promptly despatched his brother, Peter de Courtenay, accompanied by the count of Clermont, William des Barres, the lord of Montmorency, and other barons, to represent him at the knighting of his son-in-law.[20] In all probability Louis expected his brother to perform the ceremony in his place, but instead Prince Henry chose his tutor in the customs of chivalry, William Marshal. In the presence of the young king's entourage and the French prince and his companions, William girded the sword of a knight on his young master.[21] To receive his king into the order of chivalry was a signal honor for a landless knight. Nothing could demonstrate more clearly the high place William had gained in his master's esteem.

King Louis had gone down to Chartres to watch the outcome of his intrigues against Henry II, and on March 8th Prince Henry crossed the Norman frontier and joined him there.[22] Sometime later his two younger brothers, Richard and Geoffrey, whom Henry II had left in Aquitaine in the care of their mother, arrived at the French court, but Eleanor herself, who sympathized with and encouraged her rebellious sons, was captured and imprisoned by her husband. Louis formed an alliance with his royal guests and declared war on Henry II. This action was the signal for a general rising of the barons of the Angevin domains who had long been restless under the heavy hand of King Henry. Resenting the curtailment of their feudal privileges, which had always been part of Henry's policy, the discontented baronage seized upon young Henry's break with his father as an excellent excuse for rebellion.[23] Some attempted to justify their disloyalty by recalling the oath of homage which they had taken to Prince Henry, but as they had sworn fealty to the young king against all men except his father, this argument had no validity. One must, however, sharply distinguish the position of the members of Prince Henry's household from

[20] *Ibid.*, 2123-2142.   [21] *Ibid.*, 2084-2092.

[22] *Ibid.*, 2109-2111. Benedict of Peterborough, I, 42. Eyton, *Itinerary*, p. 171.

[23] For a full account of this rebellion see Kate Norgate, *England under the Angevin Kings*, II, 131-168.

that of the other rebels. While four of the young king's entourage went over to his father, most of them followed him in his revolt.[24] Although William was undoubtedly a subject of Henry II, he held no fief for which he had done him homage. He was the " man " of Prince Henry who fed him, clothed him, and maintained him in every way.[25] The ties of feudal loyalty, gratitude, and affection bound him to the young king. William did not consider his support of his master's rebellion treason against Henry II, and later events indicate that the king himself did not.

The *History* says nothing of the part played by William in the rebellion. Perhaps even though he did not feel himself guilty of disloyalty towards King Henry, in his riper years he preferred to forget his armed opposition to the head of the house of Anjou. If, as seems likely, he followed his master to the French court, one can imagine William ripening his acquaintance with such famous knights as William des Barres. Possibly a young French prince, the future Philip Augustus, noticed the dashing young warrior who commanded Prince Henry's knights. This is supposition, but it is certain that in later years William was on very friendly terms with the French court. The foundations for the mutual respect that always existed between him and his life-long antagonists, the French, may have been laid at this time. Such an assumption would go far to explain the friendship between William and Philip Augustus that was to be so evident in later years.

In the course of a year and a half King Henry crushed the rebellion and forced his external enemies to sue for peace. On September 30, 1174 he came to terms with the French king and the three Angevin princes at Mt. Louis between Tours and Amboise.[26] The treaty between Henry and his sons was confirmed at a great council held at Falaise on October 11th.[27]

[24] Benedict of Peterborough, I, 43, 45-47.
[25] On the position of such knights of the mesnie see Guilhiermoz, *L'Origine de la Noblesse*, pp. 242-254.   [26] Benedict of Peterborough, I, 77.
[27] Rymer, *Foedera* (new edition, *Record Commission*), I, I, 30.

By its terms Prince Henry received two castles in Normandy and a yearly revenue of fifteen thousand pounds Angevin. Both the elder and younger kings forgave the partisans of the other and promised to bear no malice against them. William took part in the council at Falaise, and his name appears among the witnesses to the treaty of peace. In May 1175 he accompanied the two kings to England.[28] Far from injuring his position, William's part in the rebellion had increased his prestige. Not only was he the chief of Prince Henry's mesnie, but by dubbing his master a knight he had become his father in chivalry.

The comparatively quiet life in England soon palled upon young Henry and his household, and their adventurous spirits longed for the land of knightly deeds. It occurred to the prince that a pilgrimage to the shrine of St. James of Compostella along the route made famous by the legends of Charlemagne and his paladins might furnish amusement and excitement.[29] King Henry did not approve of so extended an expedition, but he gave his son leave to cross to the continent. Landing in Normandy in May 1176, Prince Henry and his knights plunged into the chivalric life of northern France in which they were soon to become central figures.

As a debutante seeks the support of an established social leader, so young Henry, desiring an auspicious introduction into the chivalric world, turned to his cousin, Philip of Alsace, count of Flanders, who was generally recognized as the age's foremost patron of chivalry. Count Philip received his royal cousin most hospitably and took him on a grand tour through his extensive domains. One day word came to Prince Henry of a tourney to be held between Gournay and Ressons in the county of Clermont. The young king and his mesnie wanted to go, but for some unexplained reason they lacked arms and war horses. This misfortune gave Philip of Flanders a splendid opportunity to display his generosity. When his guests arrived

---

[28] *Récueil des Actes de Henri II,* Introduction, p. 258.
[29] Benedict of Peterborough, I, 114.

at the scene of the tournament, they were so richly equipped that a spectator could hardly have estimated the value of their accoutrements.[30] Thus young Henry and his suite were introduced to the chivalric world by one of the foremost knights of the day and served as shining examples of his *largesse*.

This was but the first of a number of tourneys attended by Prince Henry and his knights during the course of 1176. William continued to serve his master as guardian and tutor. In the press of the combat he stayed near the prince and beat off with mighty blows anyone who might try to capture the heir to the Angevin lands. But William was more than a mere bodyguard, he was a strategist as well. It appears that Count Philip of Flanders, the flower of chivalry, took an extremely practical view of tournaments. He was accustomed to hold aloof from the combat until the contestants were thoroughly exhausted. He could then charge into the mêlée at the head of his mesnie and take many valuable prisoners at small risk to his own men. After the young king and his followers had suffered several times from these tactics, William decided to beat the count at his own game. At the next tournament Prince Henry pretended that he would take no part in the contest, but at the opportune time, he and his knights rode into the field and attacked the count's household. So successful was this stratagem, that young Henry and his men used it in many other tourneys.[31] William served his master with a clear head as well as with a strong arm.

Shortly after their visit to Flanders, Prince Henry and his mesnie attended a tournament between Anet and Sorel-Moussel in the valley of the Eure to the north of Dreux. The knights of the Angevin lands were so encouraged by the presence of their king that they drove the French from the field with their first charge. In the confusion of the pursuit William and his master became separated from their men. While riding through a street in Anet, they were suddenly confronted by three hundred foot serjeants under Simon de Neauphle, a French baron,

---

[30] *Hist.*, 2443-2496.   [31] *Ibid.*, 2715-2772.

who was apparently covering the retreat of his compatriots. Not to be disturbed by a few wretched infantrymen, William, closely followed by the prince, rode straight towards their line. The serjeants gave way before the two knights, and as he rode through their ranks, William, seizing Simon's horse by the bridle, forced the unwilling baron to accompany him. As they rode on through the town, a low-hanging water drain swept Simon from his horse. The young king, who was riding behind, saw the accident but kept it to himself. When they finally arrived at their camp William, who still led the riderless horse, proudly ordered his squire to take charge of the captured knight. Great was William's merriment when he learned how he had lost his prisoner.[32]

Early in the spring of 1177 word came to young Henry's court of a tournament which was to be held at Pleurs near Épernay in the valley of the Marne. The prince decided that it was too long a journey for him to undertake with all the baggage required by his household, but he readily gave William, who was unwilling to miss any opportunity to acquire glory, leave to go with a single companion. At Pleurs they found a splendid assembly of the chivalry of France, Flanders, and the adjacent Imperial provinces. Hugh, duke of Burgundy, Count Philip of Flanders, Count Theobald of Blois and Chartres, the counts of Clermont and Beaumont, and the valorous William des Barres were at hand to take part in the contest. The valley swarmed with knights who hoped to gain honor and profit. There one could see fine horses from Spain, Lombardy, and Sicily put through their paces. The accoutrements of the knights were so rich as to beggar description. In the tourney William gained the admiration of all by his valor and his skill in the use of arms. When the contest was over, the knights gathered together to discuss the events of the day. Some sought news of friends or relatives who had been captured, others were trying to raise money for their ransoms or to find pledges who would guarantee their payment. A lady of high rank, possibly

that famous patroness of chivalry and courtly love the Countess
Marie of Champagne in whose husband's fief the tourney was
held, presented to the duke of Burgundy a very fine pike.
Wishing to " double the honor to the lady " the duke sent the
gift to Count Philip of Flanders who in turn passed it on to
the count of Clermont. The latter, not to fall behind his peers
in courtesy, sent it to Count Theobald of Blois. As the proceeding was becoming rather ridiculous, Count Philip suggested
that they give the pike to the knight who had borne himself
most worthily in the tournament. As everyone acclaimed this
idea, the count was asked to name his candidate. He replied
that the hero of the day was a knight of the young king's household—William Marshal. Two knights were deputed to make
the presentation of this strange prize. Preceded by a squire bearing the pike, they set out for William's lodgings. There they
were informed that he could be found at the blacksmith's shop.
In the smithy they discovered William kneeling with his head
on the anvil while the smith labored with hammer and tongs
to draw off his helmet which had been beaten out of shape and
driven down on his head by the force of the blows received in
the tournament. When the helmet had finally yielded to the
smith's efforts, the two knights presented the prize to William
who received it with becoming modesty. The barons, learning
from their emissaries the strange situation in which they had
found the hero of the tourney, were greatly impressed and felt
that they had shown excellent judgment in awarding the prize
to so hardy a warrior.[33]

Apparently not even so enthusiastic a patron of chivalry as
Prince Henry could attend enough tournaments to satisfy William's craving for glory and profit. In the spring of 1177 Roger
de Gaugi, a fellow member of young Henry's mesnie, asked
William to join him in a systematic tour of all the tournaments
that might be held. William agreed, and the two knights entered into partnership for the full exploitation of their military
abilities. For two years they journeyed from tourney to tourney

[33] *Ibid.*, 2875-3164.

in search of honor and gain. In its commercial aspects at least their venture was a great success. According to a list kept by Wigain, the young king's clerk, the partners captured in the course of ten months one hundred and three knights.[34]

One day William and his partner went to a tourney at Joigni which lay in the Seine valley south of Sens. The party to which they attached themselves armed in the castle and reached the field before their opponents. There they found the countess of Joigni and her ladies who had come to watch the sport. To while away the time the knights and ladies danced to a song sung by William. When he had finished, a young minstrel who had just been made a herald gave a piece of his own composition of which the refrain was " Marshal, give me a good horse." Just at that moment the first knight of the opposing party arrived on the field. William calmly left the dancing throng, mounted his charger, dismounted the newly arrived knight, and gave his horse to the minstrel. It was a nice exploit —a combination of the two knightly virtues of generosity and prowess. Scarcely less entrancing is the picture of knights dancing in full armor. As for William, the sight of the fair ladies so raised his spirit that he carried all before him.[35]

In the course of the year 1179 William dissolved his partnership with Roger de Gaugi and returned to Prince Henry's court. The continual round of tournaments did not cease, but once more William attended them as commander of young Henry's mesnie rather than as a knight-errant. Soon after he rejoined his master, a series of three tourneys drew all good knights to the region of Dreux and Chartres. The largest of these took place in the valley of the Eure between Anet and Sorel-Moussel, the scene of a former tourney attended by William. This time Prince Henry did not go, but he sent his mesnie under William's command. When William and his companions reached the field, they found that the combat had already begun and that the French were getting the best of it. The arrival of the young king's mesnie turned the tide in favor of the knights of the

[34] *Ibid.*, 3381-3424.   [35] *Ibid.*, 3426-3562.

Angevin lands, and their opponents were put to rout. Some of the fugitives took refuge on a mound surrounded by a palisade and moat. So great was their haste that they did not stop to take their horses inside the enclosure but simply tethered them to the outside of the palisade. William, who had as usual lost his companions in the heat of the pursuit, chanced to ride by the mound and realized that here was a splendid opportunity. Leaving his mount in charge of the squire who was his sole attendant, he jumped into the moat, climbed the mound, seized two of the horses, and led them back the way he had come. As he was coaxing them up the bank of the moat, two French knights rode by. Seeing that William was dismounted and helpless, they bore down upon him and relieved him of the two horses. William realized that he was at a hopeless disadvantage and made little attempt to protect his booty. As he knew the names of the two knights, he could settle with them later.

Remounting his charger, William rode on until he came to a group of farm buildings in which fifteen French knights were being besieged by a greatly superior force. When William arrived on the scene, the hard-pressed defenders offered to surrender to him rather than to the besieging party. The latter were naturally annoyed at seeing fifteen good prisoners slip from their grasp, but as none of them cared to fight William over the matter, they were forced to withdraw. When he had escorted his prisoners to safety, William let them go and declined to accept any ransom. Considering that the besieging party must have formed part of William's own side in the tournament, this whole proceeding seems rather high-handed, but it undoubtedly earned him the friendship of the French knights and added to his reputation for generosity.

William rode back to his lodgings thoroughly satisfied with his day's work. There he disarmed and prepared to set out in search of the two horses which had been taken from him. To the modern mind it seems eminently proper that the horses he had captured should in turn be taken from him, but it was, apparently, against the laws of chivalry. Mounting his palfrey, William rode to the quarters of William des Barres who was the uncle of one of the young knights who had taken the horses. William des Barres was greatly shocked at his nephew's conduct. Had the story come from any less trustworthy man he would not have believed it. As it was he ordered the youth either to restore the horse or to leave his household. Someone suggested that William show his knightly generosity by giving the young man half the horse and then throwing dice with him to see who should have the whole animal. Accepting the suggestion, William promptly threw an eleven against his opponent's nine and won the horse. William des Barres urged William to stay, but he insisted on going after the other horse. The knight who had taken it was a member of the mesnie of a French baron. When the latter heard William's story, he commanded his vassal to return the stolen charger. Again it was suggested that he give the young knight half the horse. William agreed and asked the youth to estimate the value of the animal. Supposing that William had no money with him and realizing that he could put a low valuation on the horse, pay his half at once, and get the animal very cheaply, the young man valued the charger at only fourteen pounds though it was worth thirty or forty. Much to his surprise, William threw seven pounds on the table and went off with the horse.[36] The young knight had been caught in his own trap. William had in each case sustained his reputation for generosity and still gained his object.

Even the author of the *History,* who shared to the full his hero's joy in these knightly sports, protests that he cannot describe all the tournaments in which William took part. So great was the chivalric enthusiasm of the baronage of France that an energetic knight-errant could attend a tourney every two weeks.[37] But most of these contests were small affairs patronized by the knights of the vicinity and such assiduous jousters as Philip of Flanders and William Marshal. A truly

[36] *Ibid.,* 3884-4284.   [37] *Ibid.,* 4971-4976.

representative gathering of the chivalry of north-western Europe required the patronage of an extremely rich feudal prince and an occasion which would draw together the nobles of the land. Not only was the cost of holding a large tourney far too great for any but the most opulent lords, but few barons and knights could afford to make a long journey purely for sport. The most splendid of William's tournaments, one described by the author of the *History* as finer than any held before or since, resulted from a rare combination of favoring circumstances.

On All Saints Day, 1179, Philip, son and heir of King Louis VII of France, was crowned in Rheims cathedral by his uncle, Archbishop William. Headed by young Henry Plantagenet and Count Philip of Flanders, the vassals of the French crown were present in force to honor their new sovereign.[38] For once King Henry had loosened his purse strings, and the young king had come with an escort magnificent enough to suit even his extravagant tastes.[39] Seldom could one find so ideal an occasion for a really first class tournament. As Philip Augustus and his royal guest journeyed from Paris to Rheims and back, they passed through the fair county of Champagne. Henry, count palatine of Champagne and Brie, was one of the richest and most powerful barons of France. His wife was the daughter of Louis VII by Eleanor of Aquitaine, his sister Adela was queen of France, and his three brothers were respectively archbishop of Rheims, count of Blois and Chartres, and count of Sancerre. Count Henry and his wife Marie were noted as patrons of chivalry and courtly love. Extremely rich and a lover of knightly sports, Count Henry might well take advantage of the occasion to hold a tourney in honor of his newly-crowned nephew. For the scene of the contest he chose his town of Lagni-sur-Marne which lay on the main road from Rheims to Paris and was the site of one of the great fairs that contributed so largely to Count Henry's wealth.[40]

---

[38] Benedict of Peterborough, I, 242. Ralph de Diceto, *Opera Historica* (ed. William Stubbs, *Rolls Series*), I, 438.   [39] Robert de Torigni, p. 287.

[40] There is no positive proof that there was any connection between the

On the appointed day a truly noble concourse of knights assembled at Lagni. The *History* mentions the presence of the duke of Burgundy and nineteen counts while it estimates the number of ordinary knights at three thousand. As all mediaeval writers were inclined to be careless with round numbers, the latter figure may be an exaggeration, but it agrees with the number of combatants attending the great tournaments of the contemporary romances.[41] The young king himself had some two hundred knights under his banner. The *History* names eighty-six of Prince Henry's knights of whom sixteen were bannerets with mesnies of their own. This was not, of course, the permanent entourage of the young king, but rather the splendid escort which his father's bounty had enabled him to lead to Philip's coronation. The list includes such great barons as Robert, count of Dreux, the head of a cadet branch of the Capetians, David, earl of Huntingdon, the brother of King William of Scotland, and the counts of Eu and Soissons. Here William Marshal appears for the first time as a knight banneret.[42] Although still a landless man, he had risen to the point where he could flaunt his banner beside those of counts and barons.

The *History's* account of the actual tournament is confused and of no particular interest. The author had seen the roll of Prince Henry's mesnie and had been told of the noble gathering that graced the occasion, but he knew little of the contest itself. William had twice rescued his master from grave peril of capture, and the third son of Henry II, Count Geoffrey of Brittany, had borne himself bravely in the combat. Lances had

tourney at Lagni described in the *History* and the coronation of Philip II. I base my assumption on several facts. The tourney must be placed between October 1178, when Philip of Flanders returned from Palestine (Ralph de Diceto, I, 428; Robert de Torigni, p. 279), and Christmas 1182 (*Hist.,* 5693-4). The presence of Prince Henry with so extraordinarily large a following and as many as nineteen counts indicates a special occasion.

[41] See C. V. Langlois, *La Vie en France en Moyen Age,* I, 29.

[42] *Hist.,* 4457-4796.

been broken and mighty blows struck while acres of vines were destroyed by the trampling chargers.[43] That is about all the author of the *History* knew of the affair for he had not been present in person as he had at the tourney between Anet and Sorel-Moussel.[44] As a splendid spectacle of the assembled chivalry of France, the tournament of Lagni could have had few equals.

In the year 1180 William was at the summit of his career in the young king's court. Valued for his prowess in battle and his sagacity in counsel, he was favored by Prince Henry above all the other members of his household. While in general the possession of a fief was a prerequisite for the enjoyment of any prestige in feudal society, William was treated by his master as the peer of counts and great barons. But his eminence aroused the envy of a number of his companions-in-arms. Led by Adam de Iquebeuf, who had been a prominent member of Prince Henry's mesnie since the rebellion of 1173, they circulated the rumor that William was the lover of the young queen, Margaret of France, who was the daughter of Louis VII by his second wife, Constance of Castile. William's loyal friends such as Peter des Preaux and Baldwin de Bethune refused to believe the story. The young king himself found the tale hard to accept, but it served to poison his mind against his favorite knight. Torn between jealous suspicion and the need of William's strong arm at his side, Prince Henry hesitated to take any definite action. Meanwhile the conspirators carried their scandal to the elder king. Henry II was in a most receptive mood for rumors derogatory to William.[45] The chamberlain of Tancarville was at the time decidedly out of favor, and William was that baron's cousin.[46] Besides the king was again worried about his heir's extravagance and as William was Prince Henry's closest friend and counselor, he may well have felt that he was partially responsible for it. As a result, King Henry was prepared to regard a break between his son and

[43] *Ibid.*, 4820-4970.
[44] *Ibid.*, 3885-3886.
[45] *Ibid.*, 5095-5668.
[46] Walter Map, *De nugis curialium*, p. 232.

William Marshal with perfect equanimity. The *History* does not suggest that he believed the story, but even if he had, one cannot but doubt that it would have seriously shocked his sense of propriety. William's biographer cannot let the matter rest so cheerfully. As the seduction of the wife of one's liege lord was a most serious breach of feudal propriety, the presumption is that William, who was always most scrupulous in such matters, could not have been guilty of it. On the other hand Margaret is known to have been on very friendly terms with her half-sister Marie of Champagne, a patroness of the cult of courtly love. Did Margaret see a Launcelot in the handsome young captain of her husband's mesnie? As it was the age of courtly love, one can conceive of William as the " true knight " of the young queen, but hardly as her paramour.

Naturally William wished to put an end to these rumors and clear his name as publicly as possible. His opportunity came in the autumn of 1182. At Christmas time King Henry held high festival at his city of Caen. With him were his three elder sons, Henry, Richard, and Geoffrey, and his son-in-law, Henry the Lion, duke of Saxony and Bavaria, who had just been sentenced to a year's exile from Germany by the Emperor Frederick of Hohenstaufen. The festivities had been well advertised, and a splendid assemblage of the prelates and barons of the Angevin domains was in attendance on their king and his distinguished guest.[47] William and his cousin of Tancarville were destined to furnish most of the entertainment for this noble gathering. On Christmas day, just before the great feast, while a servant was preparing to pour water on the hands of King Henry and the princes, William of Tancarville burst suddenly into the room with a large retinue of knights, seized the vessels of water from the astounded servant, and performed the ceremony himself. Then he coolly handed the basins to one of his own attendants despite the protest of the royal chamberlains. The next day the lord of Tancarville successfully de-

---

[47] *Hist.*, 5693-5714. Benedict of Peterborough, I, 291. Walter Map, *De nugis curialium*, p. 232.

fended his somewhat precipitous action before the assembled court. As hereditary chamberlain of Normandy it was his privilege to pour water on his duke's hands on all state occasions, and he had custody of the basins used in the ceremony. He allowed no one to usurp his rights.[48]

William's appearance before the assembled court was less sensational than that of his cousin of Tancarville. While the two kings sat in state surrounded by their prelates and barons, he approached and addressed Prince Henry. Categorically denying the truth of the rumor that he was Queen Margaret's lover, he offered to prove his innocence by battle. On three successive days he would fight the three strongest of his accusers. If any one of them defeated him, his master could hang him as a traitor. When young Henry refused to accept this offer, William proposed that a finger should be cut off his right hand and that he then should be allowed to fight the strongest of his enemies. But Prince Henry had no intention of bringing the matter to trial. While his good sense made him doubt William's guilt, his jealousy urged him to get rid of a possible rival. As soon as William realized that his master's purpose was to drive him from the court, he turned to the elder king and demanded a safe conduct to the frontier of the Angevin lands. Considering this a neat solution to a most unpleasant situation, King Henry readily granted his request. William and his mesnie left Caen at once and made their way over the Norman border into the county of Chartres.[49] Throughout the whole affair William had acted with perfect propriety. If a lord refused his vassal a hearing in his court, the ties between them were severed automatically. William had demanded justice from his lord, Prince Henry, and it had been denied him. Knowing that Henry II looked on him with disfavor, William had not actually appealed to him, but the elder king by his silence seemed to sanction his son's action. If William had held a fief, the situation would have been more complicated, but as it was he could simply leave the lord who refused to fulfil his feudal obligations and seek another.

When the news spread that William had left the young king's court, many a patron of chivalry sought to attract him into his service. The count of Flanders, the duke of Burgundy, and the advocate of Bethune sent messengers in search of him with tempting offers, but they were unable to find him. Enjoying his independence, William had wandered from the lands of his old friend Count Theobald into those of the count of Champagne. At the fair of Lagni he bought for thirty pounds a splendid war horse that was well worth fifty. Early in January he heard of a tournament to be held in the county of Clermont and went north to take part in it. Attaching himself for the day to the mesnie of the count of St. Paul, he performed many brave deeds and twice saved the count from capture. After the combat the assembled barons sent for William. The count of Flanders and the duke of Burgundy each offered him an annual income of five hundred pounds for his services. The advocate of Bethune raised the bid by offering five hundred pounds a year, a town, and his daughter in marriage.[50] The *History* asserts that William declined all these offers, but as he appears some years later as the holder of a fief in Flanders, it seems likely that he accepted a grant of land from Count Philip at this time.[51] At any rate, he did not give up his freedom of action, for he promptly set out on a pilgrimage to Cologne.[52]

William's piously used vacation was destined to be of short duration. In February, 1183, fresh quarrels broke out between the Angevin princes.[53] The young king and Count Geoffrey of Brittany had gone into Poitou to support the vassals of their brother Richard in a rebellion against his authority. Finding himself in serious difficulties, Richard called on his father for

[50] *Ibid.*, 5923-6170; 6260-6277.   [51] *Rot. Chart.*, p. 46a.
[52] *Hist.*, 6176-6192.
[53] For a full account of young Henry's last revolt see Norgate, *England under the Angevin Kings*, II, 225-228, and *Richard the Lion Heart*, pp. 47-56.

aid. Early in March Henry II entered the city of Limoges and laid siege to the castle in which young Henry and Geoffrey had taken refuge. One day the two princes took counsel with their adherents to decide on their future course. Geoffrey suggested that they needed the wisdom and valor of William Marshal. The chief of the Poitevin rebels, that same Geoffrey de Lusignan whom William hated so cordially as the slayer of his uncle, Earl Patrick, supported Prince Geoffrey's advice and even offered to prove in a judicial combat that the accusations against William were false. The lord of Lusignan added that despite William's belief to the contrary, he was innocent of Earl Patrick's death. While they were discussing the matter, the chief of those who had plotted against William burst into the room and addressed Prince Henry. " Sire, your father is besieging this castle, and I am his liege-man. I dare not stay with you. I beg you to give me leave to join your father as I am bound to do." " Hear the traitor," cried Prince Henry. " This proves at last that he has slandered the marshal, the best of men." [54] As the man's interpretation of his feudal duty was probably correct—the point is a debatable one—the term traitor seems rather harsh. At any rate the desertion of the chief of his accusers convinced young Henry of William's innocence. He promptly despatched his chamberlain to find him and bring him to court.[55]

The chamberlain after a long search found William as he was returning from Cologne and gave him Prince Henry's message. William promised to join his master as soon as he could. But he had no intention of plunging recklessly into the lion's jaws. He was safe in France, and there he intended to stay until he could enter the Angevin lands under a safe conduct from Henry II. Accordingly he applied to Philip Augustus, to William, archbishop of Rheims, to Count Robert of Dreux, and to Count Theobald of Blois for letters of recommendation to king Henry. The *History* fails to state what these letters said,

---

[54] *Hist.*, 6408-6512.   [55] *Ibid.*, 6525-6552.

but they must have stressed William's good qualities and re-quested Henry to allow him to join the young king. Whatever their contents they had the desired effect. King Henry promptly sent letters to William authorizing him to join his master.[56] The *History* adds that according to report the king went so far as to give William leave to fight against him under Prince Henry's banner, but the author clearly has his doubts as to the truth of this statement.[57] Even without that addition Henry's action was sufficiently perplexing. A few months earlier the king had considered William a bad influence on his son. Had the letters of the French dignitaries altered his views? It seems more likely that he had confidence in William's essential loyalty and good sense, qualities sadly needed in the rebel camp, and hoped that he might be able to control to some extent the vagaries of the young king's behavior. William might have been responsible for his master's over-extravagant patronage of chivalry, but he could be relied on to oppose the ravaging of the countryside and the plundering of abbeys and shrines which were at the moment Prince Henry's principal activities.

As soon as he received King Henry's safe-conduct, William arranged a rendezvous at Montmirail-en-Brie, some twenty miles east of Paris, with two old companions in arms, Baldwin de Bethune and Hugh de Hamelincourt, who were also on their way to join Prince Henry.[58] As he rode to the place of meet-ing, William had an adventure which may serve to illustrate the customs of wandering knights. As William lay dozing by the roadside while his squire, Eustace de Bertrimont, kept watch, a richly dressed couple rode by on two fine palfreys. The woman murmured " Ah, God, but I am tired." This plaint from a lady in distress awoke the sleeping knight, and he asked his squire what was going on. Eustace replied that a man and woman, both very richly equipped, had gone by at full speed. William called for his horse. He wished to know who they were, where they had come from, and where they were going. Jumping on his horse in such haste that he forgot his sword, he soon came

[56] *Ibid.*, 6553-6656.   [57] *Ibid.*, 6657-6663.   [58] *Ibid.*, 6665-6676.

up with the travellers, seized the man by his sleeve, and demanded his name. Replying that he was a man, the other broke
from William's grasp and reached for his sword. William was
delighted. "You want a fight?" he cried, "you shall have it.
Eustace! my sword." These warlike words quenched the other's
ardor, and he attempted to make his escape, but William soon
caught up with him again and seized him by the cap. As the
cap came off in his hand, he saw to his great surprise that the
man was a monk. His curiosity thoroughly aroused, William
settled down for a regular inquisition. The embarrassed monk
admitted that he had eloped with the lady and was taking her
to a foreign land. William turned to the lady. "Tell me, fair
one, who you are and of what family?" "Sire, I am from
Flanders and I am sister to Ralph of Lens." "Fair lady, this is
idiotic. I advise you to give up this foolishness and I will reconcile you with your brother whom I know well." But the lady
had not the courage to face her friends again, and William let
that point drop. "Have you enough money to live on?" he
asked the monk. When the latter produced forty-eight pounds,
William pointed out that so small a sum would not keep them.
The monk hastened to explain that he did not intend to live
on the principal but to invest the money and use only the
interest. William was profoundly shocked. "At usury! By the
spear of God that will not do. Seize the money Eustace. Since
you do not wish to return to a virtuous life, go, and may the
devil guide you." When he arrived at the rendezvous, William
divided the money with his two friends and told them how he
had come by it. Hugh de Hamelincourt was for following the
two travellers and taking their palfreys and baggage as well as
their money, but William restrained his friend's enthusiasm.[59]

At first glance William's conduct appears as officious med-
dling followed by plain highway robbery, but such an interpretation is in accord neither with his known character nor with
the fact that the author of the *History* was anxious to record the
event for posterity. Both William and his biographer were dis-

[59] *Ibid.*, 6677-6864.

tinctly proud of the adventure. The solution must be sought in the mediaeval conception of the order of chivalry as a semi-official police force. One aspect of this idea is found in the romantic tradition by which knights-errant rescued beautiful ladies from wicked men or savage dragons. The more practical side of the theory is clearly exposed in the eighth chapter of the sixth book of the *Polycraticus* of John of Salisbury. Speaking of soldiers, that is knights, he says "The high praises of God are in their throats and two edged swords are in their hands . . . to the end that they may execute the judgement that is committed to them to execute; wherein each follows not his own will but the deliberate decision of God, the angels, and men in accordance with equity and public utility." [60] William had investigated a lady's cry of distress. He had found the damsel unwilling to be rescued from her abductor, but he had at the same time uncovered another wrong—their plan to live on the proceeds of usury. As a knight was the sworn servant of the church as well as the state, it was clearly William's duty to prevent a monk from living with his mistress on money gained by the sin of usury. The forty-eight pounds were simply the profits of this rather summary act of justice. Such, I believe, would have been William's justification of his action. While it is very doubtful whether it would have been acceptable to the constituted authorities, either lay or ecclesiastical, the *History's* attitude indicates that it did no violence to contemporary mores.

After dividing the spoils of William's adventure and eating a good dinner, the three knights set out on the long journey to Poitou. Young Henry had left Limoges some time before and was then in the neighborhood of the river Dordogne to the south-east of Périgueux. There William and his companions joined him. The young king's brilliant but wavering career was drawing to its end. Towards the end of May he fell sick and on June 5th he was seized with a violent fever at the castle of

---

[60] John of Salisbury, *Polycraticus* (ed. J. A. Giles, *Patres Ecclesiae*), IV, 21. Translated by John Dickinson, *The Statesman's Book of John of Salisbury* (*Political Science Classics*), pp. 190-1.

Martel on the Dordogne. On the seventh he confessed to
Gerald, bishop of Cahors, and two other prelates and leaping
naked from his bed, prostrated himself before the host, received
the sacrament, and solemnly renounced his rebellion against his
father. Four days later the attending prelates administered the
last rites of the church to their dying king.[61] But one thing
more troubled Prince Henry—he had taken a crusader's vows
and had never fulfilled them. When he had received extreme
unction, he turned to William. "Marshal, you have always
been loyal and faithful. I leave you my cross and pray you to
carry it to the Holy Sepulchre. You will acquit for me my vow
to God." [62] William took the cloak with the red cross sewn
on the shoulder and promised to carry it to Jerusalem as his
master's legate. So died the young king, the flower of chivalry.
Brave, courteous, and lavishly generous he lacked but one
knightly virtue—loyalty. He was a capable captain and a born
leader of men. His beauty of body and lovable personality won
the hearts of all who met him. But his manifold good qualities only made his utter instability of character more dangerous.
He was a magnificent patron of chivalry, but a thoroughly
worthless prince.[63] William had loved him for his virtues and
suffered from his faults.

While the young king's knights were making ready to carry
their late master's body to his father at Limoges, a most unto-
ward incident disturbed their preparations. Prince Henry had
died deeply in debt, and one of his creditors, a mercenary captain named Sancho, conceived an ingenious scheme for collecting some of the money due him. Seizing William Marshal, he
at first demanded that he pay his master's debt, but finally
agreed to release him for a ransom of one hundred marks.
William could not pay so large a sum, but he promised to sur-

[61] Geoffrey de Vigeois, in *Récueil des historiens des Gaules et de la France*
(ed. Bouquet), XVIII, 217.

[62] *Hist.*, 6891-6911.

[63] For a good contemporary estimate of Prince Henry see Walter Map, *De
nugis curialium*, pp. 139-140.

render himself as a prisoner to Sancho as soon as he had borne Prince Henry's corpse to Limoges. As this was satisfactory to Sancho, the funeral procession started on its way. When they reached the royal camp, William told King Henry of his son's illness, of his repentance, and of the resignation with which he had borne his sufferings. The king then ordered William to escort the bier to the cathedral of Rouen where Prince Henry had asked to be buried. When William explained his promise to Sancho, Henry summoned the man and paid him the hundred marks. Freed from that burden, William set out for Rouen. There on July 22nd Prince Henry was solemnly interred. In the throng of mourners was his great rival in chivalry, Philip of Alsace, count of Flanders.[64]

Having buried his master, William prepared to carry out his last request—to bear his cross to the Holy Sepulchre. King Henry readily gave him permission to fulfil his promise, but ordered him to return as soon as possible as he wanted to take him into his own mesnie. As a guarantee against any undue delay in the Holy Land the king took from William two fine horses. At the same time he gave him a hundred pounds Angevin to cover the expense of the journey. Then William paid a brief visit to England to take leave of his family—his elder brother John, the king's marshal, his sisters one of whom was married to Robert de Pont de l'Arche, a minor Hampshire landholder, and his cousin Earl William of Salisbury.[65]

A crusade was the supreme adventure. In the actual as distinct from the romantic chivalry the defence of the Holy Sepulchre played the same part as did the quest of the Holy Grail in the Arthurian romances. It was eminently fitting that William should crown his career as a knight-errant with an excursion to the Holy Land. Unfortunately there is no record of the brave deeds which he undoubtedly performed against the forces of the redoubtable Saladin. The *History* simply asserts that in two years he did more than another man could in seven.[66] One can vouch, however, for his state of mind while

[64] *Hist.*, 7003-7184.   [65] *Ibid.*, 7239-7274.   [66] *Ibid.*, 7275-7295.

engaged in his pious expedition. As befitted a crusader his thoughts were centered in securing for himself a safe and dignified passage into the next world. He entered into very close relations with the Templars and probably promised to die under the sheltering cloak of their order. He even bought two rich silken cloths to serve as a covering for his corpse.[67] Aside from these far-sighted preparations for the future. William's pilgrimage to Jerusalem must remain a lacuna in his biography.

William's visit to the Holy Land marks the end of his life as a knight-errant. For fifteen years he had been an enthusiastic devotee of the most aristocratic cult of his day. His prowess and his knightly virtues had gained him a prominent place among the stars of the chivalric firmament. Although he held no fief of any importance, he was the esteemed friend of such great feudal princes as Philip of Flanders and Theobald of Blois. He had been the favorite knight, the intimate companion, and the father-in-chivalry of young Henry Plantagenet. William's exalted position in the chivalric world makes the *History's* account of this part of his career of unusual interest to the student of mediaeval society. While the writings of churchmen and romancers describe theoretical chivalry, the *History* enables us to examine the living institution as we follow the adventures of a prominent knight-errant. This clear and unique view of a picturesque phase of twelfth century life merits particular attention.

The cult of chivalry was a fad of the ruling class. While its membership was strictly confined to those of knightly rank, the term knight did not in the twelfth century have the purely chivalric connotation that it was to achieve in later times. Knight, *miles,* still meant the adult male of the feudal class who could acquire either from his own resources or from the generosity of his lord the horse, lance, sword, shield, and hauberk that constituted the complete military equipment of the day. The order of knighthood embraced the entire no-

---

[67] *Ibid.*, 18217-18226.

bility.[68] This fact, I believe, justifies the somewhat arbitrary use made in this chapter of the term knight-errant to describe a knight who was imbued with chivalric ideas. By the last quarter of the twelfth century the vigorous propaganda of the trouvères had made this new game of chivalry highly popular in northern France. The *History* tells us who were the leaders of the movement in this region—Prince Henry, Philip of Flanders, Theobald of Blois, Robert of Dreux, the duke of Burgundy, the count of Clermont, and William des Barres. Of twelve tournaments mentioned in the *History* two were held in the county of Clermont, two in the county of Dreux, and four in the lands of Count Theobald of Blois and Chartres. Three of the remaining four took place in the domains of Theobald's brother, Henry, count palatine of Champagne and Brie. While the omission of Count Henry's name from the pages of the *History* indicates that he was not a prominent participant in the tourneys, the fact that the most magnificent of these contests were held in his lands justifies the presumption that he was an important patron of chivalry. The *History* is loud in its praise of the rich barons who by their encouragement of tournaments furnished young knights with a means of livelihood and a training for war. They were the high priests of the order of chivalry.

The members of the chivalric cult differed from their fellow knights in the possession of new interests and in the profession of new motives for following the old ones. Fighting was the principal occupation of the feudal caste, but the knight-errant was supposed to fight primarily for renown. Again and again the *History* asserts that William's first consideration was always the search for military glory.[69] The capture of horses, arms, and prisoners was an unworthy though highly profitable sideline. But while prowess was the chief qualification of a knight-errant, the newer and gentler virtues were held in high esteem. True to his character as a trouvère, the author of the *History*

---

[68] See P. Guilhiermoz, *L'Origine de la Noblesse*, pp. 370 et. seq. and pp. 393 et. seq.   [69] *Hist.*, 3010-3012.

lays particular stress on the importance of generosity. Prince Henry and William Marshal are praised for their *largesse*.[70] Courtesy was added to the knightly virtues through the influence of the cult of courtly love. It denoted not only ordinary politeness but the desire and ability to please the ladies. William could sing. He may even have become the true knight of Margaret of France. In the tourney at Joigni the eyes of fair ladies roused him to a particular display of prowess in battle and generosity to the vanquished.[71] If, as Bédier suggests, William Marshal was the Count William to whom Marie de France dedicated her fables, he must have been noted as a devotee of courtly love and romantic literature.[72]

Although a number of hardy warriors such as Richard Plantagenet and Savaric de Mauleon were so deeply influenced by courtly love that they took to the composition of poetry, there is no evidence that the softer side of chivalry affected William to any such extent. His primary interest lay in fighting for renown and profit. Thanks to his enthusiasm for warlike sports, one can obtain from the *History* a fairly clear idea of the twelfth century tournament. Some two weeks before the appointed day messengers would ride through the countryside to announce the time and place of the contest and sometimes at least the composition of the two parties. In the case of William's first tourney it was proclaimed that the knights of Anjou, Maine, Poitou, and Brittany would contend against those of England, Normandy, and France.[73] The nature of the contests varied. There were carefully prearranged affairs where even the ransoms were fixed by the rules, but these were scorned by true knights. As a rule a tournament was a regular pitched battle fought for amusement and gain. One entered when one pleased with all the knights one could muster. The victors harried the defeated over the countryside in the hope

---

[70] *Ibid.*, 5067-5072; 3557-3562.
[71] *Ibid.*, 3538-3562.
[72] Joseph Bédier and Paul Hazard, *Histoire de la littérature française*, I, 23.
[73] *Hist.*, 1208-1212.

of capturing as many of them as possible. In at least one combat Philip of Flanders used serjeants as well as knights, and on another occasion three hundred infantry were used to cover the retreat of the vanquished.[74] Only the provision of refuges where the knights could arm and repair injuries to their harness and the fact that prisoners could give their parole instead of remaining in custody differentiated these combats from ordinary battles. A great tournament might last several days. On the eve of the general engagement the young knights had an opportunity to show their skill without the competition of the more experienced warriors. After the combat the knights of both parties gathered together to discuss the events of the day and to settle the ransoms of those who had been captured. Later in the evening the knights would visit one another in their lodgings. Apparently the ladies and their romancers had not yet had their way with the tournament. In the romances the ladies are enthusiastic spectators of the combats, present the prize to the best knight, and crown the day with dancing and such feminine festivities.[75] Only in the case of the tourney at Joigni does the *History* mention the presence of ladies. Their complete conquest of this knightly sport was still in the future. William and other pure lovers of battle were still in control of the cult of chivalry.

Although William's enthusiastic and successful pursuit of renown had won him the esteem of the patrons of chivalry, it had not brought him wealth. The death of Prince Henry left him dependent on his small Flemish fief and what extra income he could gain from his prowess in the tourney. He had still to obtain the " temporal possessions, riches, and heritages " so strongly emphasized in the advice of Philip de Navarre. He was a paragon of knightly virtue, but the richest temporal rewards in western Europe were in the bestowal of two highly practical monarchs who had no great enthusiasm for knights-errant—Henry II and Philip Augustus. Fortunately in the process of earning chivalric fame William had displayed quali-

---

[74] *Ibid.*, 3247; 2829-2830.   [75] Gautier, *La Chevalèrie*, p. 701.

ties that were valued by feudal sovereigns. He was noted for his loyalty, for his general reliability. He told the truth and fulfilled his obligations. In an age when the very cohesion of society depended on the feudal oath, loyalty was a virtue highly prized by princes. Then the same prowess which had brought him success in his tourneys could be turned to more practical use in actual warfare. In his game with fortune William held three aces—his ability as a fighter, his reputation for trustworthiness, and the affection felt by Henry II for the chosen companion of his dead son.

CHAPTER IV

" FAMILIARIS REGIS "

On his return from the Holy Land in the spring of 1187 William found the king at Lyons-la-forêt.[1] Henry welcomed him cordially and took him into his mesnie. But the king did more than furnish employment to his son's companion-in-arms—he established him in the feudal hierarchy by giving him as a fief the land of Cartmel in Lancashire.[2] He also entrusted to him the custody of the person and lands of Helwis, daughter and heiress of William de Lancaster.[3] If he chose to marry the lady, William could obtain permanent possession of her fief. In the meantime as custodian he enjoyed its revenues. These combined with the thirty-two pounds a year which Cartmel yielded would enable him to support himself and his followers from his own resources. William's days of irresponsible knight-errantry were over. He held a fief for which he owed service, and he had at least the opportunity to marry and beget heirs. Still more sobering were his responsibilities as a member of King Henry's household. He was a *familiaris regis* whose duty was to serve as counselor, captain, and ambassador.[4] In this capacity he was to play an active part in the events of the last years of King Henry's reign.

The political history of France and England during the years 1187-1189 is a bewildering maze of raids, sieges, battles, conferences, and truces. Except for a brief respite when they both took the cross, the two kings continued the endless series of quarrels which had become traditional in the relations between the Capetian kings and the Norman dukes. Between the camps of the rival monarchs, now in one, now in the other, flitted the elusive figure of Richard Plantagenet, count of Poitou and heir

[1] *Hist.,* 7302.
[2] Pipe Roll 34 Henry II, *Pipe Roll Society,* XXXVIII, 50.
[3] *Hist.,* 7304-7318. [4] Benedict of Peterborough, II, 46.

to the Angevin lands. Richard's position was not an easy one. Since 1168 he had been affianced to Alis of France, a sister of Philip Augustus. While he had no desire to marry this princess, he was most anxious to retain her dowry, the great fortress of Gisors. His natural inclination was to continue to postpone the marriage—a policy which was thoroughly satisfactory to his father. As long as his heir failed to wed Alis, he was bound to be on bad terms with her brother, Philip. In the meantime Gisors was in Henry's custody. If there had been no other factor in the situation, Richard and his father could have co-operated effectively against the French king. But Henry was obsessed by his desire to provide for his youngest son, John. He had never loved nor trusted Richard and after the young king's death he lavished all his affection on John. Some years before he had made him lord of Ireland. He now wished to give him the duchy of Aquitaine which Richard considered as peculiarly his own. There were rumors that Henry even planned to have John supplant Richard as the heir to all his domains. Whatever his purpose may have been, Henry steadfastly refused to have his vassals swear fidelity to Richard as his heir. In the hope of saving his inheritance the count of Poitou sought the support of his father's suzerain, Philip Augustus. Considering this situation one can easily understand Richard's rapid changing of allegiance. When he felt particularly disinclined to marry Alis, and his father had temporarily lulled his suspicions of John, Richard was in the English camp. When his fear of disinheritance was uppermost, he went over to Philip. As Louis VII had roused the young king against his father, so Philip stirred up Richard's resentment against the favor shown to John. As a result Henry's last years were filled with continual turmoil.[5] Through his devotion to this harassed monarch William was to win his way to fortune.

Late in January 1188 Henry and Philip, moved by the elo-

[5] For a complete account of this period see Norgate, *Richard the Lion Heart*, pp. 57-90.

quent pleas of the archbishop of Tyre, laid aside their differences and agreed to combine their forces to rescue the Holy
Sepulchre from the victorious Saladin.[6] Henry immediately
crossed to England to make his preparations.[7] William accompanied him and took advantage of the occasion to see to his
own affairs.[8] He took formal possession of Cartmel and collected the year and three quarters revenue that was due him.[9]
He also engaged a new attendant, John d'Erley, who as squire
and knight was to serve him loyally all his life. In fact John's
services did not end with his master's death. By supplying the
material for the *History*, he passed his lord's name and deeds
on to posterity.

Soon after Henry left the continent, Richard plunged into
a quarrel with Count Raymond of Toulouse. The latter appealed to his suzerain for aid, and by the middle of June Richard and Philip were at war. Henry promptly raised a force of
Welsh mercenaries and crossed to Normandy early in July.
The French king replied by sending the bishop of Beauvais to
raid the Norman marches while he himself invaded Maine.
King Henry hesitated to attack his suzerain and brother crusader no more than six months after they had sworn eternal
amity in God's service. He therefore sent the archbishop of
Rouen, the bishop of Evreux, and William Marshal to find
Philip and demand that he make restitution for the damage
done to the Angevin lands. Philip cheerfully informed the
ambassadors that he meant to continue the war until he had
conquered Berry and the Norman Vexin. Henry's legates then
presented their master's formal defiance, and the war was on
once more.[10]

By the middle of August the two kings had concentrated

---

[6] Benedict of Peterborough, II, 29-30.

[7] *Ibid.*, pp. 32-3.

[8] *Calendar of Charter Rolls 1327-41*, p. 337. *Récueil des Actes de Henri II*,
II, 287.

[9] Pipe Roll 34 Henry II, *Pipe Roll Society*, XXXVIII, 50.

[10] Benedict of Peterborough, II, 34-46.

their forces in the Vexin.[11] After a futile parley on the Norman frontier near Trie-Chateau, Henry occupied Gisors while Philip retired to Chaumont-en-Vexin. The next morning the French king advanced to Gisors. He drew up his army in battle array on the eastern bank of the river Epte while the English issued from the town and faced their enemies across the stream. King Philip was in a merry mood. He sent two members of his household to suggest to Henry that the questions at issue between them be settled by a combat of four champions from each side. The counts of Flanders, Clermont, and Dreux, and Dreux de Mello, all good knights, would fight William fitz Ralph, the seneschal of Normandy, William de la Mare, Richard de Villequier, and Richard d'Argences. As William fitz Ralph was too old for battle and the other three notoriously incapable, no one could doubt Philip's humorous intent. Henry was annoyed at his suzerain's mockery, but he solemnly agreed to seek the advice of his barons. William Marshal pointed out that the contest should be held in a neutral court—that of the Emperor or of the king of Navarre. Then of course Henry had the right to choose his own champions. William thought that he himself, Earl William de Mandeville, John de Fresnai, and Osbert de Rouvrai would make an excellent team. When the fiery Count Richard of Poitou protested at being omitted from the list, William pointed out that it would never do to risk the heir to the throne in such an affray. In short William advised his master to ignore Philip's joke and to suggest a serious combat. Henry was delighted with this solution and ordered William and Earl William de Mandeville to carry the proposition to Philip. At the river they were met by the counts of Flanders, Dreux, and Blois. Count Philip assured William that he had no intention of fighting him—that would be too serious a matter—but he readily agreed to carry the ambassadors' message to the king. Philip, of course, angrily rejected the offer. His original suggestion was a joke, and it had gone far enough.

[11] *Hist.*, 7368-7372. Benedict of Peterborough, II, 47. Ralph de Diceto, II, 55.

The French king then ordered Robert of Dreux to drive back a party of English who had crossed the stream. This resulted in an indecisive skirmish during which the French infantry chopped to pieces a great elm. By this time Philip's martial ardor was satisfied. He retired across the frontier and disbanded a large part of his army.[12]

When William learned of the French king's action, he saw a chance for a really profitable raid. He advised Henry to disband his army, but issue secret orders to have it reassemble at Paci-sur-Epte a few days later. This plan was carried out, and on August 30th the English swept over the border and ravaged the country as far as the walls of Mantes. As he had plundered and burned fifteen villages and acquired a large amount of booty, Henry was well pleased with his raid. William Marshal was a sound counsellor.[13]

Throughout the summer and early autumn the war went on in a desultory way. The French barons hesitated to support their master in his contest with a fellow crusader, and Philip himself saw his best course in negotiating with Richard. So successful was he that by November the count of Poitou was ready to marry Alis to obtain Philip's assistance in assuring his succession to the Angevin lands. On the 18th of that month a conference was held at Bonmoulins near Mortain.[14] Richard and Philip, who arrived together, had already come to an agreement. They demanded that Henry surrender to his son his fiancée Alis and formally recognize him as his heir. When Henry demurred, Richard was convinced that his suspicions were well founded. Turning to Philip he did homage to him for all the continental fiefs of the Angevin house. Then after agreeing to a truce until the following January, the three princes separated.[15]

Henry was deeply troubled by his son's behavior. Although

[12] *Hist.*, 7429-7781. Guillaume le Breton, *Philippidos* (ed. H. F. Delaborde, *Société de l'Histoire de France*), pp. 69-72.

[13] *Hist.*, 7782-7852. Benedict of Peterborough, II, 46, *Philippidos*, pp. 76-7.

[14] Benedict of Peterborough, II, 50.   [15] *Ibid.*

in doing homage to Philip Richard had reserved the faith he
owed his father, the king feared that the hot-headed prince
planned open rebellion. He asked counsel of his entourage
as to what course he should pursue. William advised him to
send someone to persuade Richard to return and explain his
actions. Henry accepted this suggestion and dispatched William and Bertram de Verdun to bring back his son. Riding
south along the route taken by Richard, they arrived at Amboise where he had passed the night. There they learned that
Richard had left for Aquitaine. During the night he had sent
out over two hundred letters summoning his supporters to his
standard. William and his companion realized that their mission was hopeless and returned to Henry to warn him of his
son's rebellion.[16]

King Henry and his court passed the winter and spring in
Anjou and Maine. In March at Le Mans Henry had the first
serious attack of the disease that was soon to cause his death.[17]
Ill, deserted by his eldest son and many of his barons, the king
grew fonder of those who had remained faithful to him. William in particular received proof of his favor. Henry promised
him the second richest heiress in England, Isabel, daughter of
Richard fitz Gilbert de Clare, earl of Pembroke.[18] This eighteen
year old girl was the heiress to extensive fiefs including the
lordship of Striguil in the Wye valley, the county of Pembroke
in West Wales, and Leinster in Ireland. By marrying her
William would become one of the most powerful barons of
England. Having provided William with a richer prize, Henry
gave the heiress of Lancaster to Gilbert fitz Roger fitz Renfrew,
another of the little group who were with him at Le Mans.[19]
A comparison of the importance of these two heiresses shows
how decidedly William had risen in King Henry's esteem. The
fief of Helwis de Lancaster consisted of a single knight's fee

[16] *Hist.*, 8202-8266.
[17] Giraldus Cambrensis, *Opera (Rolls Series)*, VIII, 259.
[18] *Hist.*, 8303-8305.
[19] *Early Lancashire Charters* (ed. William Farrer), p. 395.

which was held of the king not *in capite* but of the honor of Lancaster.[20] Isabel de Clare owed the service of sixty-five and one-half knights for her English fiefs alone without counting her extensive possessions in Wales and Ireland.[21] In the spring of 1187 Henry had planned to make William a minor tenant of the honor of Lancaster—two years later he was willing to place him in the front rank of the English baronage.

At the conference of Bonmoulins the three princes had agreed to meet again on January 13th, but Henry's illness postponed this parley. Towards the end of March Philip and Richard grew so impatient of this delay that they launched a raid into his lands.[22] Henry decided to try to separate his two opponents. William Marshal and Ralph, archdeacon of Hereford, were sent to persuade Philip to make peace at the expense of Richard, but they were outmanoeuvred by the latter's agent, the wily William de Longchamp, and forced to return to Henry empty-handed.[23] The rest of the spring was occupied by a series of fruitless conferences on the frontier of Maine. After the failure of the final meeting which was held at La Ferté-Bernard in early June, both sides prepared for war.[24] While Henry massed his forces in Le Mans, Philip and Richard set about reducing the castles to the north east of that city.[25] Considering the speed with which these fortresses were captured, one is inclined to suspect that their constables had already been won over to Richard.

On June 10th Philip and Richard were at Montfort-le-Rotrou about fifteen miles to the east of Le Mans.[26] In the hope of taking Henry by surprise they decided not to march directly on Le Mans but to divert his attention by crossing the river Huisne and making a feint towards Tours.[27] That evening King Henry

[20] *Red Book of the Exchequer*, pp. 444, 568.
[21] *Ibid.*, p. 288.
[22] Benedict of Peterborough, II, 61.
[23] *Hist.*, 8311-8334.
[24] See Norgate, *Richard the Lion Heart*, pp. 85-87.
[25] Benedict of Peterborough, II, 67. Ralph de Diceto, II, 62-3. *Hist.*, 8362-8380.   [26] *Ibid.*, 8377-8380.   [27] Benedict of Peterborough, II, 67.

learned that his enemies were headed toward the south. As he suspected this movement to be a strategem, he decided to send out scouts to reconnoitre.[28] Early next morning William Marshal and four other knights crossed the Huisne and rode south in search of the allied army. They soon met a part of the enemy riding north towards Le Mans. As William and his companions had discarded their hauberks in order to move more quickly, they were forced to retire hastily. One of the knights wished to return at once to warn Henry of the enemy's advance, but William insisted on ascertaining the whereabouts of the main body of the hostile army. Turning to one side to avoid the advance-guard, they rode up a small hill from which they could obtain a view of the surrounding country. From there they saw, spread out before them within crossbow range, the entire host of the king of France and the count of Poitou. Then at last William was satisfied and turned back towards Le Mans. As they were passing the hostile vedettes, one of the knights suggested that they charge them to see if they could capture some horses, but William refused to consent. Their duty was to carry their information to their master with the least possible delay.[29] For once more serious considerations turned William from a gallant adventure. The knight-errant was becoming a captain.

When King Henry learned of the approach of the enemy, he destroyed the bridge over the Huisne and drove stakes into the fords to make them impassable. The hostile army soon appeared and pitched camp on the south bank within bow shot of the river. The English, who believed that they had effectively blocked the passages over the stream, retired within the walls of Le Mans. That night King Henry and his barons held a council of war. They decided that if the enemy should succeed in crossing the river, they would set fire to the suburbs to the south of the town to impede their advance. Early the next morning Henry summoned a number of knights to join him in a reconnoitring expedition. William appeared fully

[28] *Hist.*, 8381-8395.   [29] *Ibid.*, 8396-8478.

equipped for battle at the rendezvous near the south gate of the town. As this precaution annoyed Henry who had neglected to put on his armor, he ordered William and the other knights of the party to disarm. William protested. His armor did not bother him, and he wished to be prepared for any emergency that might arise. The king did not insist, but he refused to take him on the scouting expedition. While Henry and his companions advanced toward the river to view the enemy's camp, William stayed by the gate.

When the king and his party reached a point from which they could see the river, they noticed that a troop of French knights were sounding with their lances at the site of the bridge which had been destroyed the day before. To the great surprise of the English, who had never suspected that there was a ford under the bridge, they found the water shallow and easily rode across. King Henry and his unarmed knights were forced to retire in haste. Pressing close on the heels of the king's party, the enemy approached the gate where William stood. He took his helmet from his squire, John d'Erley, and prepared to hold the gate. Soon Baldwin de Bethune, Renaut de Dammartin, and a half dozen other knights came to his assistance. There followed one of those delightful little mêlées in which all true knights delighted—a miniature tournament fought on the ground in front of the gate. William succeeded in capturing André de Chauvigni, one of Count Richard's favorite knights, but as he was leading him through the gate a volley of stones was thrown upon them from the top of the wall. One broke André's arm while another hit his horse and frightened the animal so much that it broke away and carried its injured master to safety. William captured three more knights, but two of them escaped by detaching the reins from their horses' bridles as John d'Erley was leading them through the gate. So absorbed did William become in this pleasant combat that he completely forgot the plan to set fire to the suburb. As he was leading his last prisoner through the gate, he met King Henry who pointedly reminded him of his omission. William exchanged his horse, which had hurt its foot on a piece of broken lance, for that of the captured knight and followed his master into the suburb to carry out their plan.[30]

Unfortunately the fire could not be confined to the suburb. No sooner had the king and his men entered the city than they found it in flames. When all attempts to check the conflagration proved ineffectual, Henry decided to evacuate Le Mans and retire toward Fresnai. The French wasted no time in taking advantage of their enemy's retreat. Count Richard of Poitou was so eager for the pursuit that he neglected to don his hauberk and led the chase wearing no other armor than an iron cap. Thus lightly equipped, Richard and his knights soon caught up with the English rear-guard. Two knights of Henry's household, William des Roches and William Marshal, promptly turned back to cover their master's retreat. While his companion broke a lance with Philip de Colombières, William rode at Count Richard. "By the legs of God, Marshal, do not kill me," cried the count, "that would not be right for I am unarmed." "No, let the devil kill you for I shall not," replied William as he deftly shifted his aim and ran his lance through Richard's horse. The count's followers soon raised him to his feet, but his enthusiasm for the pursuit was thoroughly quenched.[31]

That night Henry rested at Fresnai, a castle belonging to the viscount of Beaumont, but most of his army went on to Alençon. The next morning the king ordered William to go to Alençon to take command of the Norman barons who were mustering there while he himself, accompanied by his illegitimate son Geoffrey, turned south toward Anjou. A few days later Henry reached his fortress of Chinon. There he learned that Philip and Richard had occupied Tours. Henry realized that he was beaten. Racked by illness and deserted by many of his vassals, he could not hope to hold his own against his enemies. His only course was to make the best peace he could. But he needed the counsel of the one man in whom he felt complete confidence. A letter was despatched to Alençon summoning William to Chinon. He was ordered to take with him only the knights of his mesnie and to leave the rest of the army to cover the Norman frontier.[32]

Soon after William's arrival at Chinon King Philip proposed a conference between Tours and Azay-le-Rideau. Henry agreed on the advice of his barons. On July 4 the king set out from Chinon to meet his victorious enemy and rebellious son. When he reached the commandery of the Templars at Ballan, he was so exhausted from the pain of his disease that he had to go to bed. The rest revived him sufficiently so that William was able to get him to the scene of the conference. Philip was so moved by the obvious suffering of his old enemy that he called for a cape and asked Henry to sit down on it, but the latter refused. He had come to learn what he must pay for peace.[33] The terms offered him were extremely humiliating. He must surrender his continental lands to Philip who would then re-grant them to him in return for his homage. Philip was to receive an indemnity of twenty thousand marks. Richard was to marry Alis and receive the homage as his father's heir of all the barons of England and the continental fiefs of the Planta-genet house. Henry's barons were to swear to support Richard and Philip against him if he violated this treaty. As an added guarantee the allies were to hold certain castles until the terms were completely carried out.[34] Trembling with rage and illness, Henry accepted these harsh terms, gave Richard the kiss of peace, and returned to Chinon to nurse his plans for future revenge. Two days later he died.

To few monarchs has fate vouchsafed a less dignified end. Only one of his sons, the bastard Geoffrey, was at his side dur-ing his last days.[35] William Marshal, Gilbert Pipard, Gilbert fitz Renfrew and a few other loyal knights were the sole vassals of the English crown who stood by their dying master. Even they were absent at the last moment. Henry Planta-

[32] Ibid., 8877-8920.
[33] Ibid., 8935-9028.
[34] Benedict of Peterborough, II, 70.
[35] Giraldus Cambrensis, Opera, IV, 370.

genet died surrounded by servants who pillaged his chamber and even removed the clothing from his stiffening corpse.[36] Only when the news of the king's death had spread through the town did William and his fellow knights arrive to take charge of his body. That night they watched the bier, and the next morning the barons of Anjou and Touraine began to arrive at Chinon. The poor of the countryside gathered by the bridge over the Vienne to await the almsgiving which always accompanied a prince's death. But the knights of the household had no money to give. William sought out Stephen de Marcai, the seneschal of Anjou, who had custody of the Angevin treasury, and asked him to give the usual alms. Stephen replied that the treasury was empty. William then suggested that the seneschal must have money of his own which he could use for so pious a purpose, but Stephen pleaded complete poverty. The most powerful monarch of the century was dead, . . . and the poor howled in vain for the customary disbursements. Finally the barons dressed their master's body in his robes of state and bore it to the abbey of Fontrevault. There the abbess and her nuns received the corpse of their benefactor and watched over it throughout the night in the great abbey church.[37]

While King Henry's body lay in state, the barons who had attended the corpse from Chinon discussed their prospects. As all these men had supported Henry against his rebellious son, they had grave doubts as to how Richard would receive them. All agreed that William, who had slain Richard's horse at Le Mans, had most to fear from his anger, and each one offered him aid if the new king should confiscate his property.[38] To this William replied " Lords, it is true that I slew his horse, and I do not regret it. I thank you for your offers, but I would be ashamed to take your gifts if I were not sure of being able to return them. Ever since I was made a knight, God, by his great mercy, has cared for me so well that I trust in him for the future. His wishes will prevail." [39] As a matter of fact

[36] *Ibid.*, VIII, 304. *Hist.*, 9135-9143.
[37] *Ibid.*, 9146-9244.
[38] *Ibid.*, 9253-9276.
[39] *Ibid.*, 9276-9290.

William was at the crisis of his career. Because of his long and faithful service to Henry II and his eldest son he had been given the lady of Lancaster. Her he had given up for the greater prize, Isabel de Clare, but he was not in possession of the lady. If Richard proved his enemy, he would once again be an almost landless knight. The old king had promised him one of the richest heiresses in England—would the new one fulfil the pledge?

While the barons were conversing, Count Richard of Poitou arrived at Fontrevault. Leaping from his horse, he entered the church and stopped by his father's bier. Without showing the slightest sign of emotion he stood for a long time at the head of the corpse deep in thought. At last he called for William Marshal and Maurice de Craon. When they had joined him, he said, " Montez, let us go outside." Once on the open ground outside the abbey church, he turned to William, " Marshal, good sir, the other day you wished to kill me, and you would have done it if I had not turned your lance aside with my arm." To this William replied, " Sire, I had no intention of killing you nor have I ever tried to do so. I am still strong enough to direct my lance. If I had wished, I could have struck your body as I did your horse. If I had slain you, I would not consider it a crime, and I still do not regret having slain your horse." " Marshal, I pardon you, and I will bear you no rancor." [40] In his frank and outspoken answer William without doubt was relying on his knowledge of Richard's character. The idea of honoring a man who had aided his father against him and actually slain his horse in battle appealed to his somewhat quixotic nature. Besides, a king needed trustworthy servants, and who could be more reliable than those who had stood by Henry II in his misfortune. The combination of wisdom and chivalry in Richard boded well for William Marshal. Finally William was one of the most noted knights of the age, and Richard, the troubadour and lover of tourneys, must have admired him as a kindred spirit.

[40] *Ibid.*, 9291-9341.

As an immediate sign of his favor Richard informed William that he and Gilbert Pipard were to go to England in his service as soon as Henry's funeral rites had been performed.[41] By that time the old king's chancellor, Geoffrey, had joined the group.[42] He reminded his half brother that their father had given William the heiress of Striguil.[43] " By the legs of God," said Richard, " he did not give her to him—he merely promised to. But I will give him freely both the lady and her lands."[44] The crisis was past. William had won the favor of the new king, and his future was secure. Probably at this time William suggested that he be given half the lands once held by the Earls Giffard in consideration of a suitable contribution to the royal exchequer. The last Earl Giffard had died in 1164, and his lands in England and Normandy had remained in the king's hands ever since.[45] Isabel de Clare and her cousin, Richard de Clare, earl of Hertford, had a claim to these fiefs as descendants of a sister of an earlier Earl Giffard.[46] In his journeys about Normandy William may well have cast envious eyes on the castle and fair fields of Longueville, the Norman seat of the house of Giffard. He could surely draw enough money from his wife's broad domains to pay a fine for his share of the Giffard inheritance. As for Richard, he was planning a crusade and had no intention of missing an opportunity to acquire ready money. An agreement was reached under which William was to pay a fine of two thousand marks for one-half of the honor of Giffard.[47]

The next day they buried Henry Plantagenet in the church of Fontrevault. As soon as the ceremony was over, William and Gilbert Pipard set out on their mission to England. The

[41] *Ibid.*, 9347-9354.

[42] Geoffrey was an illegitimate son of Henry II, and his chancellor.

[43] *Hist.*, 9361-9366.   [44] *Hist.*, 9367-9371.

[45] Pipe Rolls 14-34 Henry II under Buckinghamshire, *Pipe Roll Society*, XII-XXXVIII. *Magni Rotuli Scaccarii Normanniae sub regibus Anglie* (ed. Thomas Stapleton, *Society of Antiquaries of London*), I, 59.

[46] See *ibid.*, II, cxxxvii for genealogy of Clare family.

[47] Pipe Roll 2 Richard I, *Pipe Roll Society*, XXXIX, 144.

exact nature of their commission is far from clear. According
to the *History,* they were to take over the control of the kingdom and administer it until Richard arrived.[48] On the other
hand Ralph de Diceto and Benedict of Peterborough state that
Richard gave his mother, Queen Eleanor, full power in England.[49] The probable explanation is that William bore Richard's order releasing Eleanor from Winchester castle where she
had been in confinement for some years and giving her the
control of the realm. This is borne out by the fact that on his
arrival in England William went to Winchester, saw the queen,
and then went about his own affairs—a course of action hardly
to be expected of one to whom the care of the kingdom had
been entrusted. Leaving Fontrevault shortly after the funeral,
William and Gilbert slept that night at Mouliherne, near Baugé
in Anjou, and then hastened by forced marches across Maine
and Normandy to the Pays de Caux. There William stopped
long enough to seize his share of the Norman lands of the
honor of Giffard. After passing a night at St. Vaast-d'Equique-
ville, they moved on to Dieppe to take ship for England.
Their embarkation was marred by a serious accident. So great
was the haste of their retainers to get aboard that they over-
crowded the gangplank so that it gave way. As Gilbert Pipard
broke his arm in this affair, William was forced to proceed without him.[50]

When William reached Winchester, he found Queen Eleanor
already at liberty. After giving her Richard's letters, William
turned to his own affairs.[51] The Welsh lands of his future wife
were in an extremely hazardous position. Encouraged by the
death of Henry II, Rees ap Griffith, prince of South Wales, had
invaded the English lands in Pembrokeshire.[52] Sixteen knights
and twenty-five mounted serjeants were despatched to its defence by the sheriff of Devonshire, and the sheriff of Gloucester-

[48] *Hist.,* 9347-9354.
[49] Benedict of Peterborough, II, 74.   Ralph de Diceto, II, 67.
[50] *Hist.,* 9439-9502.
[51] *Ibid.,* 9507-9512.   [52] Giraldus Cambrensis, *Opera,* VI, 80.

shire furnished thirty pounds for the same purpose on the authority of a writ of Ranulf de Glanville issued by order of Queen Eleanor.[53] In all probability before he left Winchester, William arranged with the queen for the succor of the lands he was about to acquire by marriage. These measures of defence against Rees were a mere stop-gap pending Richard's arrival in England. In early October the whole feudal array of England was called out for a punitive expedition against the Welsh prince under the command of Count John of Mortain.[54] Here at the very start of his career as a marcher lord William was given a sample of the troubles he was to encounter all his life.

From Winchester William proceeded to London to take possession of Lady Isabel who was in the custody of the justiciar, Ranulf de Glanville.[55] One would like to know what this young girl of some nineteen years of age thought as she sat in the justiciar's gloomy stronghold, the Tower of London, awaiting the husband whom the king would choose for her. She probably knew from Glanville's clerk, Hubert Walter, that Henry II had promised her to William Marshal.[56] Would it be too much to suppose that she was pleased at the prospect of marrying the foremost knight of the age even though he were over twenty years her senior? Unfortunately nothing is known of the lady's opinions—she was there, and William took possession of her. As he had no lands nor money, he intended to take her into her own domains and there wed her in fitting state, but his host in London, Richard fitz Renier, one of the sheriffs of the town, refused to permit it. When William pointed out that he could not pay for a wedding in London, Richard replied that he would arrange that.[57] Thus in London with due pomp and ceremony William married the heiress of Striguil—Isabel, " the good, the fair, the wise, the courteous lady of high degree." After the wedding he took her to the home of Enger-

---

[53] Pipe Roll 1 Richard I (ed. Joseph Hunter, *Record Commission*), pp. 130, 163.
[54] Benedict of Peterborough, II, 87-8. [56] *Ibid.*, 8303-8310.
[55] *Hist.*, 9515-6. [57] *Ibid.*, 9519-9536.

rand d'Abernon at Stokes d'Abernon in Surrey. This place, both quiet and pleasant, was well suited for a honeymoon.[58]

One may well doubt whether even in this fair retreat the charms of Isabel herself could long divert William's thoughts from her rich heritage. Its nucleus, the honor of Striguil, consisted of some three score knights' fees scattered through nine shires and the demesne manors of Weston in Hertfordshire, Chesterford in Essex, and Badgworth in Gloucestershire.[59] This represented the Domesday holding of William d'Eu.[60] Attached to the honor was the marcher lordship of Striguil which comprised some hundred square miles lying between the Wye and the Usk. The chief seat of this great barony was the castle of Striguil which still stands on the west bank of the river Wye near the town of Chepstow. The honor of Striguil had not been the sole fief of Earl Richard fitz Gilbert. At the south-westernmost extremity of Wales his county of Pembroke occupied the lowlands between the western arm of Carmarthen bay and St. Bride's bay, and its lords had certain claims in the highlands which stretched to the north toward the river Teife.[61] Directly across from Pembroke lay the southern part of the lordship of Leinster in Ireland. Comprising the present counties of Kildare, Carlow, Kilkenny, Wexford, Queens, and about a third of Kings, this slightly developed country of great potentialities was probably the most valuable part of Isabel's inheritance.[62] These extensive lands in the marches, in Wales, and in Ireland were palatinates in which the lord had complete authority. As

[58] *Ibid.*, 9537-9550.

[59] Pipe Rolls 31-34 Henry II under Striguil, and *Rotuli de dominibus, pueris, et puellis, Pipe Roll Society*, XXXV, 66, 76. In 1187 the honor paid scutage on 65½ fees *preter Walenses* (Pipe Roll 33 Henry II, *Pipe Roll Society*, XXXVII, 142). The meaning of *preter Walenses* seems to be indicated by an entry on the same page under the honor of Gloucester *et in perdonis per breve regis baronibus eiusdem honoris fiffatis in Wallia.*

[60] William d'Eu forfeited his lands in 1096. His barony passed eventually to the de Clares.

[61] For instance they claimed Kilgerran (*Annales Cambriae*, ed. John Williams ab Ithel, *Rolls Series*, p. 63) and Emlyn (*Rot. Chart.*, p. 47).

[62] See G. H. Orpen, *Ireland under the Normans*, I, 258-9, 326.

lords marchers the possessors of Striguil and Pembroke appointed their own officials and enjoyed the proceeds of government.[63] No royal justice or sheriff was at hand to curb their power, and except in ecclesiastical cases, the king's writ did not run in their lands. In short they enjoyed all the privileges of a continental baron—they were kings in their own domains. To the English crown they owed homage, fealty, and military service. As for Leinster it had been specifically granted to Earl Richard on these terms.[64] Henry II gave him all the rights he himself had in the region in return for his homage and the service of one hundred knights. The possession of these lands made William the dominant figure in south Wales and in Ireland. Their extent was great, their location was of extreme strategic value, and his authority in them was absolute. Such was the inheritance of the Lady Isabel.

In addition to the lands which had been held by Richard de Clare William obtained by his marriage the opportunity to offer the king two thousand marks for one-half of the honor of Giffard. By this arrangement he acquired the demesne manors of Crendon in Buckinghamshire and Caversham in Oxfordshire and the homage and service of forty-three knights.[65] His share of the Norman possessions of the house of Giffard comprised half the barony of Longueville with the castles of Longueville and Meullers and the service of forty or fifty knights.[66] For this fief he owed five knights to the duke's army.

The father and grandfather of Isabel de Clare had been earls. In the year 1138 King Stephen had bestowed the title of earl of Pembroke on Gilbert fitz Gilbert de Clare.[67] At about the same time Gilbert had inherited the honor of Striguil from his

[63] There is little contemporary evidence on this point except that like the palatinates of Chester and Durham, Striguil and Pembroke never appeared in the records of the English government.

[64] See below Chapter VIII.

[65] For the Marshal share of the honor of Giffard see Inquisition of 1242-3, *Book of Fees (Rolls Series)*, pp. 637-1138.

[66] *Red Book of the Exchequer*, p. 633. Teulet, *Layettes du Trésor des Chartes*, I, no. 715.   [67] Ordericus Vitalis, V, 112.

uncle, Walter.[68] His son and successor, Richard fitz Gilbert, was usually styled earl of Striguil, though in his own charters he used his father's title of earl of Pembroke.[69] This variation was a mere matter of usage with no real significance. The head of the elder branch of the De Clare family was called earl of Clare or earl of Hertford interchangeably. The important point was not the actual title, but the fact that the holder enjoyed the dignity of an earl. Although by his marriage with Isabel William obtained all the possessions of Earl Richard, he could not become an earl unless the king created him one. This honor was not accorded to him until 1199. In the meantime he was often called earl of Striguil as a courtesy, but officially he was simply William Marshal, and he so designated himself in his own charters.[70]

On August 13th the arrival in England of Richard and his brother John brought William's honeymoon to an end.[71] He had several matters to settle with the younger prince. As Richard had granted his brother the honor of Lancaster to which Cartmel belonged, William was forced to become John's vassal for that fief.[72] By a charter issued about this time John granted Cartmel to William for the service of one knight.[73] But there was a far more important matter at issue between them. As lord of Ireland John had in his custody the lordship of Leinster which belonged to Isabel's inheritance. He had treated it as if it were his own rather than a fief held in trust for the heiress of Richard de Clare and had made generous grants in it to his own men. John was extremely loath to surrender Leinster, and William was forced to ask Richard to intercede for him. At his brother's demand John agreed to give it to William on condition that his men could keep the fiefs

---

[68] For the genealogy of the Clare family see Round, *Feudal England*, pp. 472-3.

[69] *Calendar of Charter Rolls*, II, 72; III, 96.

[70] For courtesy title see Benedict of Peterborough, II, 80. For official see Ralph de Diceto, II, 90.

[71] Benedict of Peterborough, II, 75.

[72] *Ibid.*, p. 78.   [73] Farrer, *Lancashire Charters*, pp. 343-4.

he had given them. Since John had divided among his men all the land which earl Richard had not previously enfeoffed, this arrangement would leave William nothing more than the bare overlordship. At Richard's insistence John finally reduced his demands to the stipulation that his butler, Theobald Walter, should retain his fief. This Richard agreed to on condition that Theobald should hold it as William's vassal.[74] To John, as lord of Ireland, William did homage for the whole lordship of Leinster.[75]

God, who had cared for William when he was a landless knight, had made him a rich baron—surely the least that he could do was to found a monastery to His glory. At the same time he could show his gratitude to his patrons, Henry II, Henry the young king, and King Richard, by dedicating his foundation to the salvation of their souls. Finally he could gain the Divine favor for himself, his wife, and the sons and daughters whom she would bear him. He decided to make use of Cartmel, the only land he held in his own right, to endow a priory of regular canons. Soon after John had confirmed him in the possession of Cartmel, William obtained his permission to found an ecclesiastical establishment on it.[76] He then took a group of canons from the priory of Bradenstoke in Wiltshire, a house greatly favored by his ancestors, and gave them Cartmel. This new house was to remain a priory, but it was never to be subject to any other establishment. William had no desire to see his authority over his foundation disputed by some great monastic order. When a prior died, the canons were to select two candidates from whom William or his successor would choose the new prior.[77] By this act of piety William demonstrated his appreciation of God's favor to him and did what he could to secure its continuance in the future.

William Marshal, lord of Longueville, of Striguil, of Pembroke, and of Leinster was far removed from that youth, the fourth son of a minor baron, who had left England for the

---

[74] *Hist.*, 9582-9616.
[75] *Ibid.*, 10312-10340.
[76] Farrer, *Lancashire Charters*, pp. 344-5.
[77] *Ibid.*, pp. 341-2.

court of the chamberlain of Tancarville some thirty-four years before. He had completed the program laid down by Philip de Navarre. By the strength of his arm and the loyalty of his heart he had won renown and a rich heritage. In the future the storms of adversity might beat about his head, but his position was firmly based on wide domains studded with strong castles. The knight-errant had made his fortune—well might he found Cartmel to the glory of God.

CHAPTER V

ASSOCIATE JUSTICIAR

When Richard Plantagenet ascended the English throne, he wore the cross of a crusader. He had already committed himself to the pursuit of his career as knight-errant and troubadour to the detriment of his royal duties. Two months after his coronation he swore through his proxy, William Marshal, that he would meet Philip Augustus at Vézelay on April 1, 1190 prepared to start on their joint expedition against the infidel.[1] The rendezvous was later postponed to June 24th.[2] About the 27th of the month those two bright lights of English chivalry, Richard of Anjou and William Marshal, rode out of Tours on their way to Vézelay.[3] There in the rich abbey church Richard received the scrip and staff of a pilgrim, and on July 5th the two kings and their escorts set out on the first stage of their tumultuous journey to the Holy Land.

As the crusaders rode toward Lyons, William turned his face homewards. He had laid aside his youth—the knight-errant had become a baron. The whole course of William's past life suggested that he would cheerfully leave his new responsibilities, his young wife and his broad lands, to follow his sovereign in his adventurous career. Instead he turned back to England to try his hand at the unfamiliar duties of a great landholder, a sheriff, a royal justice, and a baron of the exchequer. Whether it was dictated by his own choice or by the king's command, this renunciation definitely marks a new phase in his life. Instead of falling in glorious combat against

---

[1] Roger of Hovedon, *Chronica* (ed. William Stubbs, *Rolls Series*), III, 19-20. Roger of Wendover, *Flores Historiarum* (ed. H. G. Hewlett, *Rolls Series*), I, 170.

[2] Roger of Hovedon, III, 31.

[3] *Layettes du Trésor des chartes,* no. 369. *Calendar of Charter Rolls 1300-1326,* p. 344.

the infidel or frittering the years away in profitless adventure, he was to follow the path of duty even to the regency of England.

William was returning to England to enjoy a position of considerable strength and importance. Richard had allowed him to entrench his territorial power in the west and had given him a high place in the central government of the kingdom. In the auction of public offices which had preceded the king's departure, William had bought the shrievalty of Gloucestershire with the custody of Gloucester castle and of the forest of Dean with its fortress of St. Briavells.[4] This gave him control of the roads leading from England into south Wales where lay his own fiefs of Striguil and Pembroke. The only potentate of the south marches who could rival him in power was Count John of Mortain, earl of Gloucester and lord of Glamorgan. In addition to his local authority in the west William was a member of the board of regents to whom Richard had entrusted the government of England. At the head of this body stood the king's chancellor, William de Longchamp, bishop of Ely, who wielded the double authority of justiciar of England and papal legate in England, Wales, and the part of Ireland ruled by John. To him were associated four barons noted for their devotion to the house of Anjou—William Marshal, Geoffrey fitz Peter, William Brewer, and Hugh Bardolf.[5] The associate justiciars traversed the shires of England as itinerant justices, sat in the *curia regis* at Westminster or elsewhere, and acted as barons of the exchequer. They shared these duties with other "justices of the lord king" such as Simon de Pattishal and Michael Belet. They were distinguished from the ordinary royal justices by the fact that they enjoyed to some extent the political authority which the king's absence had placed in the hands of the justiciar. The latter was apparently expected to

[4] Pipe Roll 2 Richard I, *Pipe Roll Society*, XXXIX, 58. Pipe Roll 6 Richard I, *Pipe Roll Society*, XLIII, 239.

[5] Benedict of Peterborough, II, 101, 106. Roger of Hovedon, III, 16, 28. Ralph de Diceto, II, 83, 91.

seek their advice on important questions of policy and to be guided by their counsel.[6] As Longchamp was eventually removed for ignoring his colleagues, one may surmise that during his reign the office of associate justiciar was largely an empty honor. But even though the chancellor allowed him no voice in the government's policies, as sheriff, royal justice, and baron of the exchequer William had a place in the English administration.

His influence had been extended still further by the preferments which he had obtained for his brothers. Richard had bestowed the deanship of York on Henry Marshal.[7] As the archbishop-elect, the king's illegitimate brother Geoffrey, had been neither confirmed nor consecrated, the dean was the chief ecclesiastical official of the diocese. John, the head of the Marshal family, had been appointed sheriff of Yorkshire.[8] As a further mark of his favor Richard had given him the manors of Wexcombe and Bedwin in Wiltshire and Bosham in Sussex.[9] William Marshal had not neglected to make the most of Richard's benevolence.

When he secured his dominant position in the south marches, William probably foresaw that England would not be blessed with peace and quiet during the king's absence. Richard was at best a mediocre statesman, and he had so arranged the government of his kingdom that civil war was almost inevitable. To his younger brother, Count John of Mortain, the king had given palatine authority in the counties of Nottingham, Derby, Cornwall, Devon, Dorset, and Somerset. In these shires John appointed the sheriffs, collected the revenue, and exercised all the powers of government.[10] As the husband of the heiress of Gloucester John was master of the marcher lordship of Glamorgan, and of some two hundred knights' fees scattered over England. In addition Richard had given him the honors of Lan-

[6] Ibid., p. 91. Benedict of Peterborough, II, 213-4.

[7] Ibid., pp. 85-6.

[8] Pipe Roll 2 Richard I, Pipe Roll Society, XXXIX, 58.

[9] Public Record Office C. 52, no. 21.   [10] Benedict of Peterborough, II, 78, 99.

caster, Wallingford, Tickhill, and Peverel of Nottingham with the castles of Marlborough, Ludgershall, the Peak, and Bolsover.[11] Absolute master of six counties, the prince controlled fortresses and knights' fees in the rest of England. Although John's position seriously decentralized the government, it might not have led to civil turmoil were it not for the question of the succession. Richard was childless. As the return of a crusader was at best problematical, the question as to who was the heir presumptive was of primary importance. Geoffrey Plantagenet, the third legitimate son of Henry II, had died in 1188 leaving a posthumous son, Arthur. Under the rule of representation in inheritance this boy was undoubtedly the heir to the Angevin domains, but this doctrine was not yet firmly established in 1190. In fact Norman law definitely preferred the younger brother to the son of the elder.[12] Under the circumstances Count John, the fourth son of Henry II, would have a strong claim to the throne if Richard should perish on the crusade. Before his departure the king had resolutely refused to make a declaration in favor of either John or Arthur, but in his treaty with Tancred of Sicily he mentioned the latter as his heir.[13] If Richard did not actually inform the chancellor of his decision before he left England, he certainly notified him of it during the winter of 1190-1.[14] As a result it was Longchamp's duty to be prepared in case of the king's death to hand the kingdom over to Arthur. On the other hand John's interests demanded that he make himself strong enough to secure the succession whether or not his brother favored his claim. A conflict between John and the chancellor was unavoidable.

William de Longchamp was in a most difficult position. Circumstances, as well as his own inclinations, forced him into bitter enmity with the king's brother, the most powerful man in the kingdom. At the same time the continual demands of his

[11] *Ibid.*   [12] Pollock and Maitland, *History of English Law*, II, 281-284.
[13] *Foedera*, I, I, 52.
[14] William of Newburgh, in *Chronicles of the Reigns of Stephen, Henry II, and Richard I* (ed. Richard Howlett, *Rolls Series*), p. 335.

extravagant and impecunious master obliged him to annoy the people of England by squeezing dry every possible source of revenue. The chancellor was tactless, arrogant, and avid for power. Worse yet he sprang from servile stock. These qualities alone earned him the contempt and detestation of most of the baronage. If he were to fulfil his obligations to his sovereign, he had to maintain his own power. To do this he gave shrievalties and custodianships to men whom he could trust, such as his brothers Osbert and Henry. This only increased his unpopularity with the barons. But despite his faults Longchamp was completely devoted to his master and ruled with his interests in view.

William Marshal had no easy task before him in steering his course through these troubled political seas. He was the chancellor's colleague in the government of England and was bound to assist him to maintain order and to carry out the king's commands. But John as lord of Glamorgan and feudal overlord of many of the knights of Gloucestershire was far too potent a neighbor to antagonize unnecessarily. William was the count's vassal for Leinster in Ireland and Cartmel in Lancashire, he held many fees in John's palatinates, and he needed his assistance in curbing the raids of the Welsh princes into the English fiefs in south Wales. When Richard died in 1199, William supported John's claim to the succession against that of Arthur, and there is no reason for believing that he was of a different opinion in 1190. On one side lay his duty as a member of the regency, on the other his interests and inclinations. William's devotion to Richard would probably have brought him into the chancellor's camp had not Longchamp by taking the offensive driven him into a sort of indignant neutrality.

The chancellor apparently from the very beginning of his reign suspected William of leaning toward the opposition. While the formidable lord of Striguil and Pembroke was still on his journey to Vézelay, Longchamp took measures to reduce the power of the house of Marshal. In the spring of 1190 he removed John Marshal from the shrievalty of Yorkshire on the ground of his inability to control serious anti-Semitic riots which had broken out in the city of York.[15] Although there is no reason for supposing that John was not incompetent, the substitution for him of Osbert de Longchamp forces one to suspect the chancellor's motives. Early in August Longchamp appears to have launched a more serious attack on the Marshal position. According to the account of Richard of Devizes, when Geoffrey de Lucy, bishop of Winchester, returned to England from the continent, he found the chancellor besieging Gloucester castle. The latter greeted him warmly. " I have been hoping that you would arrive, most dear friend. Should I go on with this siege or give it up." To this Geoffrey made the sage reply, " If you desire peace, lay down your arms." [16] No other chronicler mentions Longchamp's attack on the chief stronghold of William's shire. Ralph de Diceto speaks of a large assembly convoked at Gloucester by the chancellor, but states neither the nature nor the object of the gathering.[17] Richard of Devizes is a most reliable authority. If his story is accepted, one can only conclude that Longchamp hoped to seize the shrievalty of Gloucestershire before William's return from the continent. Such an outrage alone would account for the latter's hostility to the chancellor.

During the last months of 1190 complaints against his justiciar's administration reached the king in Sicily.[18] While he was not unduly disturbed by these protests, Richard was anxious to make sure of the peace of England before his final departure for the Holy Land. He was confident of Longchamp's loyalty, but the complaints cast some doubt on his ability to rule England successfully. The king decided to send Walter de Coutance, archbishop of Rouen, to support the chancellor and if necessary, supersede him.[19] This prelate was fur-

[15] Benedict of Peterborough, II, 108. Roger of Hovedon, III, 34-5.

[16] Richard of Devizes, *De rebus gestis Ricardi Primi* in *Chronicles of the Reigns of Stephen, Henry II, and Richard I* (ed. Richard Howlett, *Rolls Series*), p. 391.   [17] Ralph de Diceto, II, 83.

[18] *Hist.*, 9777-9780. Benedict of Peterborough, II, 157-8.

[19] *Ibid.* Benedict's statement that William accompanied the archbishop is an

nished with a sheef of letters patent to be used as he saw fit. One epistle was addressed to the chancellor and his four associates, Geoffrey fitz Peter, William Marshal, Hugh Bardolf, and William Brewer. It informed them that the king was sending to England to assist them in the government a man whom he knew to be prudent, discreet, and faithful—Walter of Rouen. They were to seek his advice in all matters and to follow his counsel. This letter associating the archbishop to the existing government was obviously intended for immediate use as soon as he arrived in England. Then there was a letter addressed to the four associate justiciars, one to William Marshal, and apparently similar individual ones for the other associates and a few of the more important barons of the kingdom. The recipients were directed to act only by the counsel of the archbishop. If the chancellor should refuse to follow the advice of Walter of Rouen and the associate justiciars, they were to rule without him. The archbishop was the king's chief representative—to him he had given his heart and confided all his secrets.[20] These royal letters endowed Walter de Coutance with complete power to do what seemed best to insure the tranquility of England. Late in February 1191 the archbishop left Sicily in company with the most exalted of Richard's confidants, the queen dowager, Eleanor of Aquitaine.

When Walter de Coutance arrived in England, he found the chancellor at war with Count John. Longchamp had deprived one of the prince's partisans, Gerard de Canville, of his office of sheriff of Lincolnshire and had laid siege to Lincoln castle of which Gerard was the hereditary custodian.[21] John had replied by seizing Nottingham and Tickhill, castles which pertained to his honors but which Richard had left in the chancellor's custody. The count then mustered an army and marched to the relief of Lincoln. As Longchamp was too weak to dispute

error. William was at Northampton on January 24, 1191 (*Pipe Roll Society*, XVII, 5; XI, Introduction, p. xxiii). William's name appears on no royal acts after the king left Vézelay.

[20] Giraldus Cambrensis, *Opera*, IV, 400-1. Ralph de Diceto, II, 90-1.

[21] Benedict of Peterborough, II, 207. William of Newburgh, p. 338.

John's advance, he permitted Walter of Rouen to negotiate a peace, but the arrival of a force of continental mercenaries soon encouraged him to renew hostilities. These were brought to an end by a new treaty concluded at Winchester on July 28th. The two castles were surrended to the chancellor with the provision that they should be returned to John in case of Richard's death. Gerard de Canville was reconciled to Longchamp and reinstated as sheriff of Lincolnshire. Finally, the chancellor agreed to recognize John as his brother's heir and promised to assist him to obtain the succession if Richard died.[22]

No sooner had Longchamp temporarily disposed of Count John than he was faced with another member of the Plantagenet family. For some time he had been worried by the possibility that Geoffrey might be consecrated archbishop of York and obtain a dispensation from the vow he had taken to remain out of England. His presence, especially if he could persuade the pope to grant him immunity from legatine authority, would seriously hamper the chancellor. If Geoffrey and John should combine their forces, his position would be utterly untenable. To prevent such a contingency Longchamp ordered the sheriffs of the coastal shires to arrest Geoffrey if he should attempt to land in England and to intercept any messages he might send to John.[23] The chancellor's fears were well founded. On August 18, 1191 Bartholomew, archbishop of Tours, acting on the direct orders of the pope, consecrated Geoffrey archbishop of York. The latter hastened to the coast of Flanders where he received a letter from Longchamp forbidding him to enter England. Ignoring this prohibition, Geoffrey landed at Dover on September 14th. As he knew that the constable of Dover had been ordered to arrest him, he avoided the men waiting to capture him and made his way to the church of the priory of St. Martin. There he was seized by the agents of the constable and removed to Dover castle—a clear violation of the right of sanctuary. This act not only furnished excellent ammunition to

[22] See Norgate, *John Lackland,* pp. 31-36 and Round, *Commune of London,* pp. 207-218.   [23] Roger of Wendover, I, 193.

the chancellor's enemies, but aroused the indignation of such neutral prelates as the bishop of London. The latter persuaded Longchamp to release his prisoner, and on October 2nd Geoffrey arrived in London.[24]

The violence of his agents had placed William de Longchamp at the mercy of his opponents. Count John immediately requested the associate justiciars and the prelates and barons of England to meet with him near Reading to discuss the chancellor's conduct.[25] The latter's enemies gathered joyfully. From the far north came Hugh de Puisset, bishop of Durham, burning to avenge old injuries. William Marshal hastened in from the west. Longchamp himself declined to attend the conference. He sought refuge in his chief stronghold, the Tower of London, while John and the barons took possession of the city. Walter de Coutance was forced to take action. The attack on Geoffrey had so greatly increased the chancellor's unpopularity that it was no longer expedient to leave him at the head of the government. On October 8th the archbishop of York and the bishop of Durham presented their grievances before a council held at St. Paul's. Walter of Rouen pointed out that Longchamp had ignored the king's command to seek and abide by his counsel. The associate justiciars likewise testified to his failure to consult them. Finally William Marshal read the king's letter which authorized him and his colleagues in conjunction with the archbishop of Rouen to take any steps necessary for the good of the kingdom in case the chancellor refused to follow their advice. Longchamp was deposed from the justiciarship, and Walter de Coutance put in his place. Then the assembly swore fidelity to Richard while he lived and to John as his heir if he died without issue.[26]

The loss of the office of justiciar did not subdue the proud spirit of the bishop of Ely. Although he was forced to surrender his castles and leave England in disgrace, he promptly

---

[24] *Ibid.*, 193-4. Ralph de Diceto, II, 96-7. Giraldus Cambrensis, *Vita Galfridi*, book II, chapter VI (*Opera* IV). [25] Ralph de Diceto, II, 98.
[26] Benedict of Peterborough, II, 213-4. Giraldus Cambrensis, *Opera*, IV, 400.

set to work to confound his enemies. His first step was to complain to the pope. Celestine replied by ordering the English prelates to excommunicate anyone who injured his legate. On the authority of these letters Longchamp directed his fellow bishops to publish the sentence of excommunication against Walter of Rouen, the bishops of Coventry and Winchester, all the associate justiciars except Hugh Bardolf, and fifteen barons.[27] The sentence against John himself was not to be pronounced until February. As the bishops neglected to obey these orders and the government retaliated by seizing the temporalities of the see of Ely, this manoeuvre of Longchamp's was not a great success.[28] Walter of Rouen sent agents to Rome who succeeded in persuading the pope to withdraw the excommunications, but they could not induce him to deprive the chancellor of his legatine commission.[29]

Longchamp did not stop with his appeal to Rome—his agent sought Richard in Syria.[30] He bore a letter from the chancellor which informed the king that John was plotting to steal his throne and that the barons of the realm were willing to permit it. When he had read this epistle, Richard questioned the messenger. "What! Have they all become his liege men? You who bear these messages, you are most loyal and wise. Name for me the men of greatest worth who have gone over to my brother." "Sire" the messenger replied "They speak of the Marshal and a number of others." "The Marshal! By the legs of God, I deemed him the most loyal knight who was ever born in my lands. I am trusting in your loyalty." This was too much for the messenger. "Sire, I retract. I told you what I had been ordered to." The king was much relieved. "I believe that the Marshal would never be evil or false."[31]

Undoubtedly Richard was justified in his confidence in William's fidelity, but one can easily understand Longchamp's contrary opinion. The chancellor had been the king's chosen representative in England whose duty it was to carry out his orders.

[27] Roger of Hovedon, III, 150-4.   [28] Ibid., p. 155.
[29] Ibid., p. 188-192.   [30] Ibid., p. 155.   [31] Hist., 9828-9858.

One of these commands was to secure the succession for Arthur. As Longchamp's colleague William should have supported him to the limit in the discharge of his functions. When Count John opposed the chancellor even to the extent of taking up arms against him, William should have actively assisted his chief. Instead he had leaned toward John's party. He had allowed his sympathy for the count and his dislike for the chancellor to sway him from the path of duty. But in fairness to William it should be pointed out that he probably regarded Longchamp's feud with John as a private quarrel that did not affect the king's interests. Richard had made no public pronouncement about his successor. He had never commanded the barons to regard Arthur as his heir. Until he did, they could without disloyalty favor John's claim. When the count actually did revolt against his brother, William disproved the chancellor's accusation that he would permit John to steal the kingdom. While he might equivocate in regard to the king's orders in the mouth of an obnoxious viceroy, in a clear cut issue he would never fail his sovereign.

Walter de Coutance soon discovered that he had assumed no light burden. In December 1191 Philip Augustus arrived in France. On January 20, 1192 he met William fitz Ralph, seneschal of Normandy, on the frontier of the duchy near Gisors and showed him a document which purported to be the treaty which the French and English monarchs had made at Messina before leaving Sicily for Palestine. It provided that Philip's sister Alis, who was in the Tower of Rouen, should be surrendered to him with the castle of Gisors and the counties of Eu and Aumale. The copy of the treaty of Messina preserved in the English exchequer guarantees the return of Alis to her brother one month after Richard reached home, but it leaves Gisors in the latter's possession and fails to mention Eu or Aumale.[32] As it is incredible that Richard would have agreed to the terms contained in the treaty presented by Philip, one is

[32] Benedict of Peterborough, II, 236. *Foedera,* I, I, 54. See F. M. Powicke, *The Loss of Normandy,* p. 126.

forced to conclude that the French king was making free use of his imagination, to say nothing of a little forgery. But the seneschal refused to pay any attention to the document in the absence of confirmatory orders from his master. Philip countered by writing to John to suggest that he marry Alis and, with French aid, obtain all his brother's domains. Only the energetic action of Queen Eleanor blocked this scheme. She crossed to England and joined the justiciar and his associates in forbidding John to go to the continent under penalty of losing his English lands. Count John was far from a restful neighbor. His plots with Philip and even with the exiled Longchamp continually harassed the government. To add to the problems of the justiciar and his associates, the year 1192 saw a fresh uprising of the Welsh princes.

As lord of Striguil and Pembroke and sheriff of Gloucestershire William was particularly concerned with the Welsh menace. In the summer of 1189 Rees ap Griffith, prince of South Wales, had celebrated the death of his old enemy, Henry II, by an invasion of Pembrokeshire.[33] Queen Eleanor and Ranulf de Glanville had done what they could to check this incursion, but it was evident that Rees needed a serious lesson.[34] In September Count John marched against him at the head of a part of the feudal army of England. There were, apparently, no actual hostilities, but John made peace at Worcester with several Welsh princes.[35] The next few years were comparatively peaceful in the marches. Longchamp kept the principal English strongholds in a state of defence and carried on negotiations with the native princes. He may possibly have led a force into the marches in the summer of 1190.[36] At any rate he succeeded in maintaining reasonable quiet in that tumultuous region.

[33] Giraldus Cambrensis, *Opera*, VI, 80. *Brut y Tywysogion*, p. 235.

[34] *Pipe Roll 1 Richard I (Record Commission)*, p. 163.

[35] Benedict of Peterborough, II, 87-8.

[36] Pipe Roll 2 Richard I and Mrs. Stenton's introduction, *Pipe Roll Society*, XXXIX.

In the summer of 1192 Rees once more invaded the English lands in south Wales and laid siege to the important castle of Swansea on the Gower peninsula.[37] The archbishop of Rouen and his associates took prompt and energetic measures for the relief of this fortress. The feudal levy of the kingdom was ordered to muster at Gloucester for an expedition against Rees.[38] Two of the associate justiciars, William Marshal and Geoffrey fitz Peter, took command of the operations with the assistance of Count John himself.[39] Ships were gathered at Bristol and sent to Swansea with supplies, munitions, and reinforcements for the garrison.[40] The army marched overland from Gloucester, engaged the Welsh in battle under the walls of Swansea, and forced them to raise the siege.[41] William's part in this successful expedition was very considerable, especially on the financial side. As sheriff of Gloucestershire he furnished funds from the revenues of that county to pay for the ships sent to Swansea and other necessary expenditures.[42] From his own pocket he advanced money to William de London to aid him in maintaining the castles of Kidwelly and Swansea, loaned John one hundred marks to sustain him during the expedition, and gave twenty pounds toward paying for the ships sent to Swansea.[43] These sums were later subtracted from his debt to the exchequer for the honor of Giffard.

This summer of 1192 was a particularly busy one for William. The office of associate justiciar entailed judicial as well as administrative duties. During the year 1191 he had presided with other justices at the conclusion of nine final concords and had gone on circuit in Gloucestershire in company with the bishop of Hereford and Robert de Whitfield.[44] In 1192 six

---

[37] *Annales Cambriae*, p. 58.

[38] Pipe Roll 5 Richard I, *Pipe Roll Society*, XLI, 158.

[39] *Ibid.*, pp. 113-114, 148.

[40] *Ibid.*, pp. 99, 113-114, 148.   [42] *Ibid.*, pp. 113-4.

[41] *Ibid.*, p. 93.   [43] *Ibid.*, p. 148.

[44] *Pipe Roll Society*, XVII, 5, 7, 8, 9, 11; XL, xxiii, 291; XLI, xxiv-xxv. *Register of St. Osmund* (ed. U. R. Jones, *Rolls Series*), I, 262. *William Salt Archaeological Society*, XXVII (1924), 26.

parties of justices visited all the counties of England except the palatinates ruled by the earl of Chester, the bishop of Durham, and Count John.[45] Walter de Coutance headed the justices who visited the south-eastern counties, and each of his four associates was assigned to a group. William Marshal with the bishops of Coventry and Hereford, Richard of the Peak, and master Robert of Shrewsbury visited Gloucestershire, Worcestershire, Herefordshire, Warwickshire, Shropshire, and Staffordshire.[46] Considering William's total lack of legal experience or training, his value as a justice itinerant must have been very dubious, but his position as a great baron and associate justiciar added prestige and dignity to the group.

Walter de Coutance might well review with pride his first year as justiciar of England. The country had been ruled with a firm hand and the various factions reduced to order. Count John was still a menace, but so far all his schemes had been thwarted. Rees had been driven from Swansea. On the administrative side a judicial visitation had been carried out in all the counties which were under the government's control. England was at peace, and her king was known to be on his way home. But if any illusion of security occupied the mind of the archbishop, it was to be dispelled by a bombshell. On December 28, 1192, Henry of Hohenstaufen, Holy Roman Emperor, informed his friend Philip Augustus that Richard had been captured by an imperial vassal, Leopold, duke of Austria. A copy of this letter came in some unknown manner into the hands of Walter of Rouen and served as a warning of impending trouble.[47]

Philip of France hastened to share the good news with Count John. Once more he offered to give him Alis in marriage, to accept his homage for Richard's continental fiefs, and to aid him to conquer England.[48] John was at the parting of the ways. Hitherto he had committed no act of treason against his brother. He had merely quarrelled with Longchamp over the

[45] Pipe Roll 5 Richard I, *Pipe Roll Society*, XLI.
[46] *Ibid.*   [47] Roger of Hovedon, III, 195-6.   [48] *Ibid.*, p. 203.

question of the succession—a matter in which many loyal barons such as William shared his views. John could not resist the urge of ambition. Early in January he crossed to Normandy. When the seneschal and barons of the duchy refused to do him homage, he proceeded to Philip's court. There he concluded a formal alliance with the French king and did homage for the continental lands of his house.[49]

Meanwhile the archbishop of Rouen and his associates had not been idle. The prelates and barons of England were summoned to meet at Oxford to decide what measures should be taken for the defence of the realm.[50] All the castles of the kingdom, especially the fortresses on the channel which covered the country from a French invasion, were strengthened, provisioned, and garrisoned.[51] The government was in desperate need of troops. John had a large number of Welsh mercenaries drawn from his lordship of Glamorgan, and he was certain to import others from the continent. As Wales was the only source of mercenaries which was available to the justiciars, the sheriffs of the border counties were ordered to enlist large contingents. Immediately after the Council of Oxford William mustered strong forces in the two chief strongholds of his bailiwick, Bristol and Gloucester. The former, a castle belonging to John's honor of Gloucester but at the moment in William's custody, was garrisoned by ten knights and five hundred serjeants. Gloucester held twenty knights, four hundred and fifty serjeants, and forty archers.[52] These troops not only insured the safety of the two Gloucestershire fortresses, but gave William a mobile army which he could use in case of a civil war or a French invasion.

After forming his alliance with Philip, Count John returned to England at the head of a body of mercenaries. When the justiciars rejected his demand that they recognize him as king, he retired into his palatinates to prepare for war.[53] The gov-

[49] *Ibid.*, p. 204.
[50] *Ibid.*, pp. 196-7. Pipe Roll 5 Richard I, *Pipe Roll Society*, XLI, 158.
[51] *Ibid.*, p. xvii.   [52] *Ibid.*, p. 148.   [53] Roger of Hovedon, III, 204-5.

ernment was disturbed by rumors of a projected French invasion from Flanders, but it is extremely doubtful if Philip ever seriously contemplated an expedition to England to aid John.[54] His object was the conquest of Normandy. Shortly after Easter he invaded the duchy which was valiantly defended by Earl Robert of Leicester and the Norman barons. The French king's preoccupation with Normandy left Walter of Rouen and his associates free to turn their attention to subduing John. As the price for his obedience to the justiciars' orders in 1192 the count had gained possession of the castles of Wallingford and Windsor. He had also by some means recovered his northern strongholds of Nottingham and Tickhill. Since Windsor with its command of the Thames valley seemed the most dangerous of John's southern fortresses, the archbishop decided to reduce it. The *History* states that William Marshal came out of the west with his marcher vassals.[55] The Pipe Roll shows that he led five hundred serjeants, probably Welsh mercenaries, to Windsor.[56] Geoffrey fitz Peter and William de Briouse, sheriff of Herefordshire, brought other contingents of Welsh auxiliaries to swell the besieging army.[57] The justiciars' forces must have been largely made up of these mercenary troops. While Walter of Rouen, Queen Eleanor and three of the associate justiciars lay before Windsor, the bishop of Durham laid siege to Tickhill.[58] John's two chief castles were invested by the government.

The most interesting phase of William Marshal's activities in connection with the siege of Windsor lies in the energy and ingenuity displayed by him in finding money to pay his mercenaries. By the year 1193 the financial condition of the English government was extremely bad. Since Richard's departure it had been forced to subsist on its ordinary revenues augmented slightly by the late payments on the scutage of 1189. The chancellor's conflict with John and the wars against the Welsh had constituted a serious drain on the exchequer. Toward the end

---

[54] Gervase of Canterbury, I, 514-5.
[55] *Hist.*, 9893-9904.   [56] Pipe Roll 5 Richard I, *Pipe Roll Society*, XLI, 148.
[57] *Ibid.*, pp. 87, 99.   [58] Roger of Hovedon, III, 208.

of February 1193 William received four hundred pounds from the royal treasury, but this sum was insufficient to cover his expenditures.[59] To make up the deficit he was driven to extraordinary measures. As sheriff of Gloucestershire he collected as many as possible of the debts owed to the crown by residents of the county and used the money to pay his men.[60] For instance, Robert de Berkley owed a relief of seven hundred and fifty pounds. During 1193 he gave William forty pounds to pay the serjeants sent to Windsor and furnished a similar sum to the constable of Bristol.[61] The money penalties inflicted by William and his fellow justices in their eyre were in many cases turned over to the troops.[62] In addition to anticipating in this way the Michaelmas payments to the exchequer, William borrowed from the abbot of St. Augustine of Bristol and from several Jews.[63] He seems to have advanced about one hundred and twenty pounds from his private revenues. This sum was later subtracted from his fine for the honor of Giffard. The emergency financial measures learned by William at this time were to stand him in good stead a decade later.

As the justiciars lay before Windsor several emissaries from the captive Richard sought their camp. They brought word that Henry of Hohenstaufen had agreed to release the English king for a ransom of one hundred thousand marks.[64] Obviously the first duty of Walter of Rouen and his associates was to raise the required sum and secure their sovereign's freedom. The contest with John at once lost its significance. Once his brother was at liberty, the count would be a negligible menace, but the war with him was draining the exchequer and occupying the energies of the government. A truce until November was concluded through the mediation of Queen Eleanor. John surrendered Windsor, Wallingford, and the Peak to his mother who promised to return them to him if

[59] Pipe Roll 5 Richard I, *Pipe Roll Society*, XLI, 148.
[60] *Ibid.*, pp. 119-120.
[61] *Ibid.*, p. 118.
[62] *Ibid.*, pp. 118-120.   [63] *Ibid.*, p. 148.   [64] Roger of Hovedon, III, 205.

Richard did not reach England before the expiration of the truce. Nottingham and Tickhill were left in the count's possession, much to the disgust of Hugh of Durham who had almost reduced the latter stronghold.[65] The restoration of peace permitted the justiciars to concentrate their attention on collecting the huge ransom demanded by the Emperor. According to feudal custom this was one of the occasions on which a lord could levy a special " aid " from his vassals. This was the " scutage for the redemption of the lord king " assessed at one pound for each knight's fee. Certain non-feudal taxes were levied by the government—such as the demand for a quarter of every man's yearly income. Various monastic establishments were ordered to give a year's crop of wool, and the gold and silver in church treasuries was requisitioned.[66] In addition to the actual taxes everyone was urged to give as much more as possible. The *History* suggests that William contributed so generously that Richard in his gratitude gave the see of Exeter to Henry Marshal.[67] The ransom reached the frontiers of the empire by December 20th, and on that day Henry VI set January 17th as the date for Richard's release.[68]

As soon as the king's freedom was assured, Queen Eleanor and Walter of Rouen set out for Cologne. Hubert Walter, who had been recently elevated to the archepiscopal seat of Canterbury, succeeded to the office of justiciar. Count John had retired to France, but the archbishop and his colleagues were completely in the dark as to his intentions. But early in February they intercepted a messenger from whom they learned that John planned to resist his brother. Hubert promptly summoned a council which ordered the confiscation of all the count's lands and castles. The justiciar laid siege to Marlborough, Hugh of Durham returned to his attack on Tickhill, and the earls of Huntingdon, Chester, and Derby invested Nottingham.[69] William Marshal seized the town of Bristol and some property of

---

[65] *Ibid.*, pp. 207-8.
[66] *Ibid.*, pp. 210-211.   Gervase of Canterbury, I, 519.
[67] *Hist.*, 10000-10008.   [68] Roger of Hovedon, III, 226-7.   [69] *Ibid.*, pp. 236-7.

John's in Dorsetshire and Somersetshire.[70] Except for the castles of Nottingham and Tickhill, the count's power was completely reduced before Richard reached England.

On March 13, 1194 Richard Plantagenet landed at Sandwich—the regency was at an end. Hubert Walter remained justiciar, but his four associates passed from the political stage. On the whole they had performed a difficult task remarkably well. Working from the beginning under severe handicaps, they had carried on the government and were able to hand over the kingdom intact to their master. While the evidence is too scanty to permit one to form a satisfactory estimate of the part played by William Marshal, he must receive his share of credit for the success of the government of which he was a member. If the erstwhile knight-errant did not greatly distinguish himself as an administrator, he acquired experience that was to be of untold value to himself and to England. The best proof of his actual performance lies in the fact that he retained his high place in the confidence and favor of his sovereign.

---

[70] Pipe Roll 6 Richard I, *Pipe Roll Society*, XLIII, 194, 241.

CHAPTER VI

THE KING'S MARSHAL

By the spring of 1194 William must have been heartily tired of his administrative duties as associate justiciar. Except for an occasional expedition against the Welsh or the vassals of Count John it was a most unsatisfactory occupation for a knight who was still in the prime of life. Eagerly he awaited the return of the master who so completely shared his views. Then there would be fewer solemn councils and more good battles. The last five years of Richard's reign were to fulfil his fondest hopes. In the midst of almost continuous warfare these two kindred spirits were to be drawn still closer together and to rise still higher in each other's regard. Richard was to learn that William would defy him when he believed him in the wrong and would calm him when he lost control of his fiery temper. Richard, the tactician, was to find a captain who would implicitly obey his orders, while Richard, the headstrong knight, would find a rival in deeds of reckless daring. Richard, the diplomat, was to have in William an envoy who was known and trusted throughout Normandy, France, and Flanders. Above all, in him the king had an ever faithful servant who not only loved but understood him. When a cross-bow bolt from the walls of Chalus struck down Richard Plantagenet, William obeyed his late master's wishes and his own inclinations by aiding Count John to secure the heritage of the house of Anjou. These years form one of the most interesting chapters of William's life and one of the most varied. They provide a remarkably clear view of the multiple activities of a great baron—his master's agent, captain, envoy, counselor, and friend.

William was in the Welsh marches at his castle of Striguil when he learned of Richard's arrival in England. At the same time a messenger informed him that his elder brother, John Marshal, was dead. He did not know whether to lament or rejoice at these tidings. He mourned his brother, but his grief was assuaged by the king's return.[1] John Marshal appears on the record of history as a rather colorless and ineffective figure. Practically nothing is known about his career before 1189 when William's influence gained him preferment. Created royal escheator by Richard, he soon lost that office and was appointed sheriff of Yorkshire.[2] Longchamp removed him from the shrievalty because of his inability to handle the anti-Semitic riots at York in the spring of 1190. As he was replaced by Osbert de Longchamp, John may in this case have been a victim of politics as much as of his own incapacity.[3] After the overthrow of the chancellor he was made sheriff of Sussex and retained that office until his death.[4] When he died, he still owed the exchequer £28 14s 11d on the escheats which he had held during his short term as royal escheator.[5] These debts were passed on to William as his heir, but they did not weigh very heavily on his conscience. Out of five items on this account all were still due in 1199, four in 1201, three in 1202, and two were unpaid when William himself died in 1219 and were settled by his executors.[6]

By his brother's death William inherited the family lands and the dignity of master marshal of the king's court. The original function of the marshal's office seems to have been the care of the king's horses as a subordinate of the *comes stabuli* or constable. Round has made the very acceptable suggestion that the *magistratum in curia regis de liberate prebende* which John fitz

---

[1] *Hist.*, 10018-10048.

[2] Pipe Roll 2 Richard I, *Pipe Roll Society*, XXXIX, 58.

[3] *Ibid.* Roger of Hovedon, III, 34.

[4] Pipe Roll 4 Richard I, *Pipe Roll Society*, XL, 204.

[5] *Ibid.* 6 Richard I, *Pipe Roll Society*, XLIII, 40, 204, 252.

[6] *Memoranda Roll 1 John*, Public Record Office, E 370-1/3; *Chancellor's Roll 3 John* (*Record Commission*), p. 343; Pipe Roll 4 John, *William Salt Archaeological Society*, II, 109; *Compotus W. Marescalli Senioris*, Public Record Office, E 364/1, M. 3.

Gilbert held should be translated as the office of issuing feed.[7] Out of this responsibility for the king's horses there developed for both the marshal and his superior the constable important military functions such as keeping rolls of those who performed their military service.[8] Various other duties devolved upon the marshal as an officer of the household. He supervised all expenditures made by the king's officers and kept account of all payments made from the royal treasury and chamber.[9] It was his duty to maintain order in the palace and to guard the door to the king's hall.[10] The *Constitutio Domus Regis* which gives the perquisites of the master marshal towards the end of the reign of Henry I was still in force in the 14th century.[11] If he took his meals outside the court, he was entitled to two shillings a day, a loaf of bread, a sextary of household wine, one taper, and twenty-four candle ends. When he ate at the household table his allowance was reduced to fourteen pence a day, half a sextary of wine, and a whole candle.[12] When the king held court in great state on some special occasion such as the coronation of the queen, the marshal received a saddled palfrey from every earl and from every baron who had been knighted by the king.[13] There is no evidence that William ever performed the functions or received the emoluments of his office. The *Constitutio* presumes the close association of the marshal with the king's household. But after 1139 John fitz Gilbert never resided at Stephen's court and but rarely at Matilda's. What information there is about John and his successor during the reign of Henry II shows them living in England while the king passed

[7] *Magnum rotulum scaccarii, 31 Henry I*, p. 18; Round, *The King's serjeants and officers of state*, pp. 82-90.

[8] *Ibid.*   [9] *Red Book of the Exchequer*, p. 812.

[10] *Red Book of the Exchequer*, p. 759. There is a better text in Round, *Commune of London*, p. 312.

[11] *Calendar of Close Rolls 1313-1318* (*Rolls Series*), p. 558.

[12] *Red Book of the Exchequer*, p. 812.

[13] A fourteenth century Anglo-French translation of this passage says that he received a palfrey " from each baron and each earl made a knight on that day." I cannot read this meaning into the original. For both texts see Round, *Commune of London*, pp. 303, 312.

most of his time on the continent. Although William Marshal followed the court far more assiduously than his brother, he was absent for extended periods. From this one may conclude that after 1139 the master marshals rarely if ever performed their duties in person. William may have filled his office when he was actually at court, but it is probable that he served only on state occasions. The office had become largely an honorary and ceremonial one.

The lands of the Marshal family were not particularly extensive. The manors of Wexcombe and Bedwin in Wiltshire and Bosham in Sussex had been granted to John Marshal by King Richard in 1189 to be held in fee farm by him and his heirs.[14] By his marriage with the daughter of Adam de Port the younger John had acquired the manor of Speen in Berkshire which he held from his father-in-law for the service of one knight.[15] In Worcestershire he possessed the manor of Inkberrow as a fief of the bishop of Hereford who in turn held it of the bishop of Worcester.[16] Upleden in Herefordshire was also part of John Marshal's estate.[17] Tidworth in Wiltshire is known to have been held by John fitz Gilbert and by William Marshal by serjeantry of their office of master marshal, and it probably belonged to John the younger.[18] The manor of Hampstead in Berkshire may have been held by the same tenure.[19] This list is undoubtedly incomplete. The Marshals' methods of acquiring land combined with the fact that as ex-officio barons of the exchequer they were exempt from scutage makes it practically impossible to trace their possessions. For instance Mildenhall in Wiltshire had originally been held by Patrick of Salisbury as a fief of the abbey of Glastonbury.[20] By William's

[14] Cartae Antiquae, Public Record Office, C 52.
[15] *Hist.*, 10062. Pipe Roll 2 Richard I, *Pipe Roll Society*, XXXIX, 121.
[16] *Calendar of Patent Rolls 1354-1358*, p. 197. *Calendar of Charter Rolls 1327-1341*, p. 337.   [17] *Book of Fees*, p. 100.
[18] *Récueil des actes de Henri II*, II, 114; *Red Book of Exchequer*, p. 487.
[19] *Book of Fees*, p. 298. See Round, *King's Serjeants*, p. 90.
[20] *Feodary of Glastonbury, Somerset Record Society*, XXVI (1910), p. 22. W. H. Jones, *Domesday for Wiltshire*, p. 31.

time the overlordship of Glastonbury had been calmly forgotten.[21] The most important of the family possessions was the manor of Bosham which lay on the coast just west of Chichester. From its harbor Harold Godwinson had sailed on his ill-fated visit to Normandy, and in William's time it was still used as a port of departure for the continent.

As soon as William heard of his brother's death, he despatched the knights of his household to Marlborough to escort the body to Cirencester where he planned to join them himself. There in the abbey church the funeral ceremonies were performed. Then, leaving all but three of his knights to accompany the corpse to its burial place in Bradenstoke Priory, William hastened to join his master. Richard was on his way north to reduce Nottingham, the last of John's castles which still held out. When William joined him at Huntingdon, the king received him graciously and thanked him warmly in the presence of all the assembled barons for his loyalty to him during his absence. He and the other loyal barons had defended the realm from those who wished to seize it and had bent every effort to obtain their master's release from captivity. William replied that they had only done their duty to their liege lord.[22]

On March 28th the garrison of Nottingham castle surrendered, and two days later Richard opened in that town a council of the prelates and barons of his realm.[23] The first day was devoted to making various changes in the personnel of the royal administration. Several considerations seem to have governed the redistribution of the shrievalties. Once more Richard was in desperate need of money. The war with John had drained the royal treasury, and the payment of the preliminary installment of the king's ransom had severely taxed the resources of the country. Fifty thousand marks were still due the Emperor before the hostages whom he held would be released, and in addition, Richard needed funds for a campaign against Philip Augustus. He was forced to give the offices at his disposal to those who were able and willing to pay for them. Then William de Longchamp, still in high favor, had returned to England in the king's train burning to avenge himself on his enemies. By his influence his old foe Gerard de Canville lost his office of sheriff of Lincolnshire and was indicted for robbery and treason.[24] Still the king's finances did not suffer. Gerard's successor paid an increment of one hundred pounds on the half year's farm and made the king a gift of forty marks for having the county.[25] Gerard himself gave the king five hundred and sixty pounds for his pardon for the crimes he was charged with.[26] This same combination of the chancellor's influence and the king's need of money governed the fates of Geoffrey fitz Peter, William Brewer, and William Marshal, all loyal servants of Richard who had aided in Longchamp's overthrow in 1191. Geoffrey lost the shrievalties of Essex and Hertfordshire and of Northamptonshire, William Brewer that of Oxfordshire, and William Marshal that of Gloucestershire.[27] In each case the new sheriff made contributions in the shape of increments on the farm of the county and of gifts to the king.[28] William was recompensed for the loss of Gloucestershire by being appointed, without promising an increment or making a gift, to succeed his brother as sheriff of Sussex.[29] Longchamp himself obtained the shrievalty of Essex and Hertfordshire while his brothers, Osbert and Henry, received Norfolk and Suffolk and Worcestershire respectively—in return for generous contributions.[30]

The *History* records an interesting incident of this council. Count John had been disseised of all his English lands, but he still retained the domains in Ireland which his father had given him. Richard, apparently, doubted his authority to take the lordship of Ireland away from his brother. Longchamp viewed the matter differently and finally gained the king's permission to

[24] *Ibid.*, p. 242.
[25] Pipe Roll 6 Richard I, *Pipe Roll Society*, XLIII, 103.
[26] *Ibid.*, p. 120.
[27] *Ibid.*, pp. 28, 68, 88, 231.   [29] *Ibid.*, p. 226.
[28] *Ibid.*, pp. 30, 68, 89, 232.   [30] *Ibid.*, pp. 30, 47, 127.

try to persuade the Irish barons to do homage to Richard for their fiefs. One day after the morning mass, in the presence of the king and barons, he approached Walter de Lacy, lord of Meath, and informed him that Richard desired his homage for his Irish lands. Walter discreetly complied with this request. The chancellor then made the same demand of William Marshal. William declined with indignation. He had done homage to John for Leinster, and it would be felony for him to obey Richard's command.[31] The king and all the barons applauded this reply, much to the chagrin of the chancellor. "You are planting vines," he said to William. In other words William was sowing a crop that he hoped to harvest if John became king. "Plant vines or a garden, if you wish, lord chancellor," replied William, "but I shall never be a sycophant. I tell you that if any man should wish to take Ireland, I would support to the best of my ability my liege lord whose man I am. I have loyally served our lord the king for the land I hold from him, and I fear nothing.[32] From this it is clear that William considered Ireland an independent land of which John was lord and which he did not hold from his elder brother. William was John's man for Cartmel in Lancashire, yet when the count rebelled against his suzerain, Richard, William aided the justiciar to reduce his power and seize his lands and castles. Richard was king of England, and to him was due the primary allegiance of the barons of the realm. On the other hand, John was lord of Ireland by the gift of Henry II, and William had done him homage for Leinster. If Richard himself tried to invade Ireland, William would be bound to aid John. This passage proves without a doubt that Richard, William, and the assembled barons considered Ireland a kingdom completely separate from the English crown. In England William served Richard, in Ireland John. He was not only scrupulous in his interpretation of his feudal obligations, but also courageous in performing them.

---

[31] *Felonie*—infidelity to his oath of homage. See Godefroy, *Lexique de l'Ancien Français*. [32] *Hist.*, 10289-10340.

Richard was in great haste to depart for Normandy in order to recapture the lands taken from him by Philip Augustus. On May 12th he crossed from Portsmouth to Barfleur to take up the struggle with the perpetual enemy of the house of Anjou.[33] William accompanied his master to Portsmouth, but it is not certain that he crossed with him. In his accounts as sheriff of Sussex there appears an item of £4, 10s for two ships to carry him and his knights to the continent, but there is no evidence that these vessels formed part of Richard's fleet.[34] At any rate, William joined Richard in Normandy with enough knights to fill two ships. He probably welcomed with joy the opportunity to resume his old trade of war. He loved fighting, and he had a stake in Normandy—his broad lands of Longueville. Unfortunately, the next five years are among the most obscure of his life. He appears now as a warrior, now as a counselor, now as an envoy, but his biography becomes little more than a series of brilliant episodes.

For five years the attention of a fair part of western Europe was centered in the struggle between Richard and Philip Augustus.[35] The pope considered it disgraceful that these two great monarchs should exhaust their strength over a few frontier castles while the Holy Land stood in need of christian swords. Through his influence a number of truces were arranged, but neither king considered them permanent, and they were promptly broken. The Emperor, who was only too pleased to see the kings of France and England well occupied with each other, urged Richard on whenever the latter seemed inclined to peace. This was not a war of extensive campaigns nor of long sieges, but of fierce border raids, minor battles, and assaults on frontier castles. It was the heyday of such inveterate raiders as Philip of Dreux, bishop of Beauvais, the terror of the Norman marches. Richard's skilful diplomacy extended the

---

[33] Roger of Hovedon, III, 251.

[34] Pipe Roll 6 Richard I, *Pipe Roll Society*, XLIII, 226.

[35] The best secondary account of this struggle is in F. M. Powicke, *The Loss of Normandy*. Norgate's, *Richard the Lion Heart*, and A. Cartellieri, *Philipp II August*, are very useful.

theatre of warfare by arousing against Philip such great feuda-
tories as the counts of Flanders and Toulouse. Seldom does
one find two worthier opponents than these two kings—and
seldom a more bitter conflict than their struggle for Normandy.
In this William served his master well and rose still higher in
his esteem.

When Richard arrived in Normandy in May 1194, he found
Philip laying siege to the fortress of Verneuil. By cutting the
communications of the French army Richard forced Philip to
raise the siege on May 28th.[36] The English king then moved
south into Touraine to reestablish his authority in that region.
While he was capturing the great fortress of Loches, Philip
continued his attacks on Normandy and destroyed the town of
Evreux. The French king then decided to curb his enemy's
activities in the south. Early in July he advanced down the
valley of the Loir toward Vendôme and the frontier of Maine,
while Richard hastened north to meet him. The evening of
July 3rd the English army pitched its camp before Vendôme,
which was unfortified, while Philip stayed at Fréteval some
miles up the river Loir. The latter sent word to Richard that
he would visit him the next day in hostile guise. Richard replied that he would expect him, but if he failed to come, he
himself would seek him at Fréteval. As the next morning
brought no sign of the French army, Richard advanced up the
valley of the Loir to meet his enemy. Philip, who had little
enthusiasm for battles, decided to retire, but the English came
up before the French could get out of reach.[37] Richard immediately decided on a pursuit, but he was far too skilful a tactician not to make provision for a possible rally of the French
troops. William Marshal was ordered to hold together the men
under his command in case the enemy turned to give battle,
while Richard himself led the remainder of the army after the
fleeing French.[38] The pursuit was eminently successful. Many
of the enemy were taken or slain, and Richard captured his

[36] Roger of Hovedon, III, 252. *Hist.*, 10464-10496.
[37] Roger of Hovedon, III, 253-255. [38] *Hist.*, 10608-10612.

rival's treasury and camp equipment. Philip himself only missed capture by hiding in a church while the pursuit rolled by.[39] Meanwhile, William and his men had made no attempt to share in the plunder, but had held themselves in readiness for any emergency. As Richard rode back from the pursuit, he assured William that the enemy had no intention of fighting. William, however, refused to leave the field until all the English had returned from the chase. When the last of the pursuers had started back to Vendôme, he formed his knights behind them as a rearguard.[40] The idea of having a fresh reserve kept in formation while the rest of the army scattered in pursuit of the enemy was a mark of Richard's skill as a tactician, but its successful execution showed William's rare qualities. It is sufficiently hard for a born warrior to stay behind himself, but it is far more difficult to hold a group of knights together while the rest of the army is enjoying a splendid chance to plunder. William not only obeyed Richard, a sufficiently rare quality in mediaeval warriors, but he was able to make his men obey him. That evening as the various barons were boasting of their booty and brave deeds, Richard praised William. " The Marshal did better than any of you. In case of need he would have succored us. I esteem him because he has done more than any of us. When one has a good reserve, one does not fear one's enemies." [41]

The next military exploit of William's which the author of the *History* saw fit to recount took place in May 1197. Richard was conducting a series of raids from his frontier castle of Gournay. One day he led a considerable force against the castle of Milli, near Beauvais, with the intention of taking it by storm. His men placed ladders against the walls and swarmed up them to the assault. The garrison defended themselves so vigorously that one ladder was thrown down with its load of knights and serjeants and the assailants were driven off the others. A Flemish knight, Guy de la Bruyere, who had reached the top of

[39] Roger of Hovedon, III, 256.
[40] *Hist.*, 10632-10662.   [41] *Ibid.*, 10668-10676.

a ladder, was caught about his neck by a great fork wielded by one of the garrison and was held there, helpless. William, who was standing on the edge of the moat directing the attack, noticed the knight's predicament. Leaping into the moat, he climbed first the opposite bank and then the ladder itself, sword in hand. So fiercely did he fall upon those who were holding Guy that they fled in confusion leaving William in possession of that section of the wall. Meanwhile, Richard, who had seen William's exploit, was with difficulty restrained from following him. His men, seeing William on the wall, cheered loudly, " The castle is taken! To his aid! " and renewed the assault. While the besiegers once more rushed up the ladders, the constable of the castle attacked William. With one mighty blow William cut through his helmet, his hair, and deep into his scalp—the constable fell to the ground and lay as one dead. Then, feeling a bit tired and thinking that all in all he had done his share, William calmly sat down on his captive while the English took possession of the castle. When the combat was over William led his prisoner, who had partially recovered, to the king. " Sir Marshal," said Richard, " it is not fitting for a man of your rank and prowess to risk yourself in such feats. Leave them to young knights who must win renown. As for your captive, were he a hundred times more valuable, I would give him to you.[42] For a few moments the great baron had returned to his knight-errant days. His fifty-three years had begun to sap his strength—no longer could he climb a ladder in full armor without feeling tired—but age had not diminished his valor or his overwhelming might in battle. Such deeds as this fully as much as his work at Fréteval endeared him to his master who himself never succeeded in merging the knight-errant in the king.

Late in the summer of 1197 Richard decided to send four of his best knights to aid Baldwin, count of Flanders and duke of Hainault, who had entered into an alliance with him against Philip. For this mission he chose Peter des Preaux, Alan Basset,

[42] *Ibid.*, 11105-11264.

John Marshal, William's nephew, and William himself. Count Baldwin received them joyfully. He had collected a strong force consisting of knights and the burghers of the Flemish communes with which he hoped to recapture one of his castles which Philip held. Soon after they had invested the fortress, they learned that the French king was hastening to the relief of his garrison. The Flemish barons advised their count to put the burghers behind a barrier of carts while the knights gave battle to the French. If the knights were defeated, they could seek safety behind the wall of carts. William protested that that was no way to fight a battle. Let the burghers and their carts contain the garrison of the castle while the knights fought in the open field with no thought of retreat. His advice was accepted—a great tribute to his military reputation. But king Philip had no desire to risk a battle and retired as soon as he had ascertained that the Flemings intended to stand their ground.[43] Disappointed as he was to miss a good fight, William must have been flattered by Count Baldwin's confidence in his abilities as a general.

During the last five years of Richard's reign William's activities were not confined to military exploits. In his service of Henry II and the young king he had proved himself a wise and temperate counselor, and no king had greater need of sound advice than the impulsive and hot-tempered Richard. It was due largely to William's efforts that in the summer of 1198 a serious quarrel was averted between the king and the saintly Hugh of Avalon, bishop of Lincoln, most revered of English prelates. In the autumn of 1197 Richard had ordered Archbishop Hubert to send him one third of the feudal levy of England. When the archbishop transmitted this demand to the prelates and barons assembled in council at Oxford, Hugh of Avalon refused to comply on the ground that the see of Lincoln owed knights only for service in England.[44] The enraged justiciar immediately informed the king of the bishop's obstinacy. In August 1198 Hugh crossed to Normandy in the hope

[43] *Ibid.*, 10745-10896.   [44] See Round, *Feudal England*, pp. 528-538.

of making his peace with Richard. William Marshal and Baldwin de Bethune,[45] count of Aumale, met him at Rouen and begged him to send a conciliatory message to the king. The two barons were unwilling to have the bishop appear at court until the king's wrath had been appeased. If Richard in his anger should injure the prelate in his person or dignity, it would be a serious misfortune for the interests of England. They loved both the king and the bishop and were anxious to avoid an open rupture between them. Hugh declined to give them the message they desired, because he was unwilling to involve them in the quarrel. In his war with Philip Richard needed the services of these two tried captains, and the bishop would do nothing that might estrange them from their king by making them appear as his supporters. The two barons returned to Richard and told him of their interview with the bishop. By pointing out how solicitous Hugh had shown himself for the king's welfare, they succeeded in calming the fiery monarch. A few days later Richard and the prelate were reconciled and their differences compromised.[46] William and Baldwin had by their tact and diplomacy avoided a serious breach between the king and the most beloved and respected of his prelates.

By the end of the year 1198 King Philip was exceedingly anxious for peace. As a soldier he was no match for his antagonist, and his resources could not compete with Richard's revenue from England. Moreover public opinion in general seems to have been unfavorable to him. He was in trouble with Rome over his repudiation of his queen, Ingeborg of Denmark. While only a violent partisan could claim that either Philip or Richard was completely in the right, an impartial contemporary could not but feel that the latter was the more agrieved party. Philip had, in violation of his solemn promise, attacked the Angevin lands before Richard returned from the crusade. He

[45] Baldwin had recently married the countess of Aumale. Powicke, *The Loss of Normandy*, p. 165.

[46] *Magna Vita St. Hugonis Episcopi Lincolniensis* (ed. James F. Dimock, *Rolls Series*), pp. 257-259.

had even schemed to keep his rival in a German prison. Richard was fighting for the integrity of his inherited domains. The idea that Philip was working for French unity would have had little appeal to the men of his day. On the advice of his barons the French king asked the pope to mediate between him and his over powerful vassal. Innocent III was only too willing to accede to this request. One of the dominant ambitions of this pontiff was to free the Holy Land from the unbeliever, and the war between these two christian princes was a serious impediment to the projected crusade. The pope immediately ordered his legate, the cardinal Peter of Capua, to arrange a peace or at least a long truce between the contestants.

In January 1199 the legate met Richard on the Norman frontier near Vernon. The king absolutely refused to consider a permanent peace while Philip held a foot of his heritage, but moved by the cardinal's pleas for the needs of the Holy Land, he agreed to a truce for five years. He proposed that during this time Philip should hold the castles then in his possession, but should give up all the lands that had formed part of the Angevin domains. For example the castle of Gisors should be held by a French garrison while the land attached to it, the castellary of Gisors, should belong to Richard. As these terms were acceptable to the legate, he felt that his chief mission was fulfilled.[47] He had, however, another affair to discuss with Richard. Philip of Dreux, bishop of Beauvais, who had for years been the scourge of the Norman marches, had been captured by the English in the spring of 1197 while leading a border raid. When Richard imprisoned him in the tower of Rouen, the bishop appealed to the pope. Celestine III gave his warlike prelate scant sympathy. He had exchanged his stole for a sword and his pastoral staff for a lance—he richly deserved the fate which had fallen on him.[48] Innocent III was more jealous of the sacred privileges of the clergy and directed his legate to procure the bishop's release. When Peter of Capua

[47] *Hist.*, 11407-11578. Roger of Wendover, I, 280-1.
[48] Roger of Hovedon, IV, 21-24.

reminded Richard that it was unlawful to detain in prison a man who had been consecrated and annointed as bishop, the king's fury knew no bounds. Philip of Dreux had not been captured as a bishop, but as a marauding knight in full armor. If it were not for the legate's inviolability as Philip's ambassador, his ecclesiastical dignity would not have saved him from a beating. " Fly from here, sir traitor, liar, trickster, and simoniac and see that I never again find you in my path " was the gentle admonition with which Richard ended the interview.[49]

While the terrified legate spurred his horse towards Philip's camp, Richard, bursting with rage, shut himself in his chamber. William alone of all his entourage dared to approach him. He entered the king's room and chided him for his foolish anger. " You must not get so worked up over a slight matter. It would be more sensible to laugh over all you have gained. You see that the king of France is at the end of his rope; he is reduced to asking for peace or a truce. Take your lands and leave him the castles, but make sure that he draws no subsistence from the lands for his garrisons. When he has to supply them from France at his own cost, it will seem to him as expensive as a war.[50] William, apparently, feared that the king in his unreasoning anger would refuse to complete the negotiations for the truce. While he soothed Richard's temper, he pointed out the advantages of the proposed terms. A few days later the two kings solemnly concluded the five year truce.

During these years William was far too busy in Normandy to pay much attention to his official duties in England. He appeared before the exchequer at Michaelmas 1194 to close his account as sheriff of Gloucestershire and answer for his new county, Sussex, but after that year all his accounts were rendered by his deputies.[51] As sheriff of Gloucestershire he had had the custody of the royal forest of Dean which lay to the east of the river Wye near his own lands. After his loss of the shrievalty he retained the custodianship of the forest at an

---

[49] *Hist.*, 11579-11622.   [50] *Ibid.*, 11655-11688.
[51] Pipe Roll 6 Richard I, *Pipe Roll Society*, XLIII, 226, 231.

annual farm of ten pounds.[52] He made at least two more visits to England during this period—once in the spring of 1196 and again in the autumn of 1198.[53] On each of these occasions he sat as a royal justice at the conclusion of final concords. In general his visits to England were brief, and his activities were centered in Normandy.

In 1194 William had taken with him to the continent enough knights to fill two ships. Two charters issued during this period enable one to name at least some of these knights and form an idea of William's household. One of these was issued in 1196 by Henry, prior of Longueville, and attested by William and a number of his household.[54] The other is an act of William himself which was issued at his castle of Meullers, near Dieppe, in 1198.[55] Among the knights who witnessed these charters were John Marshal, Nicholas Avenel, Hugh de Sanford, John d'Erley, and William Waleran. This John Marshal, who was to achieve considerable eminence during the reigns of John and Henry III, has been identified as the son of William's elder brother, but this is clearly impossible.[56] Not only is William known to have inherited all the lands which his brother had held, but he was referred to as his heir in a number of official documents.[57] John Marshal must have been the son of one of William's younger brothers. He accompanied his uncle to Flanders in 1197 and continued to be a member of his household until 1207. Nicholas Avenel held land in the lordship of Striguil and had been William's deputy as sheriff of Gloucester. Hugh de Sanford was a vassal of the honor of Giffard and one of William's most faithful followers. John d'Erley had been William's squire as early as 1188 and was at this time a knight

[52] *Ibid.*, p. 239.

[53] *Ibid.*, XVII, 110. *Feet of Fines 1195-1214* (*Record Commission*), p. 176.

[54] *Newington-Longueville charters* (ed. H. E. Salter, *Oxford Record Society*), p. 54.

[55] *Récueil des actes de Henri II*, Introduction, p. 493-4.

[56] See Powicke, *The Loss of Normandy*, pp. 367-369 and Meyer, *Hist.*, III, 143, note 4 and his correction *ibid.*, p. clviii.

[57] *Rot. Chart.*, p. 47. *Curia Regis Rolls*, I, 50.

of his household. William Waleran was a witness to a number of William's charters. In addition to the knights there were his chaplain, Eustace, his chamberlain, Osbert, and three clerks, Joscelin, Michael, and Pentecost. Then there was William de Herecuria, the seneschal of Longueville. Finally, the fact that William's charter of 1198 purports to have been issued with the consent of the Countess Isabel indicates that she may have been in Normandy at this time.[58] Thus one can picture William in his rare moments of leisure living in his own castles with his family and household.

The first week of March 1199 found Richard in the valley of the Loir attended by the bishops of Salisbury and Chester, Count John of Mortain, Earl Robert of Leicester, William Marshal, William de Briouse, and other knights, barons and clerks.[59] One day an embassy arrived from one of the least reliable of Poitevin barons, Aimar, viscount of Limoges. A marvelous treasure consisting apparently of a gilded shield decorated with golden figures and a number of ancient coins had been unearthed on the land of one of Aimar's vassals, Achard, lord of Chalus. The viscount was sending his suzerain his due share of the treasure-trove. Richard, who was always in need of money and who had a well-founded dislike of Aimar, refused to be satisfied and demanded the entire find.[60] According to Norman law the king's claim was justified, but the customs of Anjou which appear to have been similar to those of Poitou permitted a baron to keep silver while he turned over gold to his suzerain.[61] Probably Poitevin custom allowed Aimar the coins which were in all likelihood of silver, but gave the gilded shield to Richard as overlord. Nevertheless the king

[58] William's eldest son was born in Normandy (*Hist.*, 16209).

[59] *Calendar of Charter Rolls 1327-1341*, p. 164.

[60] Roger of Hovedon, IV, 82. Rigord (ed. H. F. Delaborde, *Société de l'histoire de France*), pp. 144-5.

[61] *Le Très Ancien coutumier de Normandie* (ed. E. J. Tardif, in *Coutumiers de Normandie*, vol. I, part I, *Société de l'histoire de Normandie*), p. 64. *Coutume de Touraine-Anjou* (ed. P. Viollet, in *Etablissments de St. Louis*, vol. III, *Société de l'histoire de France*), p. 52.

insisted on his right to the whole treasure, and the viscount refused to surrender it. Richard promptly set out for the Limousin with his mercenaries and a few tried knights of his household to punish his disobedient vassal. As he suspected that the remaining treasure had been concealed in Chalus, he laid siege to that castle. On March 26th as the king rode gaily before the walls of Chalus, armed only with headpiece and shield, taking pot-shots with his cross-bow at any member of the garrison who exposed himself, a well aimed bolt struck him down. On April 6th he died of the wound.[62]

When Richard left Chateau-du-Loir on his fatal Poitevin expedition, his brother John had gone into Brittany to visit his nephew, Arthur, and William Marshal had returned to Normandy to observe the activities of Philip Augustus. On April 7th William was at Vaudreuil with the archbishop of Canterbury, the bishop of Bath, the seneschal and constable of Normandy, and a number of Norman barons.[63] A courier riding hard from the south spurred into Vaudreuil, sought out William and the archbishop, and appraised them of the king's desperate state.[64] William was ordered to take command of the Tower of Rouen which apparently contained the state treasure of Normandy.[65] These two favorites and faithful servants of the dying king rode mournfully to Rouen. There William occupied the castle, while the archbishop took up his residence in the priory of Notre Dame du Pré on the other side of the Seine.[66]

As they waited at Rouen for news of Richard's condition, William and the archbishop had far more to think of than their personal anxiety for a beloved sovereign. The king of England lay dying, and the question of the succession was still unsettled. The *History* records a conversation between them on this subject which it places after they had received word of the king's death.[67] As Richard on his death-bed declared John his

[62] See Norgate, *Richard the Lion Heart*, pp. 325-329.
[63] *Hist.*, 11791-11800. *Abbreviatio Placitorum* (*Record Commission*), p. 88.
[64] *Hist.*, 11802-11805.			[66] *Ibid.*, 11844-5.
[65] *Ibid.*, 11776-11784.			[67] *Ibid.*, 11853-11908.

heir, it seems likely that the discussion, in which no mention is made of this circumstance in John's favor, took place somewhat earlier. Undoubtedly the prelate and baron, the only ones in Rouen who knew of Richard's mishap, devoted much thought to the vexed question of the succession.[68] Hubert Walter and William each considered the matter from two distinct angles— which of the two, John or Arthur, was the rightful heir to the Angevin domains and which would make the more satisfactory king. The first question was one to which the legists of the day could give no definite answer. Hubert Walter, accepting the representative principle, argued that Arthur as the son of John's elder brother should succeed to the throne. William on the other hand claimed that John had more right to the land which his father and brother had held than the son of a brother who had never been in possession of the family domains. As he expressed it, " the son is nearer to the land of his father than the nephew is." [69] Both of these opinions can be supported from contemporary law books. William's view was in full accord with Norman custom as expressed in the *Très Ancien Coutumier*—" the younger son is the nearer heir to the inheritance of his father than the child of the elder brother who died before his father." [70] This probably represents the attitude of primitive German law.[71] The treatise on English law generally ascribed to Ranulf de Glanvill but which may have been written by Hubert Walter himself is far less positive. The author admits that grave doubt exists as to which of the two, uncle or nephew, the law prefers and gives the arguments on both sides. He himself is inclined to favor the nephew's claim.[72] Bracton leans still more strongly in this direction—but he still has some doubts.[73] After his time the representative principle was fully

---

[68] The *History* states definitely that the news was given solely to William and the archbishop. *Hist.*, 11804-5.

[69] *Ibid.*, 11900-1.   [70] *Très Ancien Coutumier*, XII, 1, pp. 12-13.

[71] Pollock and Maitland, *History of English Law*, II, 281.

[72] Glanvill, *De Legibus et Consuetudinibus Regni Anglie* (ed. G. E. Woodbine), VII, 3, pp. 101-104.

[73] Bracton, *De Legibus* (ed. T. Twiss, *Rolls Series*), I, 512.

accepted in English law.[74] It is clear that William was voicing the traditional viewpoint and Hubert Walter the modern trend. William then went on to discuss the qualifications of the two candidates. Arthur was haughty, easily angered, and as a friend and protégé of Philip Augustus he had no love for the English, while John with all his faults was an Englishman. Neither the archbishop nor William can be said to have had any enthusiasm for either candidate—they simply disagreed as to which was the lesser of two evils. Hubert Walter finally gave way to William with the warning that he would repent his advocacy of John's cause. But he did not change his views as to the rightful heir. In his coronation speech some months later he carefully pointed out that John was king by election rather than by inheritance.[75] William Marshal and Hubert Walter did not give John the succession—Richard's death-bed decree and the acquiescence of the prelates and barons of the Angevin domains made him his brother's heir—but the influence of the primate of England and the most powerful baron of the realm must have drawn many a lesser man into John's party.

It was on the eve of Palm Sunday, April 10th, 1199, that the messenger bearing the tidings of Richard's death reached the Tower of Rouen.[76] While William had in all probability already decided to support John's claim to the succession, he was confirmed in this intention by the news that the dying king had declared his younger brother his heir. William was in somewhat of a quandary as to what steps he should take. It was clearly his duty to hold the Tower of Rouen until he received the commands of his new master who was in Brittany at the time, but it was extremely important that someone should go to England to inform the justiciar, Geoffrey fitz Peter, that Richard was dead and that he had declared John his heir. This mission he entrusted to his favorite knight, John d'Erley, who

---

[74] For a discussion of the principle of representation see Pollock and Maitland, *History of English Law*, II, 281-284.

[75] Matthew Paris, *Chronica Majora* (ed. H. R. Luard, *Rolls Series*), II, 454-5.

[76] *Hist.*, 11836-11840.

immediately departed for England.[77] William himself and Archbishop Hubert awaited John's commands in Rouen.[78] Meanwhile the barons of Anjou, Maine, and Touraine had declared for Arthur, and John's first task was to reduce them to obedience.[79] He therefore ordered William and Hubert Walter to proceed to England at once while he marched on Chinon to secure the Angevin treasury.[80] When they arrived in England, William and the archbishop, in conjunction with the justiciar, ordered everyone to swear allegiance to John. While most of the kingdom was willing to accept the Count of Mortain as Richard's heir, there was a group of powerful barons who wished to force him to purchase their support. These included David, earl of Huntingdon, brother of king William of Scotland, Richard de Clare, earl of Hertford, Ranulf, earl of Chester, William de Ferrars, earl of Derby, Waleran, earl of Warwick, and Roger, constable of Chester. The justiciar and his two associates summoned these great lords and others who were disaffected to meet them at Northampton. It is by no means clear what these barons of the north and midland counties desired, but they were satisfied when John's representatives promised in his name that each one would receive his " right " —that is, every privilege he was entitled to. They all took the required oath of allegiance to John.[81]

King William of Scotland did not anticipate that England would accept John so readily, and he hoped to sell him his support at a high price. As soon as he heard of Richard's death, he despatched messengers to Normandy to offer John his adherence in return for the counties of Northumberland and Cumberland. The messengers were intercepted in England, and William, the primate, and the justiciar refused to permit them to proceed to Normandy. They, apparently, feared that John might be tempted to accept King William's offer. Instead they sent the earl of Huntington to inform his brother that he must

[77] Ibid., 11909-11916.
[78] Ibid., 11917-8.
[79] Roger of Hovedon, IV, 86-7.   [80] Ibid., p. 86.   [81] Ibid., p. 88.

await John's arrival in England before presenting his demands.[82] When William felt that the allegiance of England was amply secured, he returned to Normandy. On May 21st he was with John at Dieppe, and four days later they landed at Shoreham.[83]

While William was by no means responsible for John's succession to the English throne, he had rendered him great assistance in securing his kingdom. His power, his prestige, and the general confidence that everyone had in him undoubtedly contributed much to the ease with which the disaffected English barons were appeased. John was duly grateful for these services and did not delay in rewarding them. Although William had held for a decade the estates of Richard de Clare, earl of Pembroke, he had never been formally created an earl. On the day of his coronation the new king solemnly girded him with the comptal sword.[84] Roger of Hovedon states that he was created earl of Striguil, but the designation earl of Pembroke was always used by William himself and is far more common in official documents. The significance lay less in the actual title than in the fact that its holder enjoyed comptal rank. Bracton explains that the earls were called *comites* because they were the companions of the king, the men whom he had chosen as his counselors—a definition drawn from Roman Law.[85] The rank of earl was a distinct dignity but little more. Its sole pecuniary attribute was the earl's right to the third penny of the pleas in the county court. This heritage from the Anglo-Saxon origins of their title was not enjoyed by all earls and seems to have been conferred by a special grant from the crown. As Pembroke was a county palatine in which he was entitled to all the proceeds of government, the third penny was of no interest to William. His comptal rank merely increased his social prestige.

[82] Roger of Hovedon, IV, 88-9.
[83] *Ibid.* Round, *Calendar*, no. 112.   [84] Roger of Hovedon, IV, 90.
[85] Bracton, *De Legibus*, I, 36. For the Roman origins of the comptal title see Fustel de Coulanges, *Les Origines du Système Feudal* (6th edition), ed. by C. Jullian), pp. 227-35.

John showed his appreciation of William's service in a more practical manner by appointing him sheriff of Gloucestershire with the custody of the castles of Gloucester and Bristol.[86] With this he retained the custodianship of the forest of Dean and the shrievalty of Sussex to which pertained the custody of Chichester Castle.[87] The Memoranda Roll of 1199 raises an interesting question regarding his appointment as sheriff of Gloucestershire. When William's deputy appeared before the barons of the exchequer, the earl himself being with John in Normandy, they demanded that he pay an increment of one hundred marks on the farm of the county. The clerk replied that his lord, William Marshal, had not agreed to pay an increment and did not intend to do so. The barons thereupon requested the justiciar to write to the king to learn his pleasure.[88] It will be remembered that when William was displaced as sheriff in 1194, his successor agreed to pay an increment of one hundred marks a year on the old farm of the county. The barons expected to continue to collect this sum from William, but he insisted that he had only contracted to pay the old farm. William seems to have won the argument, as he never paid any increment on the farm of Gloucestershire.[89]

When in the spring of 1194 William had refused to do homage to Richard for his lordship of Leinster, the chancellor had accused him of "planting vines." His support of John's claims to the succession in 1199 might be considered as a sedulous cultivation of these vines in anticipation of the crop. Still, this would not be fair to William. He had refused to do homage for Leinster because he believed that Richard had no control over John's lordship of Ireland. When Richard died, he supported John as the legal heir and as the least objectionable of the claimants. He knew John's faults, but he nevertheless preferred him to Arthur. Therefore, he did what he could to aid

[86] *Pipe Roll 1 John,* Public Record Office, E 372/45.
[87] *Ibid.*
[88] *Memoranda Roll 1 John,* Public Record Office, E 370-1/3.
[89] *Chancellor's Roll 3 John* (*Record Commission*), pp. 34-5.

John in securing his kingdom. In recognition of his services the new king not only created him an earl, but increased his official position in the English administration. During the last five years of Richard's life William had steadily risen in his esteem—the accession of John seemed about to raise him still higher in the royal favor.

CHAPTER VII

LORD OF LONGUEVILLE

There could be no better testimony to the dominant personality of Richard Plantagenet than the course of events in the continental possessions of the Angevin house after his death. To the casual observer the balance between the Capetians and their rivals would seem to have been changed in only one respect by the tragedy at Chalus—because of his claim to the English throne the intrigues of Arthur of Brittany and his mother Constance were a more serious menace to John than they had been to his brother. The new king was slightly if at all inferior to his predecessor in military capacity and was probably a more able administrator. He inherited the support of Richard's allies, the counts of Flanders and Boulogne and the powerful house of Guelf. John's deficiencies lay in a lack of force and stability of character. This is most clearly shown by the part played in the first years of his reign by his mother, Eleanor. While the strong hands of Henry and Richard held the reins of government, she had remained in the background, but under John she became one of the staunchest bulwarks of the throne. The case of Constance of Brittany was somewhat similar. She had intrigued against Richard without success—she succeeded in drawing Brittany out of John's sphere of influence. John needed the support of Eleanor and could not handle Constance. A more serious sign of his weakness was his utter inability to retain the confidence and loyalty of his barons. Outside of a few protégés, clerks and mercenary soldiers of low birth, he never completely trusted anyone. When Richard forgave a penitent rebel, the offence was, apparently at least, forgotten. The slightest suspicion would cause John to demand hostages and guarantees from his most loyal vassals. Suspicion breeds suspicion, and no one had much faith in John. When one combines these considerations with the continuous and skilful aggression of Philip Augustus and John's occasional periods of torpor, one has the explanation of the loss of Normandy.

At first John was fairly successful.[1] In May 1200 he concluded a reasonably favorable peace with King Philip. Arthur gave up his claims to Maine and Anjou and was to hold Brittany as a fief from John. Philip obtained the Norman Vexin, with the exception of the region about Les Andelys, and the city and about half the county of Evreux. The English king promised to give up his alliance with the counts of Boulogne and Flanders and to pay his suzerain a relief of 20,000 marks for his continental fiefs. The agreement was sealed by the marriage of Philip's heir, Louis, to John's niece, Blanche of Castille. Richard would never have accepted such terms, but a genuine peace might have been worth the sacrifices involved. John then turned his attention to strengthening his position in Anjou and Poitou. The ablest and most powerful of the Angevin baronage, William des Roches, was reconciled with the king and accepted the office of seneschal. Poitou, that most turbulent of fiefs, was a more serious problem. The district had been torn for years by the rivalry between the counts of Angoulême and the house of Lusignan. Except when they allied to rebel against their duke, their strife kept Poitou in continual confusion. No suzerain could hope to keep on good terms with both of them—Richard had simply succeeded in keeping both in semi-subjection to his authority. John, moved partly by a good healthy lust for a most charming young girl and partly by policy, formed a marriage alliance with the count of Angoulême. As the lady Isabel, daughter and heiress of Ademar of Angoulême, was already affianced to the son of Hugh de Lusignan, count of La Marche, John earned the undying enmity of the Lusignans. More serious yet, the stealing of a girl under his vassal's protection was a serious breach of feudal law and gave the Lusignans a valid excuse for an appeal to King Philip. From

---

[1] For good secondary accounts of the conquest of Normandy see Powicke, *The Loss of Normandy*, Chapter VI; Norgate, *John Lackland*, Chapter III; and Cartellieri, *Philipp II August*, Vol. IV.

this developed John's condemnation by the French king's court which, theoretically at least, deprived him of his continental fiefs.

Little is known of William's part in the affairs of these first years of John's reign. He accompanied the king to Normandy in June, 1199, and during that year and the next he seems to have been almost continuously in attendance at the court. His name appears as a witness or guarantor on all the important treaties of the period.[2] In June, 1200, he was one of the ambassadors despatched from Chinon to escort the count of Angoulême and his half-brother of Limoges to Lusignan for a conference with the king.[3] Despite his confirmed hatred for the house of Lusignan, William's sense of feudal propriety was probably too strong to permit him to urge John's marriage with Isabel, but one may suspect that it gave him considerable secret satisfaction. He had never forgotten nor forgiven the killing of his uncle, Earl Patrick. But the author of the History who may be supposed to reflect William's sentiments feels called on to disapprove of John's violation of feudal law.[4]

In the spring of 1201 the Lusignans rose in revolt, but were soon forced to make their submission. The king seized their lands and refused to give their complaints a proper hearing in his court. Pleading denial of justice, they promptly appealed to Philip as John's feudal suzerain. In March 1202 the French king ordered the duke of Aquitaine to appear before his court to answer the charges of his Poitevin vassals. When John refused to obey, he was declared contumacious and deprived of all the fiefs he held of the French crown.[5] King Philip immediately set about enforcing the decree of his court—the conquest of Normandy had commenced.

In order to understand William's part in the defence of Normandy it is necessary to have some idea of the geography of

[2] *Foedera*, I, I, 77-80. *Rot. Chart.*, p. 31. *Layettes du Trésor des Chartes*, I, no. 578. L. Delisle, *Catalogue des Actes de Philippe Auguste*, no. 606-612.
[3] *Rot. Chart.*, p. 97.
[4] *cel larrecin, Hist.*, 11996.   [5] See Norgate, *John Lackland*, p. 81-84.

that part of the duchy which lay north of the river Seine. From the channel to the river the north-eastern frontier of Normandy was defended by a line of fortresses. At the extreme northern point of the duchy stood the town of Eu which with Aumale some thirty miles further up the river Bresle guarded the actual frontier on that side. But as Ralph of Exoudun, count of Eu, was one of the de Lusignan brothers, this line was of little value. Some twenty miles within the Norman border lay the main line of defence consisting of the castles of Arques, Drincourt, and Gournay. The region between Gournay and the Seine had originally been covered by the great fortress of Gisors, but as this had been in French possession for some years, its place was filled by Lyons which lay in the center of the forest of the same name. The valley of the Seine was held by the most formidable of Norman strongholds, the castle of Gaillard with its subsidiary works.[6] To the west of the river Bethune which forms practically a straight line from Drincourt to Arques and Dieppe, lay the royal forest of Awi, and beyond it stretched the broad lands of William's county of Longueville. The safety of William's Norman fiefs depended on the success with which the great frontier castles were defended. But it was not simply as a landholder of the region that William was involved in the defence of the Pays de Caux. As early as the summer of 1200 he seems to have been the king's chief representative in the district.[7] In the following spring one of his knights, Jordan de Sackville, was strengthening the fortifications of Arques in preparation for the expected defection of the count of Eu.[8] This castle was of particular importance as it not only covered the entrance to Normandy from the side of Eu but also controlled the access to the port of Dieppe and thus one of the routes to England. As soon as the war began in earnest, the command of this region became a post of great re-

---

[6] For a complete description of the Norman defences see Powicke, *The Loss of Normandy*, Chapter VII.

[7] *Rotuli Normanniae* (ed. T. D. Hardy, *Record Commission*), p. 23.

[8] *Ibid.*, p. 35.

sponsibility. Considering his personal interest in the safety of the Pays de Caux and his high reputation as a soldier, it is easy to understand why John entrusted this task to William Marshal. Early in April 1202 before hostilities had actually commenced, John took steps to remove Eu from the control of the rebellious Ralph of Exoudun. On the pretense that he had learned of the death of Ralph's wife in whose right he held the county the king sent one of his knights, John of Eu, to take possession as the rightful heir. William Marshal was directed to send to his aid as many knights and serjeants as he could spare.[9] These measures were of no avail. With the assistance of the count of Boulogne and probably of King Philip himself Ralph of Exoudun easily overran the country between the Bresle and the Bethune and recovered his strongholds of Eu and Drincourt. William was authorized to seize the Norman possessions of the count of Boulogne including the castle of Lillibonne.[10] These he parcelled out at the king's direction to various Norman barons whose lands had been occupied by the enemy.[11] William apparently held Lillibonne until June when he turned it over to Earl William de Warren whose Norman fief was in the hands of the count of Boulogne.[12]

William's position in the Pays de Caux was officially confirmed by letters patent issued at Les Andelys on April 25th. The inhabitants of the bailiwicks of Arques and Caux were ordered to obey him as the king's representative.[13] The next day he received a sum of money from the *camera* to enable him to provision the castle of Arques and to strengthen its garrison.[14] A month later he was given one hundred marks to increase still further the force of knights and serjeants in this important fortress.[15] During the latter part of May one hundred and fifty marks were issued from the *camera* to pay these

[9] *Rotuli Litterarum Patentium* (ed. T. D. Hardy, *Record Commission*), p. 8 b.
[10] *Ibid.*, p. 9 b.   [12] *Ibid.*, p. 47.
[11] *Rotuli Normanniae*, p. 45.   [13] *Rot. Pat.*, p. 9 b.
[14] *Miscellaneous Records of the Norman Exchequer*, 1199-1204 (ed. S. R. Packard, in *Smith College Studies in History*, vol. XII, October 1926-July 1927), p. 67.   [15] *Ibid.*

troops.[16] Meanwhile King Philip had taken Lyons and laid siege to Gournay. William redoubled his efforts to put Arques in a state of defense. Between June 3rd and 28th the very considerable sum of one thousand six hundred pounds Angevin passed through his hands or those of his deputies for improving the fortifications and paying the garrison of the castle.[17] William did not take command of Arques in person. William de Mortimer and William Martel acted as constables while William Marshal had general supervision over the whole district.[18]

Early in July Gournay capitulated, and Philip marched against Arques. John ordered the barons of the Cinque Ports to prevent the French army from receiving supplies by sea.[19] At the same time he gave William four hundred pounds for the garrison of the castle.[20] This sum was apparently insufficient, as the earl was forced to borrow another hundred pounds from the mayor of Rouen.[21] While William de Mortimer valiantly defended Arques, William Marshal, William Longsword, earl of Salisbury, and Earl William de Warren at the head of a mobile force harassed the besiegers.[22] The king himself had gone to Le Mans to watch Arthur's activities. That young man had done homage to Philip for Brittany, Aquitaine, Anjou, and Maine and had set out with a French army to conquer these fiefs. At Le Mans John learned that his nephew and the de Lusignans were besieging Queen Eleanor in Mirabeau. With one of those terrific bursts of energy that made him at times so formidable an antagonist the king swept down upon Mirabeau and captured or destroyed Arthur's entire army. The count of Brittany himself and two of the de Lusignan brothers were made prisoners. It was a signal victory. The Poitevin revolt was crushed, and John was left free to devote all his attention to Philip Augustus.

[16] *Miscellaneous Records of the Norman Exchequer*, p. 67.
[17] *Ibid.*   [18] *Ibid. Hist.*, 12052-12054.   [19] *Rot. Pat.*, p. 15.
[20] *Miscellaneous Records of the Norman Exchequer*, p. 67.
[21] *Rot. Pat.*, p. 15 b.   [22] *Hist.*, 12119-12132.

Immediately after the victory John despatched a monk to convey the news to William. The good tidings were received with profound joy by the three earls in their camp near Arques, for it meant that Philip would be forced to raise the siege. William was particularly delighted, but his pleasure could not be complete until he had shared the news with the third of the de Lusignans, Ralph of Exoudun, who was with King Philip. Much against his will the monk was sent on to the French camp to inform the count of Eu of his brothers' misfortunes. Meanwhile, Philip had learned of the capture of his protégé Arthur and his Poitevin allies. He was already discouraged by the stern resistance of William de Mortimer and his men, and the knowledge that John was free to concentrate all his forces against him persuaded him to raise the siege. After striking their tents and dismantling their siege engines, the French marched away in good order. This movement was observed by William's scouts. The three earls were too weak to risk an attack on the retreating army, but they decided to go out with their cavalry to watch the enemy's march. As they had no intention of fighting, they laid aside their helms and hauberks, and so being lightly armed they quickly arrived in full view of the French host. Philip knew that their force was too small to be dangerous, but it occurred to him that if he could capture these three earls, he could exchange them for men whom John had taken at Mirabeau. Summoning William des Barres he told him to take three hundred knights, ride down a valley which would conceal his movements, and attempt to surprise the English party. But the fully armed French knights were easily outdistanced by the more lightly clad English. As observing a vastly superior force seemed too hazardous an amusement, William and his companions rode towards Rouen whither they had previously sent their baggage and infantry. At the gates of the city they were received by the mayor and his principal burghers. The good citizens were greatly disturbed by the sudden appearance of the three earls. Had Arques fallen, and was Philip marching on Rouen itself? William decided to take advantage of their fears to procure entertainment in Rouen which the privileges of the town prevented him from demanding. He informed the burghers that the French were near at hand. Solicitude for the safety of the city had moved him to come to its defence. The grateful citizens entertained the troops lavishly with the best of food and drink. The three earls sat in a hostelry while their hosts placed before them their choicest delicacies and rarest vintages. There were wines clear and sparkling, sweet and dry; wines perfumed with cloves, and spiced wines. For dessert there were pears, apples, and nuts.[23] William's diplomacy must have seemed exceptionally brilliant to the tired soldiers. A good dinner at the expense of the fat burghers—what could more thoroughly delight the heart of any knight?

While the three earls were enjoying the discomfiture of King Philip, John was disposing of the prisoners taken at Mirabeau. The Middle Ages knew few more delicate problems of state than the proper use of important captives, especially when those captives were rebels who had a fairly just cause of revolt. John seems to have made every possible mistake. At first he treated all his prisoners with extreme severity and so quite unnecessarily irritated both them and their friends. Then he took hostages from the de Lusignan brothers and released them. Arthur disappeared into Falaise, then into Rouen, and eventually in all probability into the Seine.[24] The de Lusignans were capable, dangerous, and incorrigible rebels. It would have been wise to have kept them in confinement until the end of the war. Arthur on the other hand was far more dangerous in prison than at liberty. He had no great ability and with due care could easily have been confined to this county of Brittany. But this scion of the house of Anjou had powerful and devoted friends. The proud and turbulent Breton baronage was only too ready to rally to the support of its lord. Still more formidable was William des Roches whose ability and vigor had

[23] *Ibid.*, 12132-12400.
[24] On Arthur's fate see Powicke, *The Loss of Normandy*, Appendix I.

maintained John's power in Touraine and Anjou. William was ambitious, but not unscrupulous. He considered Arthur the rightful heir to the old Angevin lands—Touraine and Anjou—and had supported him as such at Richard's death. He had gone over to John in the hope of establishing permanent peace within the royal house and incidentally improving his own position. The king had made him seneschal of Anjou and Touraine and had promised to follow his advice in all affairs pertaining to the region and in his relations with Arthur. Now he calmly ignored his protests against the treatment accorded the prisoners. When one considers that William des Roches and his men had formed the largest part of the army that John had led to Mirabeau, one can comprehend the seneschal's chagrin. He promptly went over to Philip, and the same strong hand which had held the district for John soon secured it for his new master. The defection of William des Roches combined with the immediately renewed rebellion of the de Lusignans meant the end of English rule in Maine, Anjou, Touraine, and Poitou. Meanwhile in Normandy John dallied with his fair young wife. Dreaming of aid from pope and emperor, the king displayed an incredible lethargy while Philip reduced his fortresses. A wild contagion of treason spread through the Norman baronage. They had lost all confidence in John—all hope in his cause. Count Robert of Alençon and Hugh de Gournay went over to Philip. Robert fitz Walter and Saher de Quency surrendered without a struggle the stronghold of Vaudreuil.

William spent most of the spring and summer of 1203 following King John about his rapidly diminishing domains. In December 1202 he had been at least temporarily relieved of his responsibility for the Pays de Caux by letters patent which gave the custody of the castle of Arques and the bailiwicks of Arques and Caux to William de Mortimer and William Martel.[25] There is little or no evidence as to what William Marshal's activities were during this dismal period. Small sums

---

[25] *Rot. Pat.*, p. 22.

were issued to him from the *camera* to expend in the king's service.[26] The castellan of Gaillard was ordered to permit the passage of a cargo of wine consigned to him.[27] King John did little or nothing, and William was usually in his train. One day while Philip was besieging Conches, the king sent William to the French camp to attempt to make peace. The earl soon discovered that Philip would make no terms, but before leaving his court, he remonstrated with the king for his encouragement of the Norman traitors. " Fair Sire," he said, " I would like to know, if you please to tell me, why traitors who in days gone by were burned, cut to pieces, and torn apart by horses in France, are now so deeply rooted in the land that they are all lords and masters." " By my faith," replied the king, " that is but natural; it is now a matter of business. They are like torches which one throws in the latrine when one is done with them." [28] Philip would discuss the propriety of his policy with an old friend, but he would not make peace with John.

By August Philip had taken Vaudreuil and Radepont. Only Chateau-Gaillard with its gallant garrison under the command of Roger de Lacy, constable of Chester, blocked the road to Rouen. Late in that month the French king occupied the peninsula formed by a bend of the Seine opposite Les Andelys, threw a pontoon bridge over the river, and laid siege to the walled town of Andeli at the foot of the castle rock. The investment of Gaillard had begun. John made one ineffectual attempt to relieve the fortress and then abandoned it to its fate. One authority asserts that William Marshal commanded this expedition, but no other source mentions his name in connection with it.[29] It seems incredible that the author of the *History* with his taste for battles would have neglected to mention this combat if William had taken part in it.[30] William le Breton

---

[26] *Miscellaneous Records of the Norman Exchequer,* p. 68.

[27] *Rotuli Normanniae,* p. 65.   [28] *Hist.* 12675-12704.

[29] *Philippidos,* book VII, line 144 et seq. In describing this same incident in his prose chronicle William le Breton makes no mention of William. (*Gesta Philippi Augusti,* pp. 213-216.)   [30] See Meyer's note *Hist.,* III, 173, note 5.

probably used poetic license in attaching a well-known name to one of the most colorful passages of his *Philippidos.*

John's inability to relieve Gaillard was the last blow to the confidence of the Norman barons. Those who had remained loyal were convinced that the conquest of the duchy by Philip was inevitable. In these circumstances their interests demanded peace at any price. If a treaty were made, Philip might allow them to retain their lands as his vassals—if he conquered the country by force of arms, their Norman possessions were doomed. William fully shared this point of view. His own lands at Longueville were still safe, but they could not be held indefinitely. In fact at his camp before Gaillard Philip promised to give one of William's castles to the count of Boulogne as soon as it should come into his possession.[31] But if peace were made, the earl felt certain that his friendship with the French king would assure him his Norman fiefs. Early in October he advised John to come to terms with his enemy, but the king insisted that he would continue the contest for at least a year. The earl even had the temerity to point out to his master that it was his own fault that he had no friends. The king had irritated his barons—he had better make peace with his enemies.[32] Although he was unquestionably loyal, William was urging the surrender of Normandy. It was the first portent of his fall from royal favor.

On December 5th both William and the king sailed from Barfleur for England.[33] Except for a few isolated strongholds such as Gaillard, Rouen, and Arques, Normandy was lost. The earl's part in the defence of the duchy had not been particularly brilliant, but so utterly ineffective a campaign rarely raises generals to fame. What glory was to be distributed to John's supporters went to such loyal and gallant castellans as William de Mortimer, Roger de Lacy, and Peter des Preaux who conducted magnificent defences of single fortresses. Still, William Mar-

---

[31] Delisle, *Catalogue des Actes de Philippe Auguste,* no. 787a.
[32] *Hist.,* 12721-12742.
[33] *Ibid.,* 12829-12830. Roger of Wendover, I, 318.

shal, either through his own energy and ability or through good fortune, had been remarkably successful in holding the region entrusted to him. His mobile force must have seriously hampered the army besieging Arques—at the same time that it protected his own lands from Philip's foragers. With the channel patrolled by the ships of the Cinque Ports and with William's troops hovering on his flanks the French king must have found it difficult to provision his army. As the field officer in charge of the threatened district a part of the credit for its successful defence must go to William. His own lands were never actually conquered, but this may have been due in part to Philip's forbearance. After the fall of Gaillard and the enemy's advance on Rouen, their position was hopeless. William had been loyal and more successful than most of his fellow commanders in John's service. On the political side there is no evidence as to William's influence on or responsibility for the king's policy. The *History* makes clear that the earl disapproved of John's freeing of the de Lusignans, of his treatment of William des Roches, and of his general attitude toward his barons. If he tendered wise counsel, it had no great effect. Doubtless when he urged the king to make peace, he was considering his own interests and those of his fellow barons. Believing the king's cause hopeless, he wanted to save his own fiefs. John was not a master to inspire much unselfish devotion.

The French conquest of Normandy forced the Anglo-Norman barons to make their choice between the two monarchs and content themselves with their possessions on one or the other side of the channel. In general, as one would expect, they followed their major interests and entered the allegiance of the sovereign who controlled the larger part of their lands.[34] No English baron of any importance went over to Philip, and the lands seized by John as *terrae Normannorum* were comparitively insignificant. But those English families which had held considerable fiefs in Normandy could not be easily reconciled

[34] For a discussion of the fate of the Norman baronies see Powicke, *The Loss of Normandy*, Appendix II.

to their loss, and their insistance on the return of their continental possessions was to be for many years an important factor in Anglo-French relations. During the years following John's retirement from Normandy they formed a strong party favoring a definite peace which would allow them to hold their fiefs on both sides of the sea. Earl Robert of Leicester probably had the greatest stake in Normandy of any English baron, but William Marshal because of his power and prestige in England, his favor at John's court, and his friendship with Philip Augustus became the leader of this group. Opposed to them were those who had no personal interests on the continent. This party, led by Archbishop Hubert Walter, argued that peace with Philip would involve the formal surrender of John's rights in the conquered territory. It was better to have a claim without actual possession than to have neither. England's honor would be abased if she resigned her rights. These two parties struggled to control John's policy in his relations with Philip.

In the spring of 1204 John still had some hope of making a compromise with Philip. While Rouen, Arques, Verneuil, and the fortresses of the west held out, the French king might not feel completely certain of his ultimate success. In April John sent an embassy consisting of the archbishop of Canterbury, the bishops of Norwich and Ely, and the earls of Leicester and Pembroke to attempt to conclude an honorable peace.[35] When they reached the French court at Bec, they discovered that Philip would not listen to any terms acceptable to John. He demanded that either Arthur or his sister be surrendered to him to hold from him all the continental domains of the house of Anjou. The king turned a deaf ear to all the counter suggestions of the English ambassadors. While he was not certain as to Arthur's fate, he probably suspected the truth. According to Ralph de Coggeshal he threatened to devote his life to driving John from the English throne if it were true that Arthur

[35] *Hist.*, 12854-12858. Ralph de Coggeshall (ed. J. Stevenson, *Rolls Series*), pp. 144-5.

had been murdered. Philip finally announced that any baron who wished to hold lands in Normandy should do him liege homage. The two earls were in a quandary. They dared not risk the loss of their English lands by doing homage to Philip without John's permission, yet they were exceedingly anxious to retain their Norman fiefs. At length they reached a compromise with the king by which they were given a year in which to make their final decision. For this respite each of them was to pay Philip five hundred marks.[36] The exact terms of the agreement between William and the French king have been preserved.[37] The earl was to surrender at once his castle of Orbec, and Philip would put a garrison in it. The castles of Longueville and Meullers were to be turned over to Osbert de Rouvrai, a Norman knight in Philip's service, who was to hold them until June 24th when they also were to receive French garrisons. If within a year William did liege homage to Philip for his Norman fiefs, they were to be returned to him to be held for the customary service. For this delay he would give the king five hundred marks—two-thirds to be paid on June 24th and the rest on August 1st. If he failed to pay the money or to do homage before the end of the year, his lands and castles would be forfeited to Philip. William was betting five hundred marks that within a year he could persuade John to make peace or at least give him permission to do homage to Philip.

In the spring of 1205 William succeeded in stealing a march on the party opposed to peace by persuading John to send him with Hugh, archdeacon of Welles, to negotiate with Philip.[38] Before he left the king, William brought up the question of his Norman fiefs. "Sire, I am not certain that I can make peace, and the respite for my Norman lands is nearly over. If I do not do homage to the king, I shall suffer great loss." John replied, "I know you to be so loyal that no consideration would draw your affection from me. I wish you to do the homage to save yourself from loss, for I know that the more land you

---

[36] *Hist.*, 12891-12898.

[37] *Layettes du Trésor des Chartes*, I, no. 715.   [38] *Hist.*, 12935-12946.

have, the better you will serve me." [39] The king gave William
letters which informed Philip that he was authorized to perform the required homage.[40] The two envoys found the French
court at Compiègne. Philip showed a disposition to negotiate
and agreed to discuss the matter in eight days at Anet. But
meanwhile Hubert Walter, who had been kept in ignorance of
the plan to make peace, learned the nature of William's mission. Ralph d'Ardern was just setting out on a royal errand
across the sea, and the archbishop took the occasion to send a
private message to Philip to the effect that William and his
fellow envoy had no power to make peace.[41] Ralph gave this
information to the count of Boulogne who passed it on to the
king. When the ambassadors appeared at Anet, Philip refused
to negotiate and reproached them for deceiving him as to their
powers.[42] Despite William's initial advantage, the archbishop
had won the game.

Although William's official mission had ended in failure, he
was successful in settling his private affairs. After he had presented to Philip John's letters authorizing the ceremony, he did
him " liege homage on this side of the sea " for his Norman
fiefs.[43] The exact meaning of this most unusual expression is
far from clear. Bracton in explaining that Frenchmen could
not ordinarily plead in England pointed out that William Marshal and several others could plead in both England and France
because they owed fealty to both kings. If the two countries
should go to war, these men would serve in person the king to
whom they had sworn allegiance and send to the other the
service owed by their fiefs.[44] Glanville also used the term allegiance to designate the relationship between a vassal and the

[39] *Ibid.*, 12948-12966. Gervase of Canterbury, II, 96.
[40] See statement made by William's son in 1220. (*Layettes du Trésor des Chartes*, I, no. 1397).
[41] *Rotuli Litterarum Clausarum* (ed. T. D. Hardy, *Record Commission*), I, 28.
[42] *Hist.*, 12995-13020.
[43] *hominagium ligium citra mare, Layettes du Trésor des Chartes*, I, no. 1397.
[44] *fidem* contrasted with *ligeantiam.* Bracton, *De Legibus*, VI, 374-376.

chief of several lords.[45] Both of these writers show that homage
and fidelity could be separate from allegiance which involved
a close personal relationship and could be due to but one lord.
But Bracton's elucidation of William's position cannot be reconciled with the latter's conception of his obligations to Philip
of France. Within a year after performing this homage William was to refuse to accompany John to Poitou on the ground
that he was the " man " of the French king.[46] To him " liege
homage on this side of the sea " obviously meant that he was
John's liege man in England and Philip's in France. If the
French invaded England, he could fight against them, but he
could not participate in John's attempts to recover his continental possessions. The earl had definitely divided his
allegiance.

When William returned to England, he found that Ralph
d'Ardern had already told John of his oath to Philip. The king
received him with a reproach, " I know beyond a doubt that
you have sworn fealty and allegiance to the king of France
and have done him homage against me and to my disadvantage.[47] " Sire," the earl replied, " whoever told you that loved
me not and lied to you. You know right well that I did nothing against you and what I did, I did by your leave." " By the
faith," said John " you did not." Despite this denial William
insisted that the king had told him to do homage to Philip
rather than lose his lands. John was not convinced and demanded a judgement by his barons, but no decision seems to
have been reached at the time.[48] The grievance remained to
rankle in the king's mind. It is impossible to ascertain where
the truth lay in this controversy. The king had not only given
William verbal permission to do homage to Philip, but had sent
the latter letters to the same effect. But John may have en-
visaged simply a secondary homage as described by Glanville

[45] Glanville, IX, I, pp. 123-126.
[46] Hist., 13134-13142.
[47] fait al rei de France feelte, ligance, et homage contre mai et pur mon
damage. Ibid., 13062-13064.   [48] Ibid., 13068-13090.

and Bracton. He had expected the earl to do homage and swear fidelity to Philip, but not to enter his allegiance. As the expression " liege homage on this side of the sea " seems to have been invented by William and the French king to fit the occasion, John could hardly have foreseen the exact obligations involved. If, as seems probable, the earl had divided his allegiance without the king realizing that he intended to do so, John had decidedly the better case. One has difficulty in believing that William was not guilty of intentional deception.

This question arose again when, in June of the same year, King John mustered his army at Portsmouth in preparation for an expedition to Poitou.[49] One day as the king and his entourage were sitting on the shore, John asked William why he had made an alliance with Philip of France. The earl replied, as he had before, that he had done nothing against John and what he had done, he had done with his leave. Once more the king denied this and demanded the judgement of the barons. Again William insisted that he had acted with the king's permission, and again John denied it. Finally the king brought the argument to a crisis. " You will go with me to Poitou," he told William, " to reconquer my inheritance from the king of France to whom you have done homage." " Ah, Sire! " replied the earl, " it would be a felony for me to go against him, for I am his man." The king called the assembly to witness that this statement of William's proved his offence. He was the man of Philip Augustus and could not follow John to battle. Still William insisted that he had acted with perfect propriety and offered to prove it in combat with any man in the realm, but John insisted on a judgement by his barons. Accepting the king's proposal, William turned to the barons, " Lords, look at me. Today I am an example and mirror for all of you. Attend closely to the king, for what he plans to do to me, he will do to you all and worse yet if he can." These words, not unnaturally, enraged the king, and he demanded a decision from his barons—had William been false to him when he did

[49] *Ibid.*, 13096-7.

homage to Philip? The barons glanced at one another and drew away without replying. They had no desire to become involved in so delicate a question. Ordinarily this should have closed the incident. John charged that William had committed a felony: William denied it, and the question was put to his peers, his fellow barons, for decision. Their refusal to answer amounted practically to an acquittal.

John, however, was not satisfied. " By the teeth of God! I see that none of my barons are on my side. I know whom I can trust. I shall converse in private with my bachelors about this treason." While the king walked off a short distance with his bachelors, William sought the counsel of his friends, but of all his familiars only Henry fitz Gerold and John d'Erley dared brave the king's wrath by speaking to him. Meanwhile John requested his bachelors' opinion of William's offence. In general, they agreed that a man who under the present circumstances refused to follow his lord to war, could not hold land from him. This view was expressed by John de Bassingbourn—" whoever fails his lord can no longer hold land." At this point William's old companion in arms, Baldwin de Bethune, count of Aumale, intervened in the discussion. " Be silent," said he, " it is not fitting for you or me to judge in court a knight of the Marshal's eminence. On all this field there is no man strong enough to prove in combat that he has failed his lord." John tried hard to find a champion willing to challenge William, but no one was anxious to face so famous a warrior, and the king was forced to let the matter drop.[50]

This whole incident is most perplexing. In general the term bachelor was used to designate either young men who were aspirants to knighthood or young knights who had not yet made a name for themselves.[51] It is used at least once in the *History* in the latter sense.[52] But neither of these definitions can apply in this case. John de Bassingbourn was a tried servant of the king whom two years later he made constable of the great

[50] *Ibid.*, 13107-13256.
[51] See Gautier, *La Chevalerie*, Chapter VI.   [52] *Hist.*, 11252.

castle of Corfe.[53] Baldwin de Bethune had served in the household of young Henry, had followed Richard to the Holy Land, and as count of Aumale ranked as an earl. Although Aumale was in the hands of Philip, Baldwin was far from landless as he held a number of fiefs in England. Apparently in this context the bachelors were men in the king's pay as semi-permanent members of his household as distinct from the barons who were present in fulfilment of their obligations as tenants-in-chief. Baldwin may have been a member of John's mesnie, but he was no untried, landless knight. This use of the term bachelor to describe any one serving under another's banner was common in England in the late thirteenth and fourteenth centuries.[54] The king was seeking from a select group of his vassals, those most dependent on him, the decision which the barons had declined to render. John de Bassingbourn was undoubtedly correct in his expression of feudal law, but Baldwin was equally so when he asserted that the bachelors could not judge William. Except for men like Baldwin himself, who was a baron as well as a member of the household, they were not his peers.

When John discovered that he could not punish William, he pretended to forgive him. As he still had grave doubts of the earl's loyalty, he demanded his eldest son as a hostage.[55] William, who had no intention of injuring the king, readily complied. Thus started the estrangement between John and William Marshal. One of the ablest and most powerful of the king's barons had done homage to his mortal enemy and had refused to follow him to war. This destroyed John's confidence in William's loyalty—therein lay the root of their quarrel. One is forced to sympathize with both these men. The king was justified in objecting to William's division of his allegiance. On the other hand John had shown himself unable to protect William's Norman fiefs, and the earl felt entitled to do what was necessary to retain them. The king should have realized that

[53] *Rot. Pat.*, p. 74.
[54] E. F. Jacob in *Chivalry*, p. 40 (ed. E. Prestage, in *The History of Civilization*). [55] *Hist.*, 13272.

William was incapable of treason, but John's suspicions always overpowered his judgement. The impartial observer must conclude that while William had not acted with complete honesty, John showed a woeful lack of comprehension of his great vassal's character.

Although William's homage to Philip Augustus was the basic cause of his estrangement from John, the more serious phases of their quarrel grew out of other circumstances. The earl's power in England and the marches of Wales had developed to an extent that the king could not view with equanimity once he had lost his confidence in its holder's trustworthiness. At the beginning of his reign John had given William the shrievalty of Gloucestershire with the custody of the castles of Gloucester and Bristol.[56] The earl had also obtained the custodianship of the forest of Dean with the castle of St. Briavells.[57] Early in 1202 the king gave him the custody of the royal fortress of Cardigan with an annual allowance of four hundred marks for its maintenance.[58] This castle, situated near the mouth of the river Teifi, was the key to the mountainous region south of that stream which was continually in dispute between the earls of Pembroke and the native Welsh princes. John had given Kilgerran, one of the most important strongholds in this region, to Maelgwyn ap Rees, prince of South Wales, but in the summer of 1204 William captured this castle and made himself master of the whole country between the Teifi and the lowlands of Pembroke.[59] Earlier in that same year the king had given him Castle Goodrich which controlled the valley of the Wye some miles below Ross in Herefordshire.[60] By the end of 1204 William's position in south Wales and its marches closely rivalled that of the earl of Chester in the north. When one considers that William was also sheriff of Sussex

[56] *Pipe Rolls* 1-8 John, Public Record Office.   [57] *Ibid. Rot Pat.*, p. 65b.
[58] *Rotuli de Liberate ac de Misis et Praestitis* (ed. T. D. Hardy, *Record Commission*), pp. 27, 71. *Rot. Claus.*, I, 54b, 68b.
[59] *Rot. Chart.*, p. 44. *Brut y tywysogion*, p. 261. *Annales Cambriae*, p. 63.
[60] *Rot. Chart.*, p. 124.

and had the custody of the important fortress of Chichester, one can easily comprehend why John feared his power once his loyalty was called in question.[61]

A still more active factor in widening the breach between William and the king was the situation in Ireland.[62] John was lord of Ireland, but this title carried little real power outside a few small districts on the east coast. The larger part of the country occupied by the Anglo-Norman invaders was under the control of barons who possessed palatine authority. Hugh de Lacy, earl of Ulster, Walter de Lacy, lord of Meath, William Marshal, lord of Leinster, and William de Briouse, lord of Limerick, were the real masters of Ireland. These feudal potentates and the minor tenants-in-chief varied their usual amusement of fighting the Irish with furious feuds among themselves. Although John's policy in Ireland was so vacillating that it is difficult to distinguish any definite purpose behind it, in general he strove, as one would expect, to maintain order and to extend the authority of his agent, the justiciar, at the expense of the palatine powers of the great barons. Soon after he ascended the English throne, John appointed to the office of justiciar one of the original group of Norman conquerors, Meiler fitz Henry. Meiler was a tenant-in-chief of comparatively small fiefs, and the bulk of his lands were held of the lord of Leinster. In the attempt to carry out the continually varying policy of his master and at the same time promote his own interests, he succeeded in quarreling with the most of the barons of Ireland. By the end of the year 1206 he was at odds not only with William de Briouse but also with the latter's son-in-law Walter de Lacy, lord of Meath. He had even infringed on the possessions of William Marshal in Leinster by seizing, with the king's consent if not by his express command, the castle and fief of Offaly.[63] But as both William Marshal and William de

[61] Pipe Rolls 1-6 John, Public Record Office.
[62] For a complete discussion of contemporary events in Ireland see G. H. Orpen, Ireland under the Normans. There is a brief summary in Norgate, John Lackland, pp. 137-145. [63] Rot. Pat., p. 72.

Briouse were absent from Ireland, the justiciar had only to contend with their vassals supported by the lord of Meath. For the moment Meiler had the upper hand.

Although William Marshal had been lord of Leinster since 1189, he probably had never visited Ireland. Now in the spring of 1207 he felt that the situation there required his presence to protect his lands and vassals. Several times the earl sought in vain the king's permission to inspect his Irish possessions.[64] Meiler had his hands full with the barons already in Ireland, and John had no desire to increase his justiciar's troubles by adding to the opposition the formidable lord of Leinster. But at length in February 1207 John gave way before William's insistent requests.[65] He issued letters patent of protection for the earl's possessions in England and for those of Henry Hose and John d'Erley who were to accompany him.[66] A few days later messengers arrived at court bearing money from the Irish exchequer and letters from the justiciar.[67] Probably Meiler insisted that the king keep William out of Ireland. He was a far more dangerous opponent than the de Lacys and was besides the justiciar's feudal suzerain. His presence would seriously hamper Meiler's activities. John repented of having given William permission to leave England and sent Thomas de Sanford to intercept him at Striguil and demand his second son, Richard, as an additional hostage. Thomas de Sanford was an old friend of William's, and his brother, Hugh, was one of his knights. When Thomas arrived at Striguil, the earl sent him to dinner while he took counsel with his countess and his knights. Although they advised him to defy the royal mandate, William insisted on obedience. When Thomas had dined, the earl took him familiarly by the hand, " Sir, you know well that if the king wished, I would willingly send him all my children, but tell me, for God's love, what he has against me." Thomas explained that John was most anxious to prevent him from visiting Ireland and was sorry that he had given him leave to

---

[64] *Hist.*, 13318-13320.   [66] *Rot. Pat.*, p. 69.

[65] *Ibid.*, 13311-13317.   [67] *Rot. Claus.*, I, 78b.

go. To this William replied that he was going whether the king liked it or not.[68] This insistance naturally served to widen the breach between him and the king.

As William had intentionally defied his wishes, John felt justified in depriving him of his positions of trust in England. Cardigan was turned over to William de London, while Richard de Mucegros received the castle of Gloucester and the shrievalty of that county.[69] The castle and forest of St. Briavells were united to the general forest administration under Hugh de Neville.[70] William had lost the office of sheriff of Sussex when he first fell in disfavor in 1205.[71] Now he was deprived of the custody of Chichester castle.[72] John also seized all the earl's castles in England and Wales as additional guarantees of his good behavior.[73] William had lost all his official positions in the English administration, his two eldest sons and his castles were in the king's hands, and he was completely out of favor at court. For the next five years his activities were to be centered in Ireland to the great benefit of his lands in Leinster.

The reasons suggested above for William's fall from royal favor may well seem insufficient. To this objection there are two possible answers, each of which partially removes the difficulty. In the first place, John's quarrel with William never grew particularly bitter as did for instance the one with William de Briouse. All through their estrangement one will find a definite restraint on both sides, an unwillingness to carry matters too far. Then the influence of the Irish question is difficult to estimate. In the absence of a thorough study of John's policy in Ireland from the point of view of the royal administration any suggestions made on this subject must be purely tentative, but one is inclined to believe that Irish affairs had a very decided influence on the king's general policy. If the supposition

[68] *Hist.*, 13355-13419.

[69] *Rot. Pat.*, pp. 70b, 71, 74b. *Rot. Claus.*, I, 81, 95.

[70] *Rot. Pat.*, p. 71.

[71] *Pipe Roll 7 John*, Public Record Office.

[72] In February 1208. *Rot. Pat.*, p. 79.   [73] *Hist.*, 14334-5.

that John had set his heart on an increase in the royal authority in Ireland at the expense of the feudal lords is correct, it goes far to explain his desire to weaken the position of the lord of Leinster. While the roots of the estrangement between William and his king are found in the closing events of the defence of Normandy, its immediate causes seem to lie in the earl's opposition to the royal policy in Ireland.

CHAPTER VIII

LORD OF LEINSTER

From one point of view the years passed by William in his lordship of Leinster were a period of exile which takes its importance from the part it played in his quarrel with the king. The earl's arrival in Ireland resulted in an open conflict with Meiler fitz Henry which further complicated his relations with John. A general reconciliation in the spring of 1208 by which the king gained at the expense of both William and the justiciar was more apparent than real. John's feud with William de Briouse and the latter's flight to Ireland caused the quarrel to break out anew. This chapter will be largely occupied with these two acute phases of the estrangement between William and his master. But William must not be regarded solely as the earl of Pembroke in exile in Ireland—he was the lord of Leinster in residence on his fief. The remarkable development of this region while it was under William's suzerainty was a decided tribute to his ability as a ruler. While the earl was engaged in his quarrel with John, he continued the extremely progressive policy which had previously been inaugurated by his seneschals under his direction.

In order to understand William's position in Ireland one must have some idea of the history of the lordship of Leinster which he acquired by his marriage to Isabel de Clare. In the year 1166 Dermot McMurrough, king of Leinster, who had been expelled from Ireland by his enemies, sought aid from Henry II and his turbulent vassals of the Welsh marches. Three years later the Norman vanguard under such leaders as Robert fitz Stephen, Meiler fitz Henry, Hervey de Montmorency, and Maurice de Prendergast arrived in Ireland to aid their ally. The chief of the Irish king's foreign auxiliaries, Richard fitz Gilbert de Clare, earl of Pembroke, reached Ireland in August 1170. A few months later he married the king's daughter, Eva, with the

149

understanding that he was to inherit Leinster at Dermot's death.[1] Of course this agreement could not be expected to have great weight with Dermot's subjects, to say nothing of the rival native kings. When Dermot died a short time after his daughter's marriage, Earl Richard was forced to maintain his right by the sword—a feat of which he was perfectly capable.[2] Meanwhile Henry Plantagenet had become alarmed at Earl Richard's success and decided to visit Ireland in person to procure its submission to the English crown. When Henry landed at Waterford in October 1171, the earl of Pembroke surrendered his conquests into the king's hands.[3] Reserving for himself the cities of Dublin, Wexford, and Waterford with the land in their immediate vicinities and the coastal region between Dublin and Wicklow, Henry granted the rest of Leinster to Earl Richard as a fief.[4] The territory included in the present counties of Kildare, Queen's, Kilkenny, Carlow, Wexford, and about a third of King's was to be held by the earl for the service of one hundred knights.[5] In 1173 the city of Wexford was added to this fief.[6] Unfortunately, the charter given to Earl Richard on this occasion has not been preserved, but its terms, can be surmised from the one by which Henry gave Meath to Hugh de Lacy.[7] Considering Earl Richard's position as the conqueror of the country and the son-in-law and designated

[1] The principal sources for the conquest of Ireland are the *Song of Dermot and the Earl* (ed. G. H. Orpen), and Giraldus Cambrensis, *Expugnatio Hibernica* (*Opera*, V, 205-411). For a full secondary account see Orpen, *Ireland under the Normans*, vol. I.

[2] Dermot died in the spring of 1171 (Giraldus Cambrensis, *Opera*, V, 263). For Earl Richard's troubles with his new subjects see *Song of Dermot*, lines 1735 et esq.

[3] *Song of Dermot.*, 2613-2622.

[4] See *ibid.* and Orpen, *Ireland under the Normans*, for maps.

[5] In 1208 John confirmed Leinster to William for the service of 100 knights and Meath to Walter de Lacy for that of 50 knights (*Rot. Chart.*, pp. 176, 178). As Henry II granted Meath to Hugh de Lacy for 50 knights, one may presume that Leinster also owed the same number as in 1208.

[6] *Song of Dermot*, 2902-3.

[7] Printed in Orpen, *Ireland under the Normans*, I, 285-6.

heir of the late king, the privileges granted him must have been fully as extensive as those of Hugh de Lacy. The earl was to enjoy all the powers which the king had or could give in return for his homage and service.[8] Thus Leinster was a real liberty in which the lord ruled as absolute master with all the privileges which the law of the time conferred on the king himself. As long as he fulfilled his feudal obligations to his suzerain, Earl Richard was practically king of Leinster.

The marcher lords who had taken part in the conquest of Leinster naturally expected to be rewarded with generous grants of land. They were not disappointed, for Earl Richard supplied them with extensive fiefs from the broad lands given him by King Henry.[9] Thus was created the baronage of Leinster—those who held from the lord in chief. When Richard de Clare died in 1176, this process of subinfeudation was by no means completed, and there was still plenty of land not yet enfeoffed. At Earl Richard's death all his domains were seized into the king's hands. In 1185 Henry II created his youngest son, John, lord of Ireland and sent him to take possession of the country. From that time until William Marshal's marriage with Isabel de Clare, Leinster was in the custody of John as the suzerain of the fief. With a fine disregard for the customs governing his position as the guardian of a minor heir, John granted fiefs in Leinster to many of his own men. It will be remembered that this question arose when William demanded Leinster from John in 1189, and that only John's butler, Theobald Walter, retained his lands, and he held them as William's vassal.[10] At that time William did homage to John for Isabel's Irish inheritance and, in all probability, he received the same palatine privileges that Henry II had given Earl Richard.

When William first obtained possession of Leinster, he sent Renault de Kedeville to seize it in his name.[11] Nothing is

---

[8] *Cum omnibus libertatibus quas ibi habeo vel illi dare possum.*

[9] The principal source of information about the sub-infeudation of Leinster is the *Song of Dermot*, 3024-3127. It has been thoroughly worked out in Orpen, *Ireland under the Normans*, I, 367-395.

[10] *Hist.*, 9600-9618.   [11] *Hist.*, 9623-9630.

known of this individual beyond the suggestion in the *History* that he did not fulfil his mission loyally. The reign of Richard forms almost a complete lacuna in our knowledge of Irish history—not even the names of the justiciars can be definitely ascertained.[12] Sometime during this period, probably about 1192, William sent to Ireland one of the ranking members of his household, Geoffrey fitz Robert. Geoffrey received a barony centering in Kells, which lay some ten miles south of Kilkenny, and was probably entrusted with the administration of the whole region.[13] By the beginning of the thirteenth century he was styled seneschal of Leinster.[14] In all likelihood it was he who constructed the castle on William's demesne manor of Kilkenny which the Irish annals say was built in 1192. If he did not actually establish the burghs of Kilkenny and Carlow, he certainly fixed the burgage fees at those places and in the walled town of Wexford.[15] His most important service to the commercial development of Leinster was the founding of the town of New Ross on the river Barrow.[16] This new port served the river traffic on the Nore and the Barrow, and a bridge thrown over the latter stream gave access to the highroad to Kells and Kilkenny. New Ross, or Rossbridge as it was then called, soon became the principal port of south Leinster and diverted a large amount of trade from the royal town of Waterford.[17] Geoffrey was active in the religious as well as the economic development of Leinster. On his own lands he founded the priory of Kells, and as William's representative he estab-

[12] See Orpen, *Ireland under the Normans,* II, 109 et seq.

[13] Orpen, *Ireland under the Normans,* II, 211, 225.

[14] There is a charter witnessed by Meiler fitz Henry as justiciar and Geoffrey fitz Robert as seneschal of Leinster. *Register of the Abbey of St. Thomas, Dublin* (ed. J. T. Gilbert, *Rolls Series*), p. 125.

[15] *Chartae, Privilegia, et Immunitates* (*Irish Record Commission,* 1889), pp. 33-4, 37, 47.

[16] In William's charter to Tintern Minor mention is made of " a burgage in Ross on the south side of the bridge." *Chartae, Privilegia, et Immunitates,* p. 80. This places the foundation of New Ross before the earl's coming to Ireland.

[17] Orpen, *Ireland under the Normans,* II, 230.

lished the monastery of Tintern Minor in accordance with his
lord's instructions.[18] Geoffrey fitz Robert was a capable administrator who carried on his master's progressive policy with
energy and ability.

In the spring of 1204 William sent his nephew, John Marshal, who had served in the French wars under both Richard
and John, to take over the seneschalship of Leinster. This action was probably due to the activities of Meiler fitz Henry.
As early as 1202 there had been some difficulty over the castle
and land of Offaly which Meiler claimed, probably on the
basis of a grant by Earl Richard which had later been revoked.
In that year Meiler appealed to John's court against Adam
de Hereford who held the disputed fief as William's vassal.
The question remained unsettled, and some years later the
justiciar seized Offaly at the king's command. As John Marshal
was a man of decided ability who stood high in the royal favor,
William hoped that he would be better able than the barons
of Leinster to cope with the justiciar. John was armed with
letters patent which directed Meiler to receive him as seneschal
of Leinster and forbade him to infringe on the palatine privileges guaranteed by William's charter.[19] Clearly the king had at
least outwardly joined with the earl in this attempt to check
the aggressions of the justiciar. There is no evidence that John
Marshal fulfilled his uncle's expectations—in fact one is inclined to believe that he was not exceptionally loyal to him.
While William was in the midst of his quarrel with Meiler,
John Marshal accepted from the king the office of marshal of
Ireland with a nice fief attached to it.[20] Suspicion of his
nephew's reliability may have been a contributing cause of the
earl's intense desire to go to Ireland in person. Offaly was in
the justiciar's hands, and the seneschal of Leinster was untrust-
worthy. His lands and his vassals required William's protection.

Early in the spring of 1207 William and his knights landed
in Ireland amid the rejoicing of most of his vassals of Leinster.

[18] *Ibid.*, p. 225.   [19] *Rot. Pat.*, pp. 40b; 42.   [20] *Rot. Chart.*, p. 173b.

The *History* asserts that this was his first visit to the great fief which formed so important a part of his wife's inheritance.[21] This statement may not be strictly accurate. According to the Irish annals found in the *Chartularies of St. Mary's, Dublin,* the earl was caught in a storm on the way to Ireland in the autumn of 1200, and when he landed in safety, founded the monastery of Tintern Minor in fulfilment of a vow made during the voyage.[22] Tintern was almost certainly established in 1200, but William's charter of foundation probably should be placed after 1207.[23] The evidence can be read either way. But even if it took place, this first visit was so brief that it has no significance either for the biographer of William or the historian of Leinster.

Immediately after his arrival the earl summoned the justiciar to appear before his court to answer for the seizure of Offaly. As Meiler was William's vassal and the land in dispute was part of Leinster, this procedure was perfectly proper, but the justiciar declined to obey on the ground that he had acted at the king's command. In taking possession of Offaly he had acted not as a baron of Leinster, but as justiciar of Ireland. Two of the great Irish lords, Hugh and Walter de Lacy, and a number of the barons of Leinster and Meath addressed a letter of protest to the king against his justiciar's contumacy. William's name does not appear, but the petition was in his interest, and he probably inspired it. On May 23rd John sent a stinging rebuke to the petitioners. He was astounded that they dared to found a "new assize" without his consent.[24] What they sought was both unjust and contrary to custom. They were immediately to cease bothering the justiciar about Offaly. No

---

[21] *Hist.,* 13316.

[22] *Chartularies of St. Mary's Abbey, Dublin* (ed. J. T. Gilbert, *Rolls Series*), II, 307-8.

[23] A charter of John dated at Hampstead on December 3 but lacking the year confirms a gift to Tintern Minor. John's itinerary and the witnesses point to the year 1200. Dugdale, *Monasticon Anglicanum* (new edition), VII, 1136. See Orpen, *Ireland under the Normans,* II, 207. William's charter for Tintern is printed in *Chartae, Privilegia, et Immunitates,* p. 80.   [24] *novam assissam.*

one who seized a fief by the king's command should answer to any one for his action. The letter closed with the suggestion that the petitioners think less about the privileges of their lord and more about the rights of the crown.[25] By this letter John definitely took the part of Meiler in his disagreement with William. But the king still hoped to settle the question peaceably. He summoned William, Meiler, John Marshal, and a number of the barons of Leinster to discuss the matter with him.[26]

The king's summons was extremely disturbing to William, for he was reasonably certain that he soon as he left, the justiciar's men would attack his lands. This danger was made more serious by the fact that the Countess Isabel, who had accompanied him to Ireland, was pregnant and would have to remain there.[27] He therefore decided to leave ten of the eleven knights who had come over from Pembroke with him to guard the countess and defend Leinster from aggression. His most loyal vassal, John d'Erley, was entrusted with the custody of part of Leinster, while Jordan de Sackville was placed in charge of the rest. Jordan was an Irish baron of considerable importance whose lands lay in Ulster. Although he does not seem to have held a fief from William in Ireland, he was his vassal for lands in Normandy and in Buckinghamshire and had been attached to his household during the French wars. In addition to John d'Erley, William left behind Stephen d'Evreux, Ralph fitz Pagan, and Mallard, his standard bearer, with six more of the knights of his household. Henry Hose alone journeyed to England with his lord. Thus he left most of his knights to guard the countess while John d'Erley and Jordan de Sackville were given general charge of Leinster. The earl instructed them to rule by the advice of Geoffrey fitz Robert, Walter Porcel, and Thomas fitz Anthony, powerful and trustworthy barons of Leinster. Finally, he summoned all his vassals to his castle of Kilkenny and addressed them. " Lords, behold the countess, the daughter of the earl who gave you your fiefs when he con-

---

[25] *Rot. Pat.*, p. 72.
[26] *Hist.*, 13436-13446. *Rot. Chart.*, pp. 171b-173.   [27] *Hist.*, 13539.

quered this land. She remains here among you, pregnant. Until God leads me back, I beg you all to guard her faithfully, for she is your liege lady, and I have no right in this land except through her." The assembled barons promised to defend their lord's wife, but here and there in the crowd were some whose loyalty was rather doubtful.[28] It was in the little knot of household knights, men who had served him in France and Wales, that William placed his confidence.

After landing in Wales on Michaelmas day, William proceeded at once to John who received him most ungraciously.[29] The king's attitude toward him was even more hostile than before, as he had recently become displeased with William de Briouse who was one of William's closest friends.[30] Early in November, Meiler arrived and was well received by the king. When the justiciar presented his complaints against William, John lent a willing ear and soon joined with him to plan the earl's destruction—or at least the seizure of his lands in Ireland. Meiler suggested that John keep William in England and summon to him John d'Erley, Jordan de Sackville, and Stephen d'Evreux.[31] In their absence he felt confident that he could easily overrun Leinster. Several barons of Leinster had accompanied Meiler to England, and they were given lands to bind them to the cause of the king and justiciar against their rightful lord. John Marshal accepted from John the office of marshal of Ireland and a fief.[32] David de la Roche and Philip de Prendergast, both vassals of William, received considerable grants from the king.[33] Thus John won to him such of William's men as could be bribed, while he summoned to England those who were loyal. By that means Meiler could be given a free hand to do what he pleased in Leinster.

[28] *Hist.*, 13464-13550.
[29] *Ibid.*, 13552-13584.
[30] *Ibid.*, 13585-13588. On William de Briouse's quarrel with John see Norgate, *John Lackland*, pp. 146-7, 149-151. See also Powicke, *The Loss of Normandy*, pp. 468-9 and *Calendar of Documents relating to Ireland* (ed. H. G. Sweetman, *Rolls Series*), no. 408.   [32] *Rot. Chart.*, p. 173b.
[31] *Hist.*, 13616-13652.   [33] *Ibid.*, pp. 172b, 171b.

Despite the fact that it was the stormy season, Meiler managed to cross to Ireland in company with the messenger who bore the king's letters summoning John d'Erley and Jordan de Sackville to England.[34] Before he left Ireland, he had instructed his men to attack Leinster as soon as William started for England. This they had done early in October and had killed twenty of the earl's men, but greatly to Meiler's chagrin, the custodians of Leinster had later captured the raiders and cast them into prison.[35] The justiciar at once summoned all William's vassals and gave them the king's letters calling their leaders to England. After a brief consultation they decided to ignore the royal mandate and to prepare to defend their lord's lands as best they could. While John d'Erley mobilized the men of Leinster, Jordan sought the aid of the lord from whom he held his lands in Ireland, Hugh de Lacy, earl of Ulster, who promptly came to their assistance at the head of sixty-five knights, two hundred mounted serjeants, and a thousand infantry. Meiler could not withstand the combined forces of Ulster and Leinster. His lands were devastated while he himself was captured and was forced to purchase his freedom by giving up his son as a hostage. Philip de Prendergast and the other disloyal barons of Leinster were likewise obliged to give hostages for their good behavior.[36]

Meanwhile, William had followed the court about England. Considering the danger to his wife and lands in Ireland and the ungracious attitude of the king toward him, he was far from happy. One day, toward the end of January, as they rode out of Guildford, the king called William to him and asked if he had had news from Ireland. As William had not, the king went on to give him a purely imaginary account of the war between Meiler and the men of Leinster. According to the story, John d'Erley had made a sorty from Kilkenny castle with all the garrison, leaving but two serjeants to hold the fortress. While he was gone, Meiler laid siege to the castle, but the countess

[34] *Hist.*, 13655-13675.
[35] *Ibid.*, 13557-13574.
[36] *Ibid.*, 13692-13786; 13873-13888.

managed to notify John and a sanguinary combat ensued. The justiciar and many of his knights were captured, but John d'Erley was mortally wounded while Stephen d'Evreux and Ralph fitz Pagan were killed. William replied, " Certainly, Fair Sire, it is a great pity about the knights. They were your men which makes the affair still more regrettable." [37] He was not, however, particularly troubled as he did not believe that the king had had any word from Ireland. At that season the passage of the Irish Sea was almost impossible, and besides, he felt that he would have received the news as soon as the king.[38] Up and down England they rode together, William and the king, each anxiously awaiting word from Ireland. John solaced himself by seizing the lands of John d'Erley and Jordan de Sackville for their disobedience of his summons, though it is rather hard to see how they could have come to England before the sea became passable.[39] Finally, late in February, messengers arrived bearing to the king and to William the news of the justiciar's discomfiture. When John summoned him and asked if he had heard from Ireland, William pretended to know nothing and gave the king the somewhat doubtful pleasure of replacing his imaginary account with the true one.[40]

The miscarriage of his plans against Leinster forced John to moderate his hostility toward his vassal. On March 7th the king despatched letters to Meiler to inform him that two days before William had come to him at Bristol of his own volition and had shown himself submissive to the royal will. There was to be a council at Winchester on the Wednesday before Lent where the affairs of Ireland would be thoroughly discussed. Meanwhile, the justiciar was to keep the peace and make what amends he could for any raids his men might have made into Leinster. William had promised to send similar directions to his vassals.[41] In short, John provided for a truce until the ques-

[37] John and Stephen were English tenants-in-chief and hence were primarily the king's men.
[38] *Ibid.*, 13787-13866.
[39] *Rot. Claus.*, I, 103, 106b.
[40] *Hist.*, 13904-13930.
[41] *Rot. Claus.*, I, 105.

tions at issue could be settled. The terms of the compromise between William and his master were formulated by March 20th. The earl agreed to accept a new charter for Leinster and promised the king a fine of three hundred marks for the return of Offaly with its castles.[42] John sent Philip of Worcester, Master Robert of Cirencester, Roland Bloet, and William Petit to inform Meiler of this agreement and to see that it was put into effect.[43] The king also turned over to William the custody of the lands of John d'Erley and Jordan de Sackville which had been seized when they failed to obey the royal summons.[44]

The real basis of the agreement between William and his king was embodied in the new charter for Leinster which was issued on March 28.[45] The earl and his heirs were to hold the fief for the service of one hundred knights. But while Henry II had given Earl Richard "all the liberties which I have or can give," John imposed important restrictions on the powers of the lords of Leinster. The pleas of the crown—treasure-trove, rape, ambush and arson—as well as all appeals for felonious breach of the peace were reserved for the king's court. In case of default of justice in the lord's court or in case of complaints against the lord himself, the question could be carried on appeal to the royal court. The regalian rights over the episcopal sees of Leinster were also reserved to the king.[46] If any tenant-in-chief of the king who held lands in Leinster should die leaving a minor heir, the lord would have the custody of the fees held of him, but the king could arrange the marriage of the heir or heiress. While this charter decidedly restricted the privileges of the lord of Leinster, it did not reduce him to the status of an ordinary English tenant-in-chief. All rights not specifically reserved to the crown were left to the lord. He still had control of the entire administration of the region—the

[42] *Rot. Chart.*, p. 176. *Rotuli de Oblatis et Finibus* (ed. T. D. Hardy, *Record Commission*), p. 434. *Rot. Pat.*, p. 80b.   [44] *Ibid.*, p. 106b.

[43] *Rot. Claus.*, I, 106b, 107.   [45] *Rot. Chart.*, p. 176.

[46] *crociis et dignitatibus adeas pertinentibus* Orpen interprets this expression more broadly, *Ireland under the Normans*, II, 233-4.

sheriffs were his officials. His courts had full jurisdiction in most cases. The custody of the fees held of him by tenants-in-chief of the crown was a right denied English barons.[47] Leinster was still a liberty, though a somewhat limited one. A month later Walter de Lacy accepted a similar charter from John.[48] Whether the king's support of his justiciar's aggressive policy was due solely to a desire to injure William or to a definite plan to reduce the power of the Irish palatine lords, he had achieved the latter result. No longer were the lords of Leinster and Meath so completely independent of the lord of Ireland.

When in April William sought leave to return to Ireland, John granted it freely.[49] He set out at once and landed at Glasscarrick near Wexford where he was met by Jordan de Sackville and John d'Erley, the latter clothed in a hauberk. William glanced at this warlike array and remarked that he thought peace had been proclaimed, but John assured him that there were some who did not observe it. As they rode inland, the two faithful knights explained to their lord the state of his land of Leinster which had been entrusted to them and told him which of his vassals had shown themselves loyal. The news of the earl's arrival spread rapidly, and the barons of Leinster hastened to greet him. Among the first to arrive were the two most prominent of those who had shown themselves disloyal to their lord and had accepted lands from John, Philip de Prendergast and David de la Roche. William saluted them with the rather dubious greeting, "God save you, if it is right that he should." When they protested that they were two of his most loyal vassals, he replied that all men both in town and countryside knew them for traitors. As Jordan and John heartily concurred in this statement, the two disloyal barons broke down and begged their lord's pardon which he granted them. The next day the Countess Isabel arrived to welcome her husband, and they returned to Kilkenny together. The countess had passed several anxious months as the result of the strife stirred up by Meiler, and she

---

[47] Bracton, *De Legibus,* II, 12. W. S. Holdsworth, *A History of English Law,* III, 64.   [48] *Rot. Chart.,* p. 178.   [49] *Hist.,* 13931-13940.

was in favor of taking summary vengeance on her enemies, but William fully realized that his rebellious vassals had really acted in accord with the king's will and in support of his justiciar. Meiler alone of the lords of Leinster could be held to account. All the other unfaithful vassals were forgiven and their hostages returned—much to the disgust of the countess. Meiler himself was soon brought to his knees by the loss of his position as justiciar which placed him practically at William's mercy as the lord from whom he held his lands. To gain the earl's forgiveness he was forced to surrender his castle of Dunamase at once and promise his lord the succession to all his lands when he died.[50] This seemed to remove the last obstacle to peace in Leinster, and William could turn his attention to the development of his lands. Probably at this time he rewarded John d'Erley and Mallard, his standard bearer, with generous fiefs.

Unfortunately, this unusual peace was not to bless Ireland for very long. William de Briouse, who had returned to his lands in Wales after his estrangement from John in the autumn of 1207, decided in the winter of 1208-9 to flee to Ireland from the king's displeasure.[51] The reasons for John's bitter quarrel with his old friend and vassal are somewhat obscure. William certainly owed vast sums of money to the exchequer, and his wife had refused to give up his son as a hostage to John.[52] Besides this, it is probable that William de Briouse knew far more about the fate of Arthur of Brittany than John cared to have published to the world. Mr. Powicke has suggested that it was he who furnished the chronicler of Margan Abbey with its peculiarly detailed information on the young prince's death

[50] *Ibid.,* 13941-14136.

[51] William de Briouse's flight to Ireland is placed in 1208 by Roger of Wendover (II, 48-9) and by the Annals in *Chartularies of St. Mary's, Dublin* (II, 310), and is listed with other events of 1208 under 1207 in *Brut y Tywysogion.* It took place in the winter (*Hist.,* 14167-8). See Orpen, *Ireland under the Normans,* II, 239, note 1.

[52] *Calendar of Documents relating to Ireland,* no. 389, 408. Roger of Wendover, II, 48-9. Norgate, *John Lackland,* pp. 149-150.

and later told the same story to William le Breton, the chronicler of the French court.[53] The author of the *History* asserts that he does not know the cause of the quarrel, and if he did, it would not be his business to tell it.[54] This seems to support the theory that there was far more to the matter than a few thousand marks owed to the exchequer or a refusal to deliver a son as hostage. At any rate, William de Briouse fled from Wales with his wife and children, and after a stormy crossing, landed at Wicklow in Ireland where, according to the *History*, William Marshal was staying at the time.[55] As Wicklow was not part of Leinster, it seems more likely that William simply went there to meet his old friend when he heard of his arrival and then escorted him into his own lands. There he sheltered the fugitives for twenty days.[56]

When John de Gray, bishop of Norwich, who had succeeded Meiler fitz Henry as justiciar, learned that the lord of Leinster was harboring William de Briouse and his family, he immediately ordered him to deliver the fugitives to him. William Marshal replied that he was harboring his lord, William de Briouse, as it was his duty to do. He knew nothing of any quarrel between his guest and the king, and it would be treason to turn him over to the justiciar. Instead he would conduct him safely to the frontier of Leinster.[57] In short William de Briouse was his lord and his guest, and he would protect him while he was in his lands. This reply of William's to the justiciar's demand is rather puzzling. One has some difficulty in figuring out how William de Briouse was William Marshal's lord.[58] It also seems most improbable that William did not know of his guest's quarrel with the king as it had started when he was in England in the autumn of 1207.[59] Apparently the real reasons

[53] Powicke, *The Loss of Normandy*, pp. 453-481.

[54] *Hist.*, 14154-14156.   [56] *Ibid.*, 14193-14198.

[55] *Ibid.*, 14186-7.   [57] *Ibid.*, 14199-14232.

[58] Orpen, *Ireland under the Normans*, II, 239, note 2. See also Norgate, *John Lackland*, p. 151, note 1. William de Briouse may have been overlord of the manor of Speen in Berkshire. *Book of Fees*, pp. 749, 846, 859.

[59] *Hist.*, 13585-13588.

which urged William to receive his old friend do not appear. This becomes more evident in the conversation that ensued in 1210 when John accused the lord of Leinster of harboring a traitor. Whatever his motives may have been, William escorted his guest safely to the borders of Meath where he was received by his son-in-law, Walter de Lacy.

William de Briouse spent the year 1209 in Ireland under the protection of the two de Lacys, and in the spring of 1210 obtained permission from the justiciar to go to Wales with the understanding that he would seek out the king and make his peace with him.[60] Meanwhile, John had decided to make an expedition to Ireland to settle the de Briouse affair once and for all and to punish the barons who had given the family shelter. While he was mustering his army, he summoned William Marshal to join him.[61] On May 31st, the king arrived at Haverford in William's county of Pembroke, and by June 3rd he was at Cross-on-the-Sea, near Pembroke, where he remained until after the 16th.[62] There William de Briouse came to him and attempted to settle their quarrel by a fine of forty thousand marks.[63] As he had been unable to pay his regular debts to the exchequer, this offer can not have been taken very seriously by the king. Furthermore, John was convinced that William's wife, Matilda, was the ruling member of the family and his promises were of little value without her concurrence. As she was still in Ireland with the equally obstinate de Lacys, John continued his preparations to go after her. In the meantime, he gave William leave to go before him to win his wife's assent to the proposed settlement, but he preferred to stay in Wales. Sometime after June 16th John set sail for Ireland to capture Matilda de Briouse and punish the barons of Ireland who had abetted her family in their contumacy. This seems a rather slight motive for so costly an expedition, but it is the only one

---

[60] Norgate, *John Lackland*, p. 151.   [61] *Hist.*, 14240-14246.

[62] *Rotuli de Liberate ac de Misis et Praestitis*, pp. 172-178.

[63] *Calendar of Documents relating to Ireland*, no. 408. Orpen, *Ireland under the Normans*, II, 241.

that John avowed. One is forced to conclude that there was some far more potent reason for John's hatred of the house of Briouse than a mere matter of debts. The forty thousand marks fine was a prohibitive sum at best. Apparently John's purpose was the destruction of the family of Briouse.

One June 20, 1210, John landed at Crook near Waterford where he was joined by his justiciar, John de Gray.[64] The next day he entered Leinster by the port of New Ross and from there proceeded to Kilkenny by way of Thomastown.[65] Accompanied as he was by William Marshal, his progress through Leinster was a peaceful one. At Kilkenny he was well received, and his whole army was entertained there two days at William's expense.[66] One wonders if this were part of John's revenge on the lord of Leinster and his barons for their contumacy in the affair of William de Briouse and their foiling of his plans in 1208. The long stay of the king in Pembroke, his advance through Leinster, and his entertainment at Kilkenny, which was William's chief seat in Ireland, must have been a great burden to the latter and his vassals. From Kilkenny John proceeded to Naas, whose lord, William fitz William, was one of William Marshal's most powerful barons.[67] Finally, on June 28th he quitted the lordship of Leinster and entered his own city of Dublin.[68] There he was met by a number of the barons of Meath who made submission to him in the name of their lord, Walter de Lacy. John refused to be mollified and moved through Meath taking possession of all Walter's castles and depriving him of his lordship. Hugh de Lacy, earl of Ulster, instead of following the pacific example of his brother, decided to defend his territories. Finding it impossible to resist the royal army, he retired to his castle of Carrickfergus, and finally, when he learned that the king was advancing against this stronghold, he fled to Scotland with Matilda de Briouse and her sons William and Reginald. Deprived of their leader and at-

---

[64] *Rotuli de Liberate ac de Missis et Praestitis*, p. 178.
[65] *Ibid.*, p. 179.   [67] *Rotuli de Liberate ac de Misis et Praestitis*, p. 181.
[66] *Hist.*, 14258-14266.   [68] *Ibid.*

tacked by all the forces John could muster, the garrison of the castle soon surrendered.[69] By August 18th, the king was back in Dublin.[70]

After he had thoroughly punished the two de Lacys, John felt that it was time to turn to William Marshal. There in Dublin, in the presence of all the barons of the army, he charged him with sheltering William de Briouse. The earl replied to the king much as he had to the justiciar a year and a half before. He had harbored his lord who had arrived at his castle in a very miserable condition. It had never occurred to him that there was any harm in this act of mercy, for William de Briouse was his lord and his old friend, and he did not know that the king had anything against him. When the earl left England, John and William were together. If anyone except the king cared to charge him with harboring a traitor, he was willing to defend himself in any way the court saw fit.[71] As usual, none of the barons showed any enthusiasm for taking up the quarrel, and John was forced to drop the matter.[72] In general, William's statement of the case was probably true. William de Briouse, his lord and old friend, had arrived on the coast of Ireland after a stormy voyage, and he had given him shelter. It is, however, impossible to believe that William Marshal was unaware of William de Briouse's quarrel with the king, especially as the *History* assures us that it affected his own position at court in 1208.[73] On the other hand, it was perfectly true that William de Briouse was at court when William departed for Ireland in the spring of 1208.[74] The earl's position was technically correct, but there could have been little doubt in John's mind that in reality William had cheerfully harbored a man whom he knew to be the king's enemy. As in the case

[69] Orpen, *Ireland under the Normans*, II, 246-260.

[70] *Rotuli de Liberate ac de Misis et Praestitis*, p. 213.

[71] *Hist.*, 14283-14314.

[72] *Ibid.*, 14314-14318.   [73] *Ibid.*, 13585-13607.

[74] He was in at least some favor with John as late as May 6th, 1208. (*Rot. Claus.*, I, 114). His complete disgrace came that summer. See Norgate, *John Lackland*, p. 150. *Rot. Pat.*, p. 86b.

of his refusal to follow him to Poitou, John could not take any action against his great vassal because his barons refused to support him. Whatever they may have felt about the rights of the question, none of them had the slightest desire to risk having to fight so doughty a warrior as William. The old knight, he was then sixty-six, found that his offer to put the question to the proof of combat still served, as it had in the past, to dampen the enthusiasm of any baron who might care to accuse him of any fault toward his king.

Despite the fact that he had been forced to drop his main charge against William, John insisted that he be given the castle of Dunamase, which the latter had received from Meiler, as a pledge for his future good behavior, and Geoffrey fitz Robert, Jordan de Sackville, Thomas de Sanford, John d'Erley, and Walter Porcel as hostages.[75] The earl replied that the king already held all his castles in England as well as his two sons, but he was willing to give him all his Irish castles and the sons of his vassals if he wanted them. He had no evil intentions toward the king and would give him whatever pledges he desired. The king answered that he only wanted the castle and hostages whom he had mentioned, and with their consent William turned over to him the only two who were present, John d'Erley and Walter Porcel.[76] The others were apparently summoned and given to the king later. John, however, was not satisfied and demanded still more hostages from the baronage of Leinster.[77] One of these lords, David de la Roche, refused to go on the ground that William had wronged him and he was not obliged to be a pledge for his conduct. At William's insistence, the king asked the barons if this charge were true, and all agreed that it was not. Sometime later, Peter fitz Herbert, a

[75] I cannot understand the inclusion of Thomas de Sanford in this list. There is no other evidence that he was a vassal of William, and he was extremely prominent in the king's service before and after this time. It seems likely that it is an error for Hugh de Sanford who was William's man.

[76] *Hist.*, 14319-14372.

[77] Probably only until the rest of those listed above could come. See *ibid.*, 14453-14465.

baron of Gloucestershire who had succeeded William as sheriff of that county in 1194, when looking for a seat, found that the only one vacant was next to David de la Roche. Peter refused to sit next to a man who had failed his lord.[78] William's hostages were sent to England and distributed among a number of royal castles—Jordan at Gloucester, Thomas at Winchester, John at Nottingham, and Geoffrey at Hereford, while Walter Porcel was entrusted to Peter fitz Herbert who entertained him royally while he was in his custody.[79]

Although William Marshal spent most of the next two years, 1211 and 1212, in Ireland, what little is known of his activities during that period belongs to the discussion of his part in the troubles of King John with the church and his barons which will occupy the next chapter. But before passing on it is necessary to form some estimate of William's work as lord of Leinster. The energy which he displayed in establishing boroughs was undoubtedly his principal contribution to the economic development of the region. He seems to have had an abiding interest in the advance of trade and commerce. When he was once more in the king's favor, he obtained free passage past Waterford for ships bound for New Ross, and later as regent of England he continued to grant favors to the merchants of Leinster.[80] Of course every increase in the volume of trade within his lands added to the revenues which he drew from them. When William's lands were divided after the death of his last son, Leinster produced the very considerable revenue of something over seventeen hundred pounds a year.[81] The earl also continued the settlement or rather the sub-infeudation of Leinster. Geoffrey fitz Robert, John d'Erley, Mallard the standard bearer, Thomas fitz Anthony, and William de St. Leger all received fiefs in the previously undeveloped county of Kilkenny.[82] Finally William showed a laudable enthusiasm for

[78] *Ibid.*, 14402-14446.   [79] *Ibid.*, 14447-14468.

[80] *Calendar of Documents relating to Ireland*, no. 648, 725, 862.

[81] *Chartularies of St. Mary's, Dublin*, II, 401-406.

[82] Orpen, *Ireland under the Normans*, II, 225-6.

establishing religious foundations. Besides the monastery of St. Mary de Voto, or Tintern Minor, he founded the abbey of St. Salvator, or Duiske, and confirmed grants made by his predecessors and vassals.[83] Leinster developed in every way under the able rule of William Marshal.

At the close of the year 1210 William was under the cloud of royal displeasure more deeply than ever. His two sons, all his castles in England and Wales, the castle of Dunamase, and the homage and service of Meiler fitz Henry were in the king's hands as pledges for his good behavior. Five of his most important vassals were held as hostages in royal castles. Still he had escaped the fate of the de Briouses and the de Lacys, and none of his lands had actually been confiscated. He had opposed John's plans in Ireland to the extent of waging war on his justiciar and had sheltered a man whom the king considered a traitor, yet officially he was in full standing as a baron of England. A sense of unreality permeates the whole course of this quarrel between William and the king—it was almost a game. John wished to reduce his vassal's overweening power while the latter resisted as best he could, but both observed scrupulously the forms if not always the spirit of feudal law. In 1207 the earl had obeyed the king's summons to England and had remained at court while Meiler returned to Ireland. He could not be held personally responsible for John d'Erley and Jordan de Sackville's defiance of the royal mandate any more than John could be for Meiler's attacks on Leinster. There could be no more intriguing picture than that of John and William travelling about England together in the spring of 1208 while their representatives, with their complete if unofficial approval, waged war on each other in Ireland. Then the two principals solemnly made peace and ordered their deputies to cease fighting. William's case was a trifle weaker in the affair of William de Briouse, yet he could and did argue that he had merely ful-

---

[83] *Facsimiles of National Manuscripts of Ireland* (ed. J. T. Gilbert), I, no. lxix; *Chartularies of St. Mary's, Dublin*, II, 158-9; *Register of St. Thomas, Dublin*, pp. 137, 356.

filled his obligations to one of his lords in perfect innocence of the fact that this lord was in enmity with John, the lord paramount. When the king summoned him to meet him in Wales in 1210, the earl obeyed promptly. Whenever the king had demanded hostages in the shape of sons, vassals, or castles, William had complied. He had never actually defied his king and suzerain. On his side John had acted throughout with rare restraint. Cheerfully disavowing the acts of Meiler, he had compromised on the question of William's palatine privileges in Leinster. In 1210 instead of punishing William with the de Lacys, he had given him the opportunity to demonstrate his loyalty by meeting him at Pembroke and accompanying the royal army to Ireland. Of course this may have been simply caution on John's part, for the combined forces of Leinster, Meath, and Ulster might well have defied him successfully. Once the de Lacys were crushed, the king did try to convict William of harboring a traitor. But John must have known from experience the futility of attempting to persuade his barons to render judgement against the earl. One is inclined to believe that the king simply used this accusation as a convenient excuse for demanding hostages. While John mistrusted William and desired to reduce his power and to insure his loyalty, he had no intention of driving him to open rebellion. The earl's wealth, his influence with the baronage, and his personal ability would make him an exceedingly dangerous enemy. He had often proved himself an invaluable servant. In such circumstances no monarch in his senses would risk his permanent disaffection. For his part William was enjoying the perquisites of his vast estates and was far too wise to give the king a valid pretext for their confiscation. Self-interest if nothing else prevented these two men from carrying their quarrel to extremes.

CHAPTER IX

EARL OF PEMBROKE

The year 1211 saw William's emergence from his retirement in Ireland to take part once more in the affairs of the English realm. King John, aglow with his recent triumphs over the de Briouses and de Lacys, planned the confusion of all his enemies. In the summer of 1211 he summoned William to join him in an expedition against the Welsh.[1] Now that he needed the earl's sword, John was willing to moderate his hostility toward him. William's castles in England and Wales and all his hostages except his eldest son were returned to him.[2] Once the Welsh princes were reduced, the king's thoughts turned to his lost continental possessions, and he began active preparations for an expedition to Poitou. As William's oath to Philip Augustus prevented him from participating in this plan, he asked leave to return to Ireland. John was still unconvinced of the earl's loyalty. He took his second son, Richard, as a hostage and demanded a guarantee that he would surrender his castles if called upon to do so. This was supplied by William's old friend, Geoffrey fitz Peter, earl of Essex and justiciar of England, who pledged himself that the fortresses would be turned over to the king on demand.[3] John was satisfied and gave William permission to go to Ireland.

John's projected expedition to the continent was part of a well-laid plan to destroy the power of Philip Augustus. The Holy Roman Emperor, Otto of Saxony, was extremely annoyed by Philip's support of the rival house of Hohenstaufen and was only too willing to ally with his English cousin against their common enemy. The counts of Toulouse, Boulogne, and Flanders, traditional supporters of the Angevins and Guelfs in

[1] *Hist.*, 14473-14475. *Rotuli de oblatis et finibus*, p. 498.
[2] *Hist.*, 14476-14478. *Rot. Pat.*, p. 94b. *Rot. Claus.*, I, 118b.
[3] *Ibid. Rot. Pat.*, p. 98b.

their struggles with the Capetians, were soon drawn into the alliance. John's diplomacy was surrounding Philip with a ring of enemies. But neither of the allied monarchs was as strong as he appeared. Otto had quarreled with the great pope to whom he owed the Imperial crown, and Innocent had excommunicated him, absolved his subjects of their oaths of allegiance, and given the papal support to young Frederick of Hohenstaufen. John had been at odds with Innocent ever since 1206 over the election of Stephen Langton to the see of Canterbury which had been inspired by the pope. On August 30, 1211, the legate Pandulf had excommunicated John in the presence of the prelates and barons of England assembled at Northampton. The king's subjects were absolved of their oaths of allegiance and were directed to lend their aid to any prince whom the pope might send to dispossess John of his kingdom. The papal sentence was particularly menacing in view of the fact that for some years the baronage of England had been seething with discontent. John knew that many of his vassals would enthusiastically support an invader fortified with the pope's blessing. The king did not lack warning of the impending storm. His excommunication so encouraged the Welsh that they rose with renewed vigor in the summer of 1212. Hastily dropping his preparations for a continental expedition, the king ordered the levies of England to muster at Chester. William Marshal and the bishop of Norwich were summoned to report there with two hundred knights and as many serjeants as could be spared from the defence of the Norman lands in Ireland.[4] John later postponed the muster and shifted its scene to Nottingham. There in mid-September gathered the English host. But sinister rumors came to the king from his daughter Joan, wife of the prince of North Wales, and from King William of Scotland. They informed him that his barons were planning to murder him. This was apparently confirmed by the action of two of his most powerful vassals, Eustace de Vesci and Robert fitz Walter, who stole away from the camp and fled the country.

[4] *Rot. Claus.,* I, 131b.

John was decidedly alarmed. He could hardly hope to hold his own against his barons, the pope, and Philip Augustus.[5]

William and the bishop of Norwich probably never actually set out for the muster of Chester, for in that same summer of 1212 they were forced to meet a serious rising of the native Irish.[6] But the earl was not unaware of the king's difficulties. He had probably been at Northampton when the legate launched his sentence, and he must have known of the attitude of his fellow barons.[7] William's loyalty was stirred by the danger to the house of Anjou and the English realm. At the same time he realized that a marked demonstration of his devotion in a time of crisis might well restore him to his old place in John's favor. With this in mind the earl persuaded the barons of Ireland to renew their oaths of allegiance to the king, and to assure him of their absolute loyalty. He himself wrote to John advising him to make peace with Innocent III, his most formidable enemy, and offering to go to England in person if he could assist in the negotiations. John was delighted. The faithful servant of his father and brothers, the great earl whose command could draw knightly swords from Buckinghamshire to the western limits of Leinster, had overlooked their quarrel and rallied to his support in his hour of need. In letters close addressed to William the king literally bubbled with gratitude.[8] He had, he wrote, already thanked his barons and men of Ireland for their faithful service and their oaths of allegiance, but he was especially grateful to William whose counsel and good will had been responsible for the attitude of his fellows. He also appreciated the earl's willingness to come to him in England, but at the moment he could not be spared from Ireland. The bishop of Norwich had greatly praised William's

---

[5] For a full discussion of John's situation see Norgate, *John Lackland,* pp. 159-172.

[6] *Annals of Loch Cé* (ed. W. M. Hennessy, *Rolls Series*), I, 247-8. Orpen, *Ireland under the Normans,* II, 289-281.

[7] This meeting had immediately followed the Welsh expedition of 1211 in which William took part.　　　　　　　[8] *Rot. Claus.,* I, 132b.

sage counsel and active co-operation and had assured the king that his presence was necessary for the safety of Ireland. He could earn the king's eternal gratitude by remaining there to assist the justiciar in forwarding the king's business. John added that he was enclosing copies of letters patent made for him by the barons of England. He would be greatly pleased if William and his fellow barons of Ireland would put their seals on similar ones. As to the earl's suggestion that he make peace with the church, the king wished his vassals in Ireland to draw up terms which might placate the pope without detriment to his own independence and royal rights. Finally John informed William that his son needed a horse and clothing. If the earl wished, the king would furnish the boy with these necessities and give him into the custody of John d'Erley or any other knight of William's who was with the court. As for the earl's fears that he planned to send his son to Poitou, John assured him that he had no such intention and had only learned of the rumor from his justiciar. This remarkable document marks William's reinstatement in royal favor. The king's appreciation of his fidelity was similarly expressed in a letter to the bishop of Norwich.[9] He also carried out his promise about the earl's son —in fact he extended it to include both of them. John d'Erley was summoned to London and entrusted with the care of the two boys. When John d'Erley insisted that one of them was enough for any man, the younger was given to Thomas de Sanford.[10]

For his part William carried to a successful conclusion at least one of the tasks which the king had entrusted to him. He persuaded twenty-six of his fellow barons to join him in issuing letters patent in the name of all the magnates of Ireland according to the form suggested by John.[11] These lords declared that they had been grieved and astonished to hear that the pope proposed to absolve the king's subjects from their oaths of fealty because he had refused to accept Stephen Langton as archbishop

[9] *Ibid.*   [10] *Hist.,* 14533-14578.
[11] *Calendar of Documents relating to Ireland,* no. 448.

of Canterbury. Everything that the pope had done in respect to the election to the see of Canterbury was contrary to the liberty and dignity of the king and crown of England. Before the Norman conquest the kings of England had chosen bishops as they saw fit, but since that time they had allowed them to be elected canonically, subject to their assent. The authors of the declaration fully realized that they and their ancestors had been nourished, enriched with wealth and honors, and granted fiefs by the king and his predecessors. The king had been faithful to his vassals and had never offended against their rights. He had resisted the pope in the election to the see of Canterbury in order to preserve intact the rights which the English crown had always enjoyed. They were prepared to live or die with the king and adhere to him faithfully to the last. While there is no positive proof that this declaration was a copy of the transcript of the "letters patent made for the king by the barons of England" mentioned by John, such an hypothesis seems highly probable. With its emphasis on the king's rights and the baron's duties and its statement that John had never violated the rights of his vassals, this document bears all the earmarks of royal inspiration. Its whole tenor is exactly what one would expect from the letters referred to in John's note to William. As for the actual letters patent which the king claimed had been issued by the barons of England, if they ever existed, they have been lost. The form sent to William may have represented not what the barons had declared but what the king hoped they might.[12] Be that as it may, the earl's success in securing the co-operation of the barons of Ireland must have strengthened John's confidence in his loyalty.

When William advised the king to make peace with the church, he undoubtedly had a clear idea of the gravity of the situation. Philip Augustus had long contemplated the conquest

[12] See Norgate, *John Lackland*, pp. 172-174 and Orpen, *Ireland under the Normans*, II, 309-311. Mr. Orpen takes this declaration to be the "oaths of allegiance" mentioned in John's letters, but its tenor seems to identify it with "the letters patent made by the barons of England."

of England with the idea of giving the throne to his son, Louis. As early as the spring of 1212 Louis and his father had settled the relationship that would exist between them after the prince had assumed the English crown. Philip was quite ready to become the sword of the church for the purpose of dispossessing John of his kingdom. In April 1213 the legate Pandulf arrived in France with the papal letters deposing John and ordering the French king to conquer England for himself and his heirs. Philip summoned his vassals to muster at Rouen on April 21st for the projected expedition. John was faced with a French invasion supported by all the power of the church at a time when but few of his barons could be relied upon.

While Philip was concentrating his army and fleet at Boulogne, the levies of England were gathering near Dover. Late in March John had summoned to his assistance William and the bishop of Norwich.[13] They arrived at Barham Down with a force of five hundred knights which must have represented the entire feudal levy of Ireland.[14] By the beginning of May both sides were fully prepared for the impending struggle. But Philip had over-estimated the sincerity of his ally, Innocent. The pope wished to force John to bow to his will and was using Philip as a threat to gain that end, but he had no desire to increase the latter's power as he knew him to be fully as intractable as John. In November, 1212, the English king, possibly acting on William's advice, had sent envoys to Rome to inform the pope that he was ready to accept the terms which had been proposed by the legate in the previous year. Innocent replied that this offer would be satisfactory if four English barons would pledge themselves that the terms would be carried out and would send letters patent to that effect to the exiled bishops. While Pandulf was urging Philip to conquer England in the pope's name, he was fully aware that Innocent was still negotiating with John. Just as the French expedition

---

[13] *Calendar of Documents relating to Ireland,* no. 455.

[14] Roger of Wendover, II, 67. William may have preceded the bishop to England. *Hist.,* 14580-14596.

was about to sail, the legate halted it while he hastened to England to give its king a last chance to submit to the church. The agreement reached between John and Pandulf is too well known to require discussion. William was a witness to the act by which the king promised to become the pope's liege vassal for the kingdoms of England and Ireland and to pay an annual tribute of one thousand marks to the papal treasury.[15] On May 24th the earl joined with eleven other barons in sending letters patent to the exiled bishops to guarantee the fulfilment by John of his agreement with the church.[16] In August William was one of the commissioners appointed to estimate the extent of the damage done to the see of London during the quarrel between king and pope.[17] The importance of the part played by William Marshal in John's reconciliation with Rome must be left to conjecture. In the summer of 1212 he had advised the king to make peace with the church and had offered his services as a negotiator. In company with a number of his fellow barons he had acted as witness and guarantor of the various agreements concluded. Whatever his influence may have been, there is little doubt that his motives were purely secular. John could not cope with pope, barons, and foreign enemies. The obvious solution was to make peace with the most formidable and least irreconcilable of these foes, Innocent III. The manoeuvre was highly successful. John obtained a staunch supporter in his quarrels with his barons, and Philip, despite his rage at what he considered papal trickery, was forced to renounce his invasion of England.

William's faithful service during the critical years of 1212 and 1213 seem to have removed John's last lingering doubts of his fidelity. In October 1213 he gave him the castle and fief of Haverford in consideration of a fine of one thousand marks.[18] This important fortress was a part of the county of Pembroke,

[15] Roger of Wendover, II, 74-76.
[16] *Rot. Pat.*, pp. 98b, 114b. *Foedera*, I, I, 115.
[17] *Rot. Claus.*, I, 164b.
[18] *Rot. Pat.*, p. 105. *Rotuli de oblatis et finibus*, p. 499.

but it had passed into the king's custody at the death of its lord, Robert fitz Richard, who was a tenant-in-chief in Somersetshire. Haverford became one of the most valuable of the demesne manors of the earl in Pembrokeshire. More decided marks of the royal confidence were to follow. John and Otto were at last ready to launch their long-planned attack on Philip Augustus that was to end so disastrously on the field of Bouvines. The Welsh were known to be potential if not actual allies of the French king, and John was extremely anxious to have them kept in check during his absence. With this end in view he restored William to his former dominant position in south Wales by giving him the custody of the strongholds of Cardigan, Carmarthen, and Gower with a grant of money to maintain them.[19] To insure still further the co-operation of the various forces watching the Welsh the king created William's nephew, John Marshal, custodian of the marches of Shropshire and Staffordshire.[20] John was also given the manor of Hengham as a fief and the office of sheriff of Lincolnshire.[21] Despite John's apparent disloyalty to his uncle in 1207, the two seem to have been on the best of terms, and John rose steadily in importance as William advanced in the king's favor. King John chose wisely in entrusting the safety of south Wales to William Marshal. His was a sword for which the native princes had a most wholesome respect. Even as he lay on his death bed in 1219, the possibility that he might march against them was enough to check a Welsh invasion of Pembroke.

While John's agreement with the church had transformed Innocent III into a staunch ally, it had increased the effectiveness of the baronial opposition. Two of the king's bitterest enemies, Robert fitz Walter and Eustace de Vesci, had been reinstated in their possessions. Still more serious was the fact that in Stephen Langton the disaffected barons found a counsellor who could teach them how to formulate and express their grievances against the royal administration. John had carried

---

[19] *Rot. Pat.*, p. 109b. *Rotuli de oblatis et finibus*, p. 522.
[20] *Rot. Pat.*, p. 109.   [21] *Ibid.*, p. 109, 109b.

out his plans for an expedition to Poitou despite the protests of a fair part of his baronage. His utter failure to accomplish anything brought to a head his vassals' discontent and materially lessened his own prestige. In November 1214 the barons met at St. Edmunds, passed around the coronation charter of Henry I which they had probably obtained from Stephen Langton, and formed a confederation to force the king to grant them the liberties guaranteed by that document.[22] In January 1215 they went to London in force to place their demands before John. The king persuaded them to postpone the discussion until after Easter, and Stephen Langton, the bishop of Ely, and William Marshal took oath that at that time John would give them full satisfaction.[23]

The confederates soon discovered that the king intended to use this respite not for consideration of their demands but for military preparation. When Poitevin levies began to arrive in England, the barons of the north demanded an explanation. John granted them letters patent of safe conduct to go to Oxford to confer with his representatives, the archbishop of Canterbury, several of his suffragans, and William Marshal.[24] Nothing is known of this meeting—in fact it may never have taken place—but on March 13th the king, after thanking his Poitevin vassals for their loyalty, ordered them to stay at home and sent back those who had already started.[25] In all probability William and the archbishop sympathized with the confederates' protests against the king's attempt to overawe them with foreign troops and persuaded John to yield.[26]

The king had failed in his attempt to gather a mercenary army, but he was most successful in mustering to his aid the spiritual might of Rome. Innocent III as suzerain of England condemned the conspiracies of the barons and ordered them to pay the scutage of Poitou to which they had objected. In order to bind the church still more firmly to his cause, John took the

---

[22] Roger of Wendover, II, 111-2.
[23] *Ibid.*, pp. 113-4.
[24] *Rot. Pat.*, p. 129.
[25] *Ibid.*, p. 130.
[26] See Norgate, *John Lackland*, p. 224.

cross. This convinced the barons that the king had no intention of granting their requests. Without waiting for the day set for the formal conference with John, they mustered their forces at Stamford and marched to Northampton. There they were met by the king's envoys, and a series of conferences took place at which the recently received papal letters were fully discussed. Innocent had suggested that John grant his vassals their " just petitions." When the confederates pressed this point, the king decided to allow them to state their grievances. On April 27th he sent Langton and William to the baronial camp at Brackley to obtain a list of the rebels' demands. But when these demands were read to him by the envoys, John absolutely refused to accede to them. Never would he concede his subjects liberties that would make the king a slave. After a fruitless attempt to persuade their master to yield, the earl and primate were forced to inform the barons that their demands had been rejected. The enraged confederates promptly marched to Northampton and laid siege to the castle.[27] The king likewise prepared for war. The earls of Salisbury, Warren, and Pembroke were sent out to rally the king's friends and put the royal castles in a state of defence.[28] William was probably despatched to meet his fellow marcher lords who were mustering in Gloucestershire at John's command.[29]

Meanwhile, the rebels had discovered that Northampton castle was too strong for them and had gone on to Bedford. As that fortress was commanded by one of their own party, William de Beauchamp, they were received in it at once. On May 17th the confederates occupied London as friends and allies of its citizens. Their next step was to attempt to secure the adherence of the barons who had remained loyal to John. The earls of Pembroke, Chester, Salisbury, and Warren, the count of Aumale, Henry fitz Count, William d'Aubigni, John Marshal, and fourteen others were summoned to join the rebellion. If they refused, the confederates would make war on them, level

[27] Roger of Wendover, II, 114-116.
[28] *Rot. Pat.*, p. 135.   [29] *Ibid.*, p. 134b.

their castles, and ravage their lands.[30] This appeal had little effect. Only the count of Aumale and William d'Aubigni, both barons of secondary importance, deserted the royal party.[31]

When William returned from his tour of inspection, he found the king's situation desperate. While the majority of the barons of England, especially those of the west, had held aloof from the rebellion, they had shown no enthusiasm for actively supporting John, and he was left to face the confederate army with a pitifully small force. In April William and Stephen Langton had urged the king to grant the demands of his vassals. They undoubtedly reiterated this advice during the first ten days of June. John finally yielded. William was sent to London to inform the barons that "for the sake of peace and the welfare and honor of his realm" the king would give them the liberties they demanded.[32]

The results of the conferences at Runnimead require no discussion here, but it is interesting to notice that the author of the *History* in his brief summary of the struggle between king and barons makes no mention of the Great Charter.[33] He may well have considered it too unimportant to mention, but there is another possible explanation. The author's patron, William Marshal the younger, was one of the confederates, and his name appears on Matthew Paris' list of the twenty-five barons who were to force John to observe the terms of the charter.[34] The author of the *History* carefully neglects to mention his young lord's part in the rebellion and his later support of Louis of France. He may have feared that a reference to the charter would have reminded young William too keenly of the follies of his youth.

Any extensive discussion of the part played by William Marshal in the phase of the contest between king and barons that

---

[30] Roger of Wendover, II, 116-7.

[31] Their names appear on the list of twenty-five barons. Matthew Paris, *Chronica Maiora,* II, 604-5.

[32] Roger of Wendover, II, 118.

[33] *Hist.,* 15031-15060.   [34] Matthew Paris, *Chronica Maiora,* II, 604-5.

culminated in the grant of the Great Charter must be based largely on supposition. The chronicles show him associated with Stephen Langton in the interest of peace. In January these two men guaranteed that the king would redress his vassals' grievances at the appointed time. To them John entrusted most of his negotiations with the confederates. In April they bore to the king the demands of the barons and urged him to accept them. Finally their names head the list of those who counselled John to grant the charter.[35] From these meagre facts one can draw a few reasonably safe conclusions. Both the earl and the primate seem to have enjoyed the confidence of both sides. Furthermore, they either actually sympathized with the barons and approved their demands or believed that the peace of the realm was worth any concession that might be necessary. Beyond this point the evidence will not carry one, and historical imagination has free rein. Several eminent authorities have credited Stephen Langton with formulating the demands of the barons, persuading the king to accede to them, and drawing up the charter.[36] The document shows rare restraint, very real qualities of statesmanship, and a thorough knowledge of the common law and the English administrative system. From what is known of the individual members of the baronial party it is incredible that they should have produced Magna Carta. But the biographer of William Marshal must hesitate to give all the credit to Stephen Langton. The earl of Pembroke was probably perfectly capable of inspiring the Great Charter. He had had the necessary administrative experience, and he was soon to show the requisite wisdom and statesmanship. His opportunities to guide and moderate the baronial policy were as great as those of the primate—greater perhaps as he had a son high in the confederate councils. Finally when it came to persuading the king to yield to his vassals, the advice of an old friend and

---

[35] Roger of Wendover, II, 118-9. W. Stubbs, *Select Charters* (8th edition), p. 296.

[36] F. M. Powicke, *Stephen Langton*, pp. 102-128. Norgate, *John Lackland*, pp. 233-4.

tried servant of the house of Anjou must have had more weight than that of a prelate who had but recently ceased to be John's implacable opponent. Until additional evidence shall clearly establish who it was that procured for England her beloved charter, William Marshal and Stephen Langton should share the honor.

While it is impossible to prove whether or not William sympathized with the demands of the barons, there can be no doubt of his attitude toward armed rebellion. He was John's liege man. He had suffered from his master's suspicious nature and had been forced to give his sons, his vassals, and his castles as pledges for his loyalty. In his quarrel with the king he had come very close to the line which separated legitimate opposition from open defiance of one's lord, but he had never crossed it. If there had been no other considerations involved, William's fine sense of feudal propriety would have kept him loyal to his king. His exemplary attitude was merely strengthened by other circumstances. The fact that the Welsh were in league with the barons inclined William and his fellow marcher lords toward the royal party. Finally, he probably believed that the path of duty was also that of wisdom. As he was once more high in favor with John, he had no temptation to fish in troubled waters. The campaign of Lincoln was to show that he had no high idea of the military capacity of the confederates. John, backed by the thunders of Rome, was much the better bet.

Despite the high hopes of its adherents the Great Charter could not save England from civil war. A number of northern barons who had left Runnimead in the midst of the conference immediately began to prepare for war on the ground that the peace had been made without their concurrence.[31] In every part of England the rebel lords were openly or secretly making ready for the renewal of hostilities. A meeting had been arranged for July 16th to discuss certain questions which had not been settled in the charter. On the fifteenth John informed the confederates that he could not attend the conference in person,

[37] Walter of Coventry (ed. W. Stubbs, *Rolls Series*), II, 222.

but would send a group of envoys of which William Marshal was one.[38] This was the last time that the earl acted as a negotiator between John and his rebellious vassals. Late in July he went into the west to supervise the defence of the marches against his old enemies the Welsh. The exact situation in south Wales in the summer of 1215 is far from clear. William held the royal castles of Cardigan and Carmarthen which covered his own county of Pembroke.[39] He also had possession of Swansea and probably of the other fortresses in Gower.[40] The chiefs of three great marcher houses, Walter de Lacy, John of Monmouth, and Hugh de Mortimer, were his staunch allies. But the loyal barons of south Wales were faced by a formidable coalition. The Welsh princes were in arms and were actively supported by Giles de Briouse, bishop of Hereford, and his brother Reginald who were anxious to avenge the wrongs of their family. Another rebel baron, Geoffrey de Mandeville, earl of Essex and Gloucester, was titular lord of Glamorgan, but it is improbable that he exercised much authority in the region.

In June or July the de Briouse brothers invaded Brecon and were joyfully welcomed by their father's vassals. Maelgwyn ap Rees and young Rees, his nephew, raided Pembroke and Gower, capturing many castles and ravaging the countryside.[41] Although they seemed unable to defend their lands with the sword, the loyal barons scored an important diplomatic victory. On October 21st Giles de Briouse made peace with John and received the custody of the castle of Swansea as well as all the lands of his house.[42] The chroniclers credit this change of heart to the bishop's fear of the thunders of Rome, and if he foresaw his own imminent death, this explanation is most plausible.[43] Still one cannot but feel that the diplomacy of William Marshal, which was in time to win over his far more intractable brother Reginald, had much to do with bishop Giles' conver-

[38] Rot. Pat., p. 149.
[39] Ibid., p. 109b.
[40] Ibid., p. 157b.

[41] Brut y Tywysogion, pp. 282-285.
[42] Rot. Pat., p. 157b.
[43] Brut y Tywysogion, pp. 284-5.

sion. At any rate the triumph was an empty one, for the bishop of Hereford died in November. Although the king promptly ordered that all his castles be turned over to the earl of Pembroke, it is probable that some at least remained in the possession of Reginald de Briouse.[44] Meanwhile Llywelyn, prince of North Wales, had reduced Carmarthen, Kilgerran, and several castles in Pembrokeshire.[45]

There is little or no information about William's part in this fairly unsuccessful attempt to defend the English lands in south Wales. Considering his seventy odd years, it is improbable that he took any very active part in military operations. The close and patent rolls indicate that during the summer of 1215 and the following winter he was the king's chief representative in the region and enjoyed vice-regal powers. To him were addressed the king's writs for the delivery of castles and lands.[46] On the Sunday after Christmas master Henry de Cern appeared before him with the pope's letters to the western bishops confirming the suspension of Stephen Langton.[47] The earl assigned manors on his own authority and even made treaties with repentant rebels.[48] While John marched about England devastating the lands of his rebellious barons, William acted as commander-in-chief in south Wales.

During this summer of 1215 the confederate barons showed their true mettle. While the king systematically ravaged their fiefs and reduced their castles, they lay supinely in London. When John laid siege to Rochester castle which was held for them by the gallant William d'Aubigni, they made only the most pitiful attempts to relieve it. They did, however, make one decisive move—they offered the crown of England to Louis of France, son and heir of King Philip Augustus. Louis agreed to send to England what knights he could muster and to follow himself at Easter. In accordance with this promise he sent over

[44] Rot. Pat., p. 159. Annales de Dunstaplia, Annales Monastici (ed. H. R. Luard, Rolls Series), III, 47.

[45] Brut y Tywysogion, pp. 286-289.

[46] Rot. Claus., I, 239b, 240, 240b. Rot. Pat., pp. 166b, 169b.

[47] Rot. Claus., I, 269.   [48] Ibid., pp. 261, 270.

two forces of one hundred and forty and one hundred and twenty knights respectively. Not even these reinforcements could stir the barons to any activity. While the French knights grumbled over the lack of wine, the English drank their ale cheerfully in the shelter of the walls of London. John continued to harry their lands with the greatest thoroughness. The confederates' only hope lay in the early arrival of Louis with his army.[49]

As this was equally apparent to John, he decided to send an embassy to Philip in the hope that he might be persuaded to forbid his son to invade England. For this mission he chose Peter des Roches, bishop of Winchester, and William Marshal. As the latter was an old acquaintance of the French king and his liege vassal for Longueville, he was peculiarly fitted for this task. The envoys were unable to come to any agreement with Philip and were forced to return to England to report their failure.[50] One thing only made Philip hesitate to give Louis leave to go to England—his fear of the wrath of Innocent III. On April 25th he received the legate Gualo at Melun and attempted to prove to him that Louis was the rightful king of England. His case was not very strong, and he completely failed to convince the legate.[51] Gualo went on to England while Philip sent envoys to Rome to plead his son's cause before the pope himself. On May 20th Louis set sail from Calais.

When William returned from his futile mission to the French court, his first care was to have a conference with his eldest son. On April 10th the king issued letters of safe conduct to permit the younger William Marshal to visit his father under the escort of Aimery de St. Maur, master of the Templars.[52] Undoubtedly the earl's avowed reason for seeking this interview was the hope that he could persuade his heir to return to the

[49] Norgate, *John Lackland,* pp. 247-263. *Histoire des ducs de Normandie et des rois d'Angleterre* (ed. Francisque Michel, *Société de l'histoire de France*), pp. 160-164.

[50] Ralph de Coggeshall, pp. 180-1.

[51] Norgate, *John Lackland,* pp. 265-267. Ch. Petit-Dutaillis, *Étude sur la Vie et le Regne de Louis* VIII, pp. 72-87.   [52] *Rot. Pat.,* p. 175b.

allegiance of John. If such was his purpose, he was unsuccessful, for the young Marshal remained with the rebels and was among the first to do homage to Louis of France when that prince arrived in England.[53] The pleas of the father could not overcome the stubborn resolution of the son. But one can imagine a different scene—that of the two men amiably planning the future policy of the house of Marshal. William served John loyally, but he had no love for him, while he had great esteem for Philip Augustus. He had also a wholesome respect for the military capacity of the chivalry of France. The earl may well have believed that Louis had an excellent chance of conquering England. With the young Marshal at Louis' court the family fortunes would be safe no matter what might happen. If John won, he could hardly be over harsh with the son of his staunchest adherent. On the other hand Louis would undoubtedly be generous to the father of his faithful partisan who was himself a friend and vassal of King Philip. These ideas may never have entered the earl's head—the suggestion may do him a grave injustice. But just such careful hedging marked his conduct during the conquest of Normandy, and his later attitude toward Louis shows that he was animated by no great hatred of the invader. The possibility that William conceived a scheme of this sort is decidedly worth bearing in mind.

On May 22, 1216, Louis' fleet appeared off Sandwich. John drew up his army on the shore prepared to give battle as soon as the enemy landed, but as he scanned the ranks of his mercenaries he was filled with doubts as to their reliability. Most of them were born subjects of Philip Augustus, and their pay was sadly in arrears.[54] William himself urged the king not to risk the fate of the realm on a pitched battle, but to retire before the invader.[55] Louis promptly advanced to Canterbury which made no resistance, took the castle of Rochester after a week's siege, and entered London on June 2nd. Meanwhile

---

[53] *Rot. Claus.,* I, 260b. *Histoire des ducs,* p. 171.
[54] Roger of Wendover, II, 180. *Hist.,* 15088-15094.
[55] *Annales de Dunstaplia, Annales Monastici,* III, 46.

the legate Gualo had solemnly excommunicated the French prince and all his partisans. After a four day halt in London Louis advanced to Winchester and laid siege to its castles while John retired toward the west. As he lay before Winchester, the French prince received the submission of the earls of Arundel, Warren, and Salisbury who represented the feudal power of Surrey, Sussex, and Wiltshire.[56] Of the English earls only those of Chester, Pembroke, Derby, and Warwick remained loyal to John while among the barons he could only count on a knot of marcher lords and a few royal officials. Leaving Louis a free hand in the eastern counties, the English king retreated to the safety of the great fortress of Corfe. By the end of July the invader was master of eastern England from the channel to the Scottish border except for a few isolated strongholds such as Dover, Windsor, and Lincoln.

By the end of June William was back in the south marches. The rolls show that throughout the summer of 1216 he was in command of that region, but little or nothing is known of his activities.[57] As the Welsh princes seem to have spent the summer quarreling among themselves, he probably enjoyed comparative peace in that quarter.[58] The earl's principal occupation was checking the depredations of Reginald de Briouse and watching for a westward movement of Louis. The latter materialized in July in the form of an expedition into Worcestershire led by the younger William Marshal. If there was a joint plan of the Marshal family, young William had been most diligent in carrying out his part of it. As Louis lay before Winchester, he had asserted his right to the marshalship, and the French prince had felt obliged to concede it to him.[59] Adam de Beaumont ceased to exercise the functions of his office, and young William became marshal of the court. When Louis obtained possession of Marlborough castle, William advanced his family's rather shadowy claim to the possession of that fortress.

[56] Roger of Wendover, II, 180-1. *Histoire des ducs,* pp. 169-174.

[57] Rot. Claus., I, 276, 280b, 282b, 283, 288b.

[58] *Brut y Tywysogion,* pp. 288-291.   [59] *Histoire des ducs,* p. 174.

This request was refused by Louis, and the castle was given to Robert of Dreux. Soon after this rebuff William departed for the west and occupied Worcester.[60] The impertinence of his heir's incursion into a region so near his own command was apparently too much for the old earl. He warned his son to leave the city. The young Marshal had sufficient discretion to accept this wholesome advice and made good his escape, while his father supported by Ranulf of Chester and Faulkes de Bréauté recaptured Worcester.[61] Except for the fact that. he continued to rule in the marches, nothing further is known of William Marshal's exploits until he hastened from Gloucester to Worcester to attend the bier of John of Anjou.

William's faithful service during these years of stress did not go unrewarded. The king showed himself particularly generous in strengthening his position in Ireland. In July, 1215, Thomas fitz Anthony who had succeeded Geoffrey fitz Robert as William's seneschal of Leinster, was granted the custody of all the county of Waterford, except the city itself, and the county of Desmond with the city of Cork.[62] On August 20th of the same year John directed two writs to his agents in Ireland in William's favor.[63] The first gave permission to all ships to go to the earl's port of New Ross, while the other ordered Geoffrey Luterel to return to William the castle of Dunamase which had been taken from him in 1210. This last order was ignored, and the resulting correspondence throws a very curious light on John's methods of government. On December 22, 1215, the king commanded the justiciar to deliver the castle to William's agent despite any countersign which they had arranged between them.[64] This command was likewise unavailing, and on May 14, 1216, a most interesting letter was despatched to the justiciar. [65] The king was greatly surprised that

---

[60] *Ibid.*, p. 175. *Annales de Wigornia, Annales Monastici,* IV, 406.

[61] *Ibid. Annales de Dunstaplia, Annales Monastici,* III, 48. *Rot. Claus.,* I, 282b.

[62] *Calendar of Documents relating to Ireland,* no. 576.

[63] *Rot. Pat.,* p. 153b.   [64] *Ibid.,* p. 161b.   [65] *Ibid.,* p. 184.

the justiciar had not obeyed his order to deliver the castle of Dunamase to William. He was commanded to turn it over without delay to the bearer of this letter who would also show him the letters patent of the earl authorizing him to receive the castle as his representative. The justiciar had informed the king, through brother Nicholas of the Hospital, that he would obey his command about the castle if he sent him a certain countersign—namely, that the king takes him or he takes the king either by the thumb or the arm; the king knows not which. The king did not doubt that the justiciar would obey him promptly. Apparently John had arranged with Geoffrey Marsh that no orders in respect to Dunamase should be obeyed unless they bore the countersign—which sign the king promptly forgot. The convenience of such an arrangement is obvious. If William demanded the return of his castle, and the king was unwilling, he could issue letters which would satisfy the earl but which would have no effect. This appears to have been a fairly common procedure with John. In September 1216 in letters patent ordering the release of some prisoners he gave his men who had them in custody the countersign of *unam balistam corneam*.[66] In this case orders had been issued previously forbidding the release of prisoners without the countersign. Other examples of this practice may be found in the rolls. It illustrates beautifully the devious methods of government that made John so generally hated and distrusted by his subjects. In the case of Dunamase, however, the king probably had no intention of deceiving William by giving him useless letters patent, but he had completely forgotten his arrangement with the justiciar. The fact that he felt obliged to follow the matter up so energetically indicates how highly he valued William.

In October 1216 King John lay dying in the episcopal fortress of Newark. About him stood a few loyal servants—bishop Peter of Winchester, John of Monmouth, Walter and Roger de Clifford, and John Marshal. The king called his followers to him and addressed them. "Lords, I must die. I cannot resist

[66] *Rot. Pat.*, p. 195b.

this disease. For the love of God beg the Marshal to forgive me the wrongs I have done him, for I repent them fully. He has always served me loyally and he has never acted against me no matter what I did or said to him. For God's sake, lords, pray him to pardon me. As I am more sure of his loyalty than that of any other man, I ask you to entrust to him the care of my son who will never succeed in holding his land unless by his aid." [67] John could no longer command—he could merely recommend to his barons that they confide the government of the infant king and his sadly harassed realm to the earl of Pembroke.

To evaluate the part played by William in the events of John's last years is practically impossible. He appears to have urged the king to become reconciled with the church, and he certainly took part in the negotiations which achieved that end. When the English barons rose in revolt, he acted as mediator between them and the king, but once it became clear that mediation was hopeless, he allied himself completely with the royal party. While the principal reason for his attitude was probably his sense of duty to his liege lord, other considerations may well have influenced his decision. The fact that the Welsh were supporting the baronial party would naturally alienate from it the sympathy of William and his fellow lords of the marches. Then these same lords, the bulk of whose lands were palatinates, had less interest in the abuses in the English administration and therefore less enthusiasm for the Great Charter. Finally, one is inclined to believe that William was far-sighted enough to see that the king, supported by the power of the church, had, in the long run, the best chance of success. Be that as it may, he stood faithfully by his master against the rebel barons and their French, Welsh, and Scottish allies. His presence in the royal party probably did much to build up and hold together that little group of marcher lords who formed its very core.

William's personal relations with his master improved

---

[67] *Hist.*, 15153-15190. *Histoire des ducs*, p. 180.

steadily during these years. His activity in urging the Irish barons to support the king in his quarrel with the pope started his rise in the royal favor. As he continued to demonstrate his loyalty, he received fresh marks of John's appreciation. His castles and hostages were returned to him, and he was once more given the custody of the great fortresses of west Wales which were so important to the safety of Pembroke. Once again he was John's most trusted servant and counsellor. So completely did he regain his master's confidence that on his death bed John entrusted to the earl of Pembroke his young son, Henry Plantagenet.

Considering the importance of the events of these six years, from 1210 to 1216, it is disappointing to know so little of William's part in them. But his very character made him utterly unfitted to shine in civil broils. His sense of duty compelled him to support his liege lord, yet his sense of justice prevented him from approving his policy sufficiently strongly to identify himself with it as completely as did such men as Peter des Roches, Hubert de Burg, and Faulkes de Bréauté. Fully in sympathy with neither party, his mark on the period was bound to be a slight one. Nevertheless he so conducted himself as to increase rather than diminish his general prestige and his position in the confidence and admiration of his contemporaries. If he had joined the rebel barons or had identified himself completely with John's policies, he would never, in all probability, have had the opportunity to demonstrate as regent his real abilities and high qualities of character. Perhaps his comparitive obscurity during this period was a benefit both to England and to his own future. This part of his life led directly to the culmination of his career—his service as regent of England.

CHAPTER X

A ROYALIST GENERAL

As soon as he learned of John's death, William hastened from Gloucester to Worcester to meet his nephew and the other barons who were escorting the corpse of their royal master from Newark. There they were joined by the legate. After interring John with due ceremony in the church of St. Wulstan, William and Gualo summoned the chief men of the royal party to assemble in council at Gloucester. Thomas de Sanford was despatched to fetch young Henry Plantagenet from his retreat in the Wiltshire stronghold of Devizes. The earl himself rode out as far as Malmesbury to meet the lord of England. The boy, who had been well instructed in his part, greeted him warmly. " Sir, you are welcome. I give myself to God and to you. May God give you his grace so that you may guard me well." " Sire," answered William, " by my soul I shall do what I can to serve you in good faith and with all my powers." The sight of the attractive, helpless boy of nine who was the heir of the house of Anjou was too much for the old servants of his family. Breaking into tears, they continued their ride toward Gloucester.[1]

As the nobles and prelates gathered at Gloucester their first care was to supply themselves with an excuse for existence as a royalist party. They had loyally served the king of England, but now there was no king.[2] One solution of the problem would have been to declare Louis of France John's successor and thus end the civil war. Such action would not have been unprecedented. King Stephen had disinherited his son in favor

---

[1] *Hist.,* 15206-15286.

[2] The theory that the king never dies had not yet developed, and there was no king between the death of one and the coronation of his successor. Richard and John used the title *Dominus Anglie* in this interval.

of Henry II. It is rather remarkable that no one seems even to have suggested this course. Not only were the barons who had remained faithful to his father determined to maintain young Henry's rights, but that weather-cock of the civil war, Count William of Aumale, cheerfully rejoined the royal party. To guard against the possibility that Louis might take advantage of John's death to assume formally the English crown, the council decided to knight and consecrate Henry immediately without even waiting for the arrival of such belated members of their party as Ranulf of Chester. To William Marshal, who was considered the foremost knight of his age and who had already received one king into the order of chivalry, was accorded the honor of performing the first ceremony. When he had been duly dubbed a knight, Henry took the customary oath, did homage to Gualo as the representative of England's suzerain, the pope, and was solemnly crowned by the bishop of Winchester.[3] This double ceremony restored the moral and legal foundations of the royal party—they had a king to serve.

A nine-year-old king might reign, but he could not rule, and some method had to be devised for carrying on the government until he came of age. A strong hand would be required for the task of driving out the invader and restoring order in the kingdom. According to the *History* John had commended his son to the care of William Marshal, and this statement is supported by another chronicle, but there is no evidence that their late master's wish carried any weight with the leaders of the loyal party.[4] A half dozen of these leaders might with good reason have aspired to the regency—the legate, bishop Peter of Winchester, the justiciar, Hubert de Burg, and the earls of Pembroke, Chester, and Derby. The legate Gualo undoubtedly realized that he could be more effective in the background. As the pope's representative he would be distrusted by the baronage and he was no soldier who could command the operations against Louis. Peter des Roches, bishop of Winchester, was an

---

[3] *Hist.*, 15287-15332. Roger of Wendover, II, 197-199.
[4] *Hist.*, 15171-15190. *Histoire des ducs*, p. 180.

able captain and an experienced administrator, but he was a Poitevin and was generally hated for his high-handed rule during John's absence on the continent in 1214. While his high office of justiciar gave Hubert de Burg a strong claim to the regency, he was simply a faithful and capable royal official, an upstart whose elevation to so great a dignity would be sure to annoy the barons. Both Peter and Hubert suffered from the additional disadvantage of being too closely connected in the public mind with John's misgovernment. The success of the new government would depend to a great extent on the ability of the regent to secure the wholehearted co-operation of the loyal barons and to win over the rebels. For this reason it was extremely desirable that he be himself a great feudal lord. Of the three earls who had actively supported John, one, William de Ferrars, earl of Derby, was a man of minor importance. The choice really lay between the two marcher earls, Ranulf of Chester and William of Pembroke. As palatine lords of vast domains both these men stood in the forefront of the English baronage in respect to rank, power, and prestige. Both of them enjoyed untarnished records of loyalty to the house of Anjou. Both were experienced soldiers who had taken part in the campaigns against Philip Augustus and in innumerable wars with the Welsh. As the younger of the two men, Earl Ranulf was the more able to bear the burdens of government, but he lacked the administrative experience which William had gained as associate justiciar during Richard's crusade. The best argument for the choice of the earl of Pembroke lay in his personal qualities which were peculiarly suited to so eminent an office as the regency. His reputation for honesty and loyalty guaranteed him the admiration and confidence of both friends and enemies. His activities on the continent as knight-errant, warrior, and diplomat made him as well known in the French court as in the English. Four kings had valued his counsel because of his wisdom and discretion. After the coronation banquet the men of rank asked William Marshal to take charge of the king and kingdom, but he insisted on postponing the discussion until after the arrival of the earl of Chester.[5] To run the risk of offending the man who controlled the palatinate of Chester and the extensive honor of Brittany would have been nothing short of idiotic.

That evening the earl summoned to his quarters in Gloucester castle his three most intimate friends, John Marshal, John d'Erley, and Ralph Musard, sub-sheriff of Gloucestershire and constable of the castle. He asked their counsel as to what answer he should give to the request that he assume control of the kingdom. John Marshal and Ralph Musard advised him to accept. While the earl's nephew stressed the honor to be gained, Ralph pointed out that William would be able to enrich all his friends. John d'Erley was less enthusiastic. The earl was old, the task was formidable, and the royal treasury was empty. The earl's energies and his private resources would be drained to the dregs. In the face of these conflicting counsels, William took the only reasonable course—he went to bed.[6]

When Earl Ranulf reached Gloucester, the men of rank gathered in council to discuss the all important question. Peter des Roches, who presided, asked the opinion of Alan Basset who replied that the choice lay between the earls of Pembroke and Chester. William insisted that he was too old and feeble for so onerous a charge and supported his argument by somewhat exaggerating his true age.[7] Let them choose the earl of Chester, and he would support him to the best of his ability. But Ranulf concurred in the general opinion that William was the man for the position. " No, Marshal," said he, " that cannot be. You are so good a knight, so fine a man, so feared, so loved, and so wise that you are considered one of the first knights in the world. I say to you in all loyalty that you must be chosen. I will serve you, and I will carry out to the best of my power all the tasks you may assign to me." As everyone seemed in agreement, the legate saw no need for continuing the

---

[5] *Hist.*, 15375-15400. [6] *Ibid.*, 15401-15464.

[7] *Ibid.*, 15510. William stated that he was over 80. He could not have been more than 72.

general discussion. Gualo, the bishop of Winchester, the two earls, and a few of the more important barons withdrew into another room. All urged William Marshal to accept the regency, but their arguments proved unavailing until the legate asked him to undertake it as a general penance for all his sins. This offer was too tempting to be refused, and William gave way.[8] Was the earl's resistance sincere or merely polite modesty? One is inclined to accept it at its face value. He was old, and the task facing him was so difficult as to be almost hopeless. In accounting for his change of mind one must not underestimate the weight of the legate's offer. His was an age of faith, and the church owed much of its wealth to the desire of feudal lords to make sure of their place in heaven. Gualo held in his hands the keys to Heaven and he offered to use them in William's behalf. For a man whose days were drawing to an end a plenary indulgence was the supreme reward.

After he had given his consent to the legate, William once more summoned the three friends whom he had consulted the previous evening. "Counsel me," he said, "for by the faith that I owe you, I see myself entering a sea without bottom or bank. May God come to my aid. They have entrusted to me an almost hopeless task. The child has no money, and I am an aged man." Overcome by his feelings the earl wept, and the others did likewise from sympathy. John d'Erley, however, knew how to cheer his lord. He pointed out to him the honor that was to be gained in so difficult a position. If all William's followers passed over to Louis, if they surrendered all the castles they commanded, if he were driven from England and forced to take refuge in Ireland, still the brave resistance would bring him honor. If a failure could be so honorable, how much greater the glory if he should succeed. No man had ever acquired such honor as would be his. John had not misjudged his lord's nature. While the great baron still hesitated on the brink of the "sea without bottom or bank," the king-errant plunged joyfully in for the sake of the honor to be gained. " By

[8] *Ibid.*, 15465-15561.

the lance of God, that counsel is good. It goes so straight to my heart that if all should abandon the king except me do you know what I would do? I would carry him on my shoulders, now here, now there, from isle to isle, from land to land, and I would never fail him even if I were forced to beg my bread." [9] The flower of chivalry was ready to embark on his last and greatest adventure.

Several extremely pressing problems confronted the newly appointed regent. As no king of England since the Conquest had come to the throne as a minor, there were no precedents to govern William's conduct. Every detail from the actual title to be borne by the regent to the forms to be used in issuing writs had to be worked out. Steps had to be taken to retain the loyalty of the barons who had remained faithful to John and to convince the rebels that the young king's government would avoid the late monarch's errors. As many as possible of the rebellious barons had to be won back to the allegiance of their rightful lord. When John died, he not only left an empty treasury, but he had failed to pay his mercenaries the wages due them at Michaelmas. If the war was to be carried to a successful conclusion these men must be satisfied and retained in Henry's service. With half the kingdom in the possession of the enemy and confusion reigning throughout, all the usual methods of raising money were out of the question and extraordinary ones had to be devised. Finally, the rebellion had to be put down and the invader driven from the realm.

During the first two weeks after his appointment as regent William styled himself justiciar, but that title did not accurately describe his position.[10] The justiciar was a royal official appointed by letters patent to act as the king's deputy.[11] His authority was purely delegated, and when he issued writs during the king's absence from the country, he did so in his own

[9] *Ibid.*, 15624-15696.
[10] *justiciarii nostri Anglie,* Patent Rolls (*Rolls Series*), I, 2.
[11] For letters appointing Peter des Roches justiciar in 1214, see *Rot. Pat.*, p. 110.

name.[12] William on the other hand had been chosen by Gualo, the representative of the overlord of England, and by the great men of the loyal party to govern the country in the king's name. With some self-imposed limitations his will was the king's— in short, he was a real regent as the term is used today. The question of his title was apparently settled at the council of loyal prelates and barons held at Bristol in the middle of November. As Louis by that time had raised the siege of Dover, Hubert de Burg was present, and he may well have objected to William's use of the title which he himself had received from John. Be that as it may, it was finally decided to designate William as *rector regis et regni Angliae*—a title which aptly described his position.[13]

Well established precedents existed for two methods of issuing writs in the absence of the king. They might be issued in the king's name under his seal and attested by the responsible official. This had been the practice of Walter de Coutance, archbishop of Rouen, when he ruled as justiciar during Richard's absence in Palestine.[14] Or the justiciar might simply issue the writs in his own name under his own seal. This had been done by William de Longchamp during 1190 and 1191 and by Peter des Roches in 1214.[15] As the young king had no seal, the first of these two methods could not be used. But writs issued in William's own name might lack the authority of those bearing the king's and would fail to express his full dignity as regent. Hence it was decided to issue the writs in the king's

[12] For the practice of William de Longchamp in 1190-1, see Gervase of Canterbury, I, 509. For that of Peter des Roches in 1214, see *Rot. Claus.*, I, 204-213. Walter de Coutance used the king's name and seal (Gervase of Canterbury, I, 509; Giraldus Cambrensis, *Vita Galfridi*, book II, chapter X).

[13] For this form see Roger of Wendover, II, 208. The form *rectoris nostri et regni nostri* appeared on the charter of liberties of November 12, 1216. (Stubbs, *Select Charters*, p. 343.) It appeared on letters patent of November 19 (*Patent Rolls*, I, 3) and the next day on letters close (*Rot. Claus.*, I, 293b).

[14] Gervase of Canterbury, I, 509. Giraldus Cambrensis *Vita Galfridi*, book II, chapter X.

[15] Gervase of Canterbury, I, 509. *Rot. Claus.*, I, 204-213.

name, but to have them authenticated by William's seal and attested by him as the person responsible for them.[16] This was the practice followed during the first two years of Henry's reign. In special cases the seal of the legate or those of other members of the council were added to William's to give greater authority.[17] A few writs which apparently bore the regent's seal were attested by others.[18] During the first three months of the reign the forms *teste me ipso* and *teste Rege* were used occasionally, but as this obviously meant nothing more than the physical presence of the king, the practice was dropped after January 1217.[19] In one case letters patent attested by the king himself were issued at Bristol under the seals of the legate and Peter des Roches at a time when the regent was at Gloucester. As the letters ordered the restoration to William of the service of Meiler fitz Henry which John had taken from him, this should simply be considered as an example of the regent's delicacy.[20] In general the business of government followed the regent, and the writs were attested by him and authenticated by his seal.

While for most purposes of government William's will was the king's, he seems to have imposed certain restrictions on his own power. He refrained from attempting to remove any officials who held John's letters patent appointing them during the king's pleasure, and he probably doubted his right to do so.[21] He realized, moreover, that he had no right to make perpetual grants which would bind the king and his successors. Such grants as he made were specifically limited to the period of

[16] *et quoniam sigillum nondum habuimus, has litteras nostras patentes, sigillatas sigillo fidelis nostri W. Marescalli, comitis Penbrochie, rectoris nostri et regni nostri, vobis mittimus.*

[17] *Patent Rolls,* I, 24.

[18] Several writs were attested by Peter des Roches (*Rot. Claus.,* I, 361, 361b) and one by Martin de Pattishal (*ibid.,* p. 364).

[19] *Patent Rolls,* I, 1, 9, 19, 24, 26. *Rot. Claus.,* I, 293, 295, 296 b.

[20] *Patent Rolls,* I, 9.

[21] See Turner, *Minority of Henry III in Transactions of Royal Historical Society,* New Series, XVIII (1904), p. 271.

Henry's minority. There are, however, several interesting exceptions to this rule. While the first charter of liberties issued by Henry was clearly provisional, that of 1217 definitely stated that it was binding on the king and his successors forever. In addition there are two grants made to ecclesiastical foundations which purport to be perpetual. Both are in the form of letters patent sealed and attested by William.[22] These examples show the regent's wisdom in delaying for two years before making a new great seal. As no perpetual grant could be valid without the great seal, the documents mentioned above, whatever their wording might be, must be considered as provisional grants. When Henry's seal began to run in the autumn of 1218, grants in perpetuity made during the minority were definitely declared invalid.[23] Thus William and his colleagues worked out each problem that arose in their unprecedented situation. The solutions arrived at bear strong witness to the regent's sound common sense.

On November 12th the adherents of Henry Plantagenet met in council at Bristol. As Louis had raised the siege of Dover, the justiciar, Hubert de Burg, had been able to join the other royalist leaders.[24] The known members of the council include the legate, seven English and four Welsh bishops, the earls of Pembroke, Chester, and Ferrars, the count of Aumale, who had just joined the loyal party, and eighteen barons.[25] After settling such minor matters as the actual title to be borne by the regent, the council authorized the issuance of a charter of liberties.[26] This document was the Great Charter of 1215 with several important omissions and minor changes. Most of the omissions were explained by a clause of the charter itself. The prelates and barons who were present announced that certain questions covered by the Great Charter were so weighty that they should

[22] *Patent Rolls.,* I, 123, 173.

[23] *Ibid.,* p. 177.   [24] Roger of Wendover, II, 199.

[25] See list of those who authorized the issue of the charter, Stubbs, *Select Charters,* pp. 340-343. *Layettes du Trésor des Chartes,* I, no. 1194.

[26] For text of charter see *ibid.* For a complete discussion of Magna Carta and its reissues see McKechnie, *Magna Carta.*

only be decided after long consideration by a full council of the realm. These included the assessing of scutages and aids, the debts to the Jews, the freedom of entering and leaving the kingdom, regulations concerning forests, warrens, and river banks, and the farms of the counties. In addition to the sections of the Great Charter covered by this statement, the new issue omitted the clause governing the distribution of the estates of men who died intestate, that governing the character of men to be appointed to royal offices, the promise to dismiss all foreign mercenaries, and all the purely temporary provisions of John's charter such as the one providing for the return of hostages. As the government was issuing this charter of its own volition, there was naturally no sanction such as the committee of barons provided for in 1215. The minor changes made in a number of sections show very clearly William's wisdom and ability. Chapter three of the Great Charter was amended to forbid a lord to take the custody of a vassal's fief before he had received the homage of the heir. At the same time the age of majority was definitely fixed at twenty-one years. Chapter five was changed so that the rules governing lay wardships were extended to the custody of vacant abbeys and sees.[27] The Great Charter permitted a widow to remain in her husband's house until her dowry was assigned to her. The new charter provided that if the house were a castle, the widow must move to another. Instead of forbidding the constable of a castle to take provisions without making immediate payment, he was allowed three weeks in which to pay for supplies taken from the *ville* in which the castle was situated. The Great Charter forbade royal officials to use a free man's carts without his consent, but the reissue simply provided that all carts should be paid for at regular rates. The explanation made by the prelates and barons of the omissions in this charter should be accepted as the truth, but not as the whole truth. No doubt the subjects enumerated seemed to William too serious and controversial for decision by what was after all but a small minority of the great men of

---

[27] It was provided, however, that ecclesiastical custodies were not to be sold.

England, but there were undoubtedly other reasons for the omissions. With an empty treasury and a war to carry on, the regency could not afford to give up such valuable sources of revenue as the debts to the Jews, increments of the farms of counties, and the estates of intestates. A number of the changes made in various sections of the Great Charter were clearly due to the requirements of war. The constable of a castle had to get food for his garrison even if he had no money. In time of war a castle was no place for a widow. A royal official in need of carts could not consult the wishes of the owners—it was enough if he paid for them. The other changes were simply attempts to clarify and make more effective various provisions of the Great Charter. In this class belongs the amendment fixing the age of majority at twenty-one years and forbidding the minor to claim release from custody at an earlier age by getting himself knighted. The only puzzling omission of the new charter is that of the clause guaranteeing freedom of election to ecclesiastical positions. Probably this was considered a controversial issue and was settled by a private agreement between the regent and the legate. While the charter of 1216 carefully omitted the most important points of dispute between John and his barons, it guaranteed that practices which were generally recognized as abuses would not be revived. As a whole the document serves as a decided tribute to the statesmanship of its authors—the regent and the legate. Issued under their seals on November 12th, this document was a definite promise that the new king's government would abjure John's errors.

When John died at Newark, his treasury was empty, and William was faced with the necessity of finding money to pay the garrisons of the royal castles and the money fiefs granted by John to his soldiers. Michaelmas had come and gone, and the government was in arrears in all its payments. This desperate situation had weighed on William's mind when he was debating whether or not to accept the regency and was John d'Erley's main reason for counseling him to refuse it.[28] In the solution

[28] *Hist.*, 15644-5, 15453-15457.

of this problem William showed admirably his energy and practical common sense. All the usual ways of raising money were out of the question, for the whole administration of the country was in hopeless confusion.[29] William was obliged to look about him for extraordinary methods. The most obvious was to make use of the jewels and rich garments stored in the various royal castles. At Devizes Thomas de Sanford had in his custody a large collection of rings set with precious stones— eighteen with the finest emeralds, seventy-three with good emeralds, sixteen with ordinary ones, one hundred and eleven with sapphires, fifteen with diamonds, twenty-eight with rubies, and nine with garnets.[30] Of these, seventy-three rings set with emeralds, twenty-three with sapphires, nine with garnets, and nineteen with rubies were given to Hubert de Burg to pay the garrison at Dover and buy supplies for the castle. The constables of Devizes and Windsor received six rings with rubies and seventeen with sapphires respectively for their garrisons. Other rings were given to the captains of mercenary troops to pay their men—for instance, to one twenty-three rings with sapphires and fifteen with diamonds to the value of five hundred and forty pounds. Then there lay in the royal castle of Corfe one hundred and nineteen garments of silk, twenty-nine of samite, and four rich *baldekins* from distant Bagdad. These were all used to make the Michaelmas payments on various money fiefs. Thus John Cretun and his brother Simon were accustomed to receive forty and twenty pounds respectively as money fiefs. The half of this sum, due at Michaelmas 1216, was paid by William by giving them thirteen silk garments. In this way all the store was distributed with the exception of one garment of silk and one of samite which were given to John Marshal who was to bear them to Worcester and there use them to cover John's tomb. These collections of rings and rich garments were the reserve fund of the English crown, and William

---

[29] The exchequer had not sat since Michaelmas 1214. Naturally no regular taxes could be collected in the territory held by Louis, and in the rest of the country war had brought confusion. [30] *Rot. Claus.*, I, 602-602b.

used them unhesitatingly in the emergency with which he was faced.[31]

As the sale of the royal treasure could not be expected to supply indefinitely the money needed by the government, the regent was forced to attempt to collect the ordinary and extraordinary revenues of the English crown. Considering the general confusion that reigned throughout the kingdom even in the districts not actually controlled by the enemy and the fact that Louis was in possession of the seat and records of the exchequer, this was no light undertaking. For the duration of the civil war the earl's wardrobe became for all practical purposes the royal exchequer.[32] Whatever could be collected on the farms of counties, or fines made with King John, or on ransoms due from prisoners of war was paid to William directly and acknowledged by his receipt.[33] Needless to say the resulting confusion between the earl's private revenues and those of the crown presented a nice problem for his executors. In the spring of 1217 the regent, probably after consultation with his colleagues, decided to attempt to raise money by taxation.[34] Orders were issued for the collection of a hidage and carucage in all the counties south of the Humber which were not actually in Louis' possession.[35] There is no evidence as to the success of this levy. In April William ordered Faulkes de Bréauté to give five hundred marks of the money collected in the counties which he controlled to Hubert de Burg for his garrison at Dover, but this may have represented merely a fond hope on the part of the regent.[36] But whatever may have been the result of any single financial enterprise, the fact remains that William Marshal was able in the face of immense diffi-

[31] This information is drawn from the accounts of William's executors entered on the Close Rolls. (*Rot. Claus.*, I, 602-602b.)

[32] *in garderoba comitis W. Marescalli Patent Rolls*, I, 83.

[33] *Ibid.*, pp. 3, 8, 10, 11, 60, 61, 63, 69. *Rot. Claus.*, I, 315. *Pipe Roll* 2 Henry III, m 7 d Public Record Office. *Memoranda Roll* 3 Henry III, m 1 d Public Record Office.

[34] See S. K. Mitchell, *Studies in Taxation under John and Henry* III, pp. 121-124.   [35] *Rot. Claus.*, I, 335b.   [36] *Patent Rolls*, I, 56.

culties to find enough money to bring the war to a successful conclusion. No better demonstration can be found of his resourcefulness, energy, and determination.

Scarcely less important than the raising of money was the winning back to their allegiance of Louis' English partisans. William undoubtedly hoped that the reissue of the charter and the knowledge that extremely generous treatment awaited repentant rebels would tempt many knights and barons from the enemy's camp. The regent used all his great personal influence to this end. He wrote to Reginald de Briouse, Hugh de Lacy, and other inveterate rebels begging them to return to the king's service and promising full restoration of their lands and privileges.[37] He literally showered safe-conducts on all who showed any willingness to talk the question over with him in a personal interview.[38] Agents were sent out with blanket letters of protection for all who would come to the king's peace through their influence.[39] Unfortunately these measures had little effect. Military success appeared to be the only argument that had any weight with the French prince's partisans. From John's death to March 1217 only one baron of any importance, Warin fitz Gerold, deserted Louis.[40] The successful campaign conducted by the regent in the latter month won over his son and Earl William of Salisbury.[41] The decisive victory at Lincoln convinced the earls of Arundel and Warren and Reginald de Briouse.[42] Despite his personal prestige and his generous offers, the regent could seduce Louis' supporters only by making his cause appear hopeless.

The success or failure of the regency depended primarily on its ability to crush the rebellion and to drive out the invader. In order to understand the plan of campaign by which William and his colleagues hoped to achieve this end, one must examine with some care the military situation at the time of John's death.

[37] *Ibid.*, pp. 4, 34. *Rot. Claus.*, I, 335.
[38] *Patent Rolls*, I, 3, 10, 15, 33, 48, 62.
[39] *Ibid.*, pp. 24-5.   [41] *Ibid.*, p. 299.
[40] *Rot. Claus.*, I, 295.   [42] *Ibid.*, pp. 312, 315b. *Patent Rolls*, I, 71.

In doing this two distinct factors must be taken into account—
the possession of fortresses, especially those of high strategic
value, and the attitude of the feudal landholders.[43] On the
Kentish coast covering the shortest route from the continent
stood the stronghold of Dover, the key to England. Under the
command of the determined and capable Hubert de Burg, this
castle had proved itself impregnable. Hubert's successful de-
defence was materially assisted by a band of adventurers and
peasants led by a certain William de Casingham who occupied
the Weald of Kent and continually harassed the forces besieging Dover. The rest of the south-eastern counties were
under Louis' domination. Not only did he hold most of the
castles of Surrey, Sussex, and Hampshire with a western out-
post at Marlborough in Wiltshire, but the great barons of the
region, the earls of Salisbury, Arundel, and Warren, and Geoffrey de Say were his partisans. In the shires on the eastern coast
between the Thames and the Tees the situation was more complicated. While the barons of these counties held the open
country for Louis, the chief strongholds of East Anglia and
Lincolnshire, Norwich, Orford, Colchester, Pleshy, Newark,
Sleaford, and Lincoln, housed royalist garrisons. If the French
prince could reduce these fortresses and gain possession of
Dover, he would be master of the richest and most populous
part of England.

Along the edge of the territory controlled by Louis lay a line
of castles which blocked his advance toward the west. Corfe
on the Dorset coast and Devizes in Wiltshire covered south-
western England while Windsor guarded the valley of the
Thames. The castles of the counties of Oxford, Buckingham,
Bedford, Hertford, Cambridge, and Northampton were under

---

[43] For the castles see *Histoire des ducs*, pp. 181, 182, 189 and *Hist.*, 15719-
15743, 15889-16032. The names of the rebel barons can be found in the lists
of *reversis* in the *close rolls*. The information as to their lands has been drawn
from the records of the aid of 1217 supplemented by the inquests found in the
Red Book of the Exchequer. For the former I am largely indebted to notes
loaned me by Professor S. K. Mitchell. See also Petit-Dutaillis, *Vie de Louis
VIII*, pp. 112-130 and Norgate, *Minority of Henry III*, pp. 17-18.

the command of that most capable of mercenary captains, Faulkes de Bréauté, and were defended by his castellans. Another staunch soldier of fortune, Philip Marc, held Nottingham. A large part of the feudal power of these counties was in rebellion. In the south, Dorsetshire and Wiltshire had followed the standard of their greatest magnate, Earl William of Salisbury. William Marshal had been unable to hold the loyalty of some of his own vassals of the honor of Striguil in this region.[44] In the shires ruled by Faulkes lay vast fiefs pertaining to the baronies of David, earl of Huntingdon, and Earl Richard de Clare. Saher de Quency, earl of Winchester, held half the honor of Leicester with the castle of Mount Sorel. The real strength of the royal party lay in the west-central counties. Earl Ranulf of Chester completely dominated Staffordshire and Shropshire, while William de Ferrars controlled his own shire of Derby. Although Henry, earl of Warwick, gave little or no active support to Henry's cause, he remained formally loyal. In Herefordshire, Worcestershire, Gloucestershire, and the adjacent marches were the fiefs of such determined royalists as William Marshal, Walter de Lacy, Hugh and Robert de Mortimer, Walter de Clifford, and John of Monmouth. But even in this region the feudal landowners were not unanimously loyal. Although the nominal master of the honor of Gloucester, Richard de Clare, earl of Hertford, had probably not gained possession of it, many of its tenants were in the rebel ranks. Still more serious was the fact that this little strip of fairly loyal country was continually menaced by Louis' Welsh allies and the fiery Reginald de Briouse. As for the rest of England, the fortresses of the far north, Newcastle-on-Tyne and the castles of the see of Durham, were held for King Henry, but Alexander of Scotland had seized Carlisle. The south-western counties might be described as open-mindedly neutral. Robert de Courtenay, an important Devonshire baron, held Exeter castle

---

[44] See lists of *conversis* and *reversis* in *Close Rolls*. For instance John de St. Quintin and John Maltravers were rebels. (*Rot. Claus.*, I, 300b). Both held of the honor of Striguil.

for Henry, but many of the magnates such as Henry fitz Count, a natural son of earl Reginald of Cornwall, were waiting to see what would happen. The two great assets of the royal party were the possession of such strategic strongholds as Dover, Corfe, Windsor, and Lincoln and the military ability of its leaders. Under the able and determined command of castellans like Nichola de la Haye of Lincoln and Hubert de Burg of Dover these fortresses formed an almost insurmountable barrier to the conquest of England. Furthermore the loyal barons, though few in number, were almost to a man tried warriors. Ranulf of Chester and his fellow marchers had passed their lives fighting the Welsh. Faulkes de Bréauté, Philip Marc, and Engerrand de Cygony were experienced and capable mercenary captains. John Marshal and Philip d'Aubigni were among the hardiest of English barons. Peter des Roches, bishop of Winchester, was to prove himself skilful tactician. In the supreme command stood William Marshal. As far as experience was concerned, he outclassed all his subordinates. Born among the commotions of Stephen's reign, he had fought the French, the Welsh, the Irish, and probably the infidel. Except in his private wars with the Welsh and Irish about which we have no information, he had never had any opportunity to display strategic ability. His tactics were simple and direct—get at the enemy and hew him down. While his military reputation rested upon his personal prowess rather than upon his qualities as a general, his prestige was sufficient to insure the respect of his subordinates among whom were several excellent tacticians. In the campaign against Louis the regent was to prove himself a capable, though somewhat over cautious, strategist.

Despite the apparent strength of his position Louis of France was faced with serious obstacles the most important of which were the royal castles which continually threatened his communications and the utter incapacity of his English allies. The rebel barons had indicated their complete uselessness as soldiers by their hopeless inactivity in London before Louis' arrival—

they were to demonstrate it even more thoroughly at the battle of Lincoln. The French prince was forced to place all his reliance on his own knights and serjeants who were excellent soldiers but comparatively few in number. His plan of campaign was to secure his communications with France by capturing Dover and then turn his attention to the royal castles north of the Thames. He would consolidate his position in the eastern counties before attempting to advance toward the west. But Dover proved impregnable, and Louis was forced to conclude a local truce until Easter with Hubert de Burg.[45] He was more successful in the second part of his plan. By the end of January he had taken Hertford, Berkhampstead, Cambridge, and all the castles of East Anglia. Some of these were reduced by siege operations, but others were surrendered as the price of short truces.[46] Louis' control of eastern England from the channel to the Tees was impeded only by Dover and the Lincolnshire strongholds. At the close of his East Anglian campaign the French prince advanced on Lincoln. The city surrendered at once, but the castle under its hereditary castellan Dame Nichola de la Haye resisted all overtures. When he returned to London, Louis despatched Hugh, castellan of Arras, to assist Gilbert de Ghent, whom he had created earl of Lincoln, to reduce the chief fortress of his shire.[47]

Meanwhile William had bided his time. The East Anglian castles, isolated in the very heart of the baronial rebellion, were of slight strategic value, and their garrisons could be used to better advantage elsewhere.[48] As soon as Louis invested one of these fortresses, the regent would surrender it in exchange for a short truce.[49] While the French prince amused himself in this manner, William concentrated his attention on securing the active support of the barons of Cornwall and Devon through successful negotiations with their leader, Henry fitz

[45] Roger of Wendover, II, 199. *Histoire des ducs*, p. 182.

[46] Roger of Wendover, II, 200-1. *Histoire des ducs*, p. 182. *Hist.*, 15717-15746.   [47] *Histoire des ducs*, p. 182.

[48] For instance the men in Norwich and Orford were sent to Dover (*Rot. Claus.*, I, 335b).   [49] *Hist.*, 15717-15746.

Count.[50] Sometime early in February, Louis, who was anxious to go to France to confer with his father and to gather reinforcements, arranged with the regent for a suspension of hostilities until a month after Easter.[51] This agreement was broken soon after it was made—in fact it seems doubtful whether William ever had any intention of observing it. The *History* asserts that the French were the first to violate the truce, and certainly the despatch of Hugh of Arras to besiege Lincoln was no peaceful manoeuvre, but the regent took advantage of the occasion to launch his first serious campaign.[52] His plan seems to have been to cut Louis off from the sea and prevent his visit to France. He may even have hoped to effect the capture of the French prince on his way from London to the channel. Early in the second week of February Hubert de Burg and John Marshal were sent to support Philip d'Aubigni in his operations on the coasts of Sussex and Kent.[53] Shortly before Louis reached Winchelsea on his way to the continent, Philip, supported by a fleet, captured Rye. Caught between the royalist forces holding the Weald and the army and fleet at Rye, Louis was in a desperate position. He was saved by the timely arrival of a French fleet and some of his knights who had hastened down from London. With these reinforcements the French prince recaptured Rye and on February 27th set sail for France. He left Engerrand, lord of Coucy, in command of his French troops with orders to remain within the walls of London until his return.[54]

The operations of Philip d'Aubigni were simply a part of William's plan of campaign. He probably hoped that Philip could keep Louis occupied until he himself could come up with the main royalist army. On February 17th the regent marched out of Gloucester at the head of all the troops he could muster and advanced through Oxford and Reading to Dorking.[55] In a letter despatched from there to encourage the men of Rye he

[50] *Patent Rolls*, I, 13, 21, 30.   [52] *Hist.*, 15747-15760.
[51] Roger of Wendover, II, 206.   [53] *Patent Rolls*, I, 32.
[54] *Histoire des ducs*, pp. 183-187. *Hist.*, 15761-15867.
[55] *Patent Rolls*, I, 33-4. *Rot. Claus.*, I, 299.

mentioned the presence in the host of the earls of Chester and Ferrars, the count of Aumale, Walter de Lacy and his fellow lords of the marches, the two mercenary captains Engerrand de Cygony and Faulkes de Bréauté, and a number of English barons.[56] When this formidable array reached the coast, William learned that Rye had fallen and Louis escaped. His plan had failed, and he was forced to content himself with turning west into Hampshire and investing Louis' castles in that county.[57] During March and April the royalists gained possession of Chichester, Porchester, Southampton, Farnham, Winchester, and Marlborough.[58]

On April 23rd Louis of France landed at Sandwich with a force of one hundred and forty knights. Three days later he was joined by the lord of Coucy with the main French army from London. The combined forces immediately set out to recover the ground lost during Louis' absence.[59] William was in no position to dispute the enemy's advance. As he had sent the earls of Chester and Ferrars, the count of Aumale, Robert de Vieuxpont, and Faulkes de Bréauté to support the castellans of Nottingham and Newark in an attack on the earl of Winchester's castle of Mount Sorel, he had at his disposal only a part of the royalist field army.[60] After dismantling all the captured castles except Marlborough and Farnham, the regent retired to Oxford.[61] But despite its rather inglorious conclusion this spring campaign of William's had not been utterly fruitless. Early in March as the regent marched from Shoreham to Farnham, he had been joined by two important members of Louis' party—William Marshal the younger and Earl William of Salisbury.[62] Although their conversion was secured at a high price in lands and privileges, it was decidedly worth the cost.[63]

[56] *Patent Rolls*, I, 108-9.   [57] *Hist.*, 15873-15904.
[58] *Ibid.*, 15905-16033. *Histoire des ducs*, pp. 187-8. *Patent Rolls*, I, 57, 62.
[59] *Histoire des ducs*, pp. 188-190.
[60] Roger of Wendover, II, 208.
[61] *Hist.*, 16048-16050. *Patent Rolls*, I, 62-3.
[62] *Hist.*, 15878-15888. *Rot. Claus.*, I, 299.
[63] *Patent Rolls*, I, 45, 86-7, 109. *Rot. Claus.*, I, 299b, 305b, 309b, 310, 311.

William Longsword was not only the king's uncle and a dominant figure in southern England, but he was practically the only
man of military capacity among Louis' English allies. His return to Henry's allegiance added a valuable captain to the royal
party and served as an excellent example to others. During the
month of March over a hundred barons and knights, mostly
from the counties of Wilts, Berks, Dorset, and Somerset, deserted the French prince's cause.[64]

On April 28th as Louis lay before Farnham, Saher de Quency
came to him to beg succor for his castle of Mount Sorel which
was about to surrender to the earls of Chester and Ferrars.
Louis gave him six hundred knights of which seventy were
Frenchmen under the command of the count of Perche. The
English knights who formed the bulk of the army were led by
the earl of Winchester, Robert fitz Walter, and other rebel
barons.[65] As soon as Earl Ranulf learned of the approach of
this relieving force, he raised the siege of Mount Sorel and retired to Nottingham. After reinforcing and provisioning the
castle, Earl Saher and the count of Perche marched eastwards
to join Hugh of Arras and Gilbert de Ghent who were besieging the citadel of Lincoln.[66] Meanwhile, Prince Louis had concentrated his forces in Kent for a new attack upon Dover. He
had brought over from France a great siege engine with which
he hoped to reduce the stubborn " key to England." [67]

The French prince had committed a serious strategic error.
As his own army and that under the earl of Winchester were
each perfectly able to cope with the royalist troops opposing
them, the division of his forces was not in itself unsafe, but
he should have watched William's movements instead of completely ignoring him. The regent on his side probably lacked
definite information about his enemy's manoeuvres. He knew
that a large force had gone north, but he was not certain

[64] *Ibid.*, pp. 299-304.

[65] Roger of Wendover, II, 209. *Histoire des ducs,* pp. 190-1.

[66] Roger of Wendover, II, 211. *Histoire des ducs,* pp. 193-4. *Hist.,* 16097-
16114.   [67] *Histoire des ducs,* pp. 188, 192. *Hist.,* 16085-16089.

whether or not Louis was in command of it. In order to keep in touch with the situation William left Oxford and advanced to Northampton.[68] With him were the young king, the legate, the bishop of Winchester, young William Marshal, the earl of Salisbury, John Marshal, Philip d'Aubigni, and a few other loyal barons.[69] Apparently Walter de Lacy and his fellow marchers had returned home, possibly to watch the Welsh. Although the regent's mobile force was probably very small, he could in case of need draw on the garrisons of the royal castles which dotted the surrounding shires.

At Northampton William learned of the relief of Mount Sorel and the concentration of the enemy before Lincoln. He also received positive information that Louis had divided his forces and that he was not with the northern army.[70] The regent immediately saw the possibilities of the situation. The earls of Chester and Ferrars with the loyal lords of the north were at Nottingham. In many a royal castle around about were hardy knights and serjeants. These scattered royalist bands could be mustered near Lincoln before Louis could learn of his friends' plight, much less go to their aid. On May 13th couriers rode out of Northampton to summon King Henry's men to assemble at Newark. Six days later the host was ready to take the field. The *History* gives its strength as four hundred and six knights and three hundred and seventeen crossbowmen.[71] Roger of Wendover estimates the crossbowmen at two hundred and fifty, but adds that the small number of knights was compensated for by an unusually large complement of serjeants. The chivalry of England was in the rebel camp, and the royalist leaders were forced to fill its place with mercenary soldiers.

The city of Lincoln occupied the crest and southern slope of a hill rising to the north of the junction of the Foss Dyke and the

[68] *Rot. Claus*, I, 308-308b.

[69] These names were obtained by subtracting those known to have been with the earl of Chester from the list in Roger of Wendover, II, 212.

[70] *Hist.*, 16115-16123.   [71] *Ibid.*, 16263-16270. Roger of Wendover, II, 212.

river Witham. It consisted of two fairly distinct parts—the old Roman camp on the summit and the lower town built on the hillside. The castle stood in the southwest angle of the Roman town and communicated with the open country on the west. The direct route from Newark approached Lincoln from the south, but to attempt to cross the Witham and climb the steep hill leading to the Roman town in the face of the enemy would have been a foolhardy venture. To avoid this William decided to make a detour to Torksey and approach the town from the west. Before the troops left Newark, the legate granted them plenary absolution and solemnly reiterated the excommunication of Louis and all his partisans, especially those who were in Lincoln. Gualo and the boy king then retired to the shelter of Nottingham castle, while the crusaders, for such they were in the eyes of Rome, set out for Torksey.[72]

On Saturday morning, May 20th, the army was drawn up for its final march on Lincoln.[73] The regent in a long harangue impressed on his men the advantage of their position. They could not lose. If they fell in battle, they were assured of places in paradise. If they gained the victory, they won glory for themselves and their descendants. The enemy was excommunicate—their dead were certainly doomed to hell's fires.[74] With this pious exhortation ringing in their ears, the troops moved towards Lincoln, joyfully as if to a tourney. The exact order of march is not quite clear. Apparently there was an advance guard of crossbowmen and mounted serjeants probably led by Faulkes de Bréauté.[75] 'The rest of the army formed four divisions under the respective commands of the earl of Chester, the regent, William of Salisbury, and Peter des Roches.[76] As William expected the enemy to sally out and

[72] *Ibid.*, p. 213. *Hist.*, 16225-16237.
[73] *Ibid.*, 16239-16242. [74] *Ibid.*, 16277-16310.
[75] *Ibid.*, 16311-16330. Roger of Wendover, II, 213-4. In lines 16314-16316 the *History* asserts that Peter des Roches led the crossbowmen, but in lines 16259-16261 it places him in command of the fourth division of the army. Faulkes led the crossbowmen in the actual battle (Roger of Wendover, II, 215).
[76] *Hist.*, 16243-16261.

attack him in the open country, probably as the army mounted the hill on which Lincoln stood, he issued his orders accordingly. At the appearance of the enemy the crossbowmen were to deploy and shoot down their horses. The two hundred mounted serjeants of the vanguard were to slay their own horses to form a barrier against the charge of the hostile cavalry.[77] The regent realized that if the enemy issued from the city and occupied the high ground to the west of the castle, they would have an immense advantage. Charging down the hill with their superior number of knights, they would have every chance for victory. William's only hope would rest in breaking up their advance before they reached his main divisions.

As the royal army approached Lincoln along the road which followed the Foss Dyke, the earl of Winchester and Robert fitz Walter rode out to reconnoitre. They reported to the count of Perche that while the enemy were drawn up in excellent battle array, they were far inferior in numbers to the combined French and baronial forces. They advised the course which William was expecting—a battle in the open field as the royalists climbed toward the castle. But the French commander was unwilling to rely on the accuracy of this report, and he himself went out to view the advancing host. According to Roger of Wendover the count was deceived by the fact that each English baron had two banners—one with his troops and another with his baggage. Be that as it may, he decided against an encounter in the open.[78] By remaining within the city walls he hoped to be able to reduce the castle before the relieving army could lend it effective aid. So certain was he that William would not dare to assault the walls that he practically ignored the advancing host. Stationing a few men to guard the city gates, he concentrated the rest of his force against the castle. This decision of the count of Perche really settled the result of the battle—it was a fatal blunder. Even if William failed to pierce the city ramparts, he could easily reinforce the

[77] *Ibid.*, 16319-16330. [78] Roger of Wendover, II, 214-5. *Hist.*, 16341-16372.

garrison of the castle. If he did succeed in carrying the walls, the battle would be fought in the narrow streets of the town where the count could make no effective use of his superior number of knights.

The regent did not fail to use the apparent cowardice of the enemy to encourage his own men. " Lords, your sworn foes have placed themselves behind their walls. That is according to God's plan. This day He gives us great glory. It is a preliminary victory for us that the French, who always have been the first at a tournament, hide from us. Let us do the right, for God wills it." [79] This use of the crusaders' war cry to hearten the men who were marching against the excommunicate disturbers of England's peace was a magnificent gesture. In fact William's delightful confidence in the efficacy of God's favor seemed highly justified. Nothing but the Divine Will could really explain the tactics of the count of Perche.

As soon as the regent was certain that the enemy did not intend to sally from the city, he sent John Marshal ahead to converse with the garrison of the castle. After talking with the deputy constable and assuring himself that troops could be sent into the castle through its postern gate, he returned to report to his uncle.[80] By that time the whole army was drawn up on the high ground to the west and northwest of the Roman town. Bishop Peter of Winchester at the head of a body of crossbowmen approached the castle wall and leaving his men outside, entered by the postern. After conversing with Dame Nichola and her deputy, he surveyed the situation from the walls of the fortress which gave him a clear view of the upper town and the disposition of the enemy's forces. Either while on his way to the castle or while he looked down from the ramparts, he noticed the old west gate of Lincoln which lay just to the north of the castle and had been loosely blocked with masonry Slipping out of the fortress by a postern on the northern side, the bishop examined this gate and found that it could be easily opened. He then returned to report to his commander.[81]

---

[79] *Ibid.*, 16381-16400.   [80] *Ibid.*, 16413-16466.   [81] *Ibid.*, 16467-16534.

Bishop Peter advised the regent to send a force into the castle to keep the enemy occupied by a sally from its main portal while the rest of the army forced its way into the town through the unguarded west gate. This mission was entrusted to Faulkes de Bréauté with the knights of his household and all the crossbowmen.[82] Meanwhile, the first division of the army, which was commanded by the headstrong earl of Chester, had grown tired of waiting and had attacked the north gate of the city.[83] This manoeuvre disgusted Bishop Peter. " They have not found the unguarded gate which I told you of," said he to the regent, " There is a breach that the enemy does not know of; come, I will lead you to it." [84] The old earl's patience was exhausted. Ranulf of Chester was hammering at the north gate, and Faulkes was sallying out of the castle while he stood inactive. " By the lance of God! My helm," he cried. Peter calmed his fervor and persuaded him to go forward with ten knights to reconnoitre the breach before advancing with his whole division.[85] The bishop wished to be certain that the men whom he had ordered to open the west gate had completed their task. As William rode toward the walls, some of Faulkes' men, whose sally from the castle had been severely repulsed, rushed out through the recently unblocked gate with the enemy in hot pursuit.[86] The earl promptly forgot that he was reconnoitring. " Charge! they will soon be conquered. Shame to him who delays longer," he cried to his little group of knights. Again Peter counselled patience—he should wait for his whole division. William refused to listen to him. He was about to spur forward into the breach when a squire reminded him that he had not yet donned his helmet. After putting this finishing touch to his armament, the old knight dashed through the breach into the ranks of the enemy while the bishop rode at his shoulder shouting, " *Ça! Dieu aide au Maréchal!* " [87] Behind

---

[82] Roger of Wendover, II, 215.
[83] *Ibid.*, 216.
[84] *Hist.*, 16542-16553.   [86] Roger of Wendover, II, 216. *Hist.*, 16572-16576.
[85] *Ibid.*, 16556-16566.   [87] *Ibid.*, 16577-16628.

their leader pressed the knights and serjeants of the second, third, and fourth divisions of the royal army.[88]

The battle of Lincoln was a grand tourney fought up and down the narrow streets of the city. The troops who occupied the upper town were caught between three fires. While Faulkes' crossbowmen raked their ranks from the castle ramparts, William and his followers poured through the breach, and Ranulf of Chester forced his way in by the north gate.[89] After a series of jousts in the streets in which the French were consistently worsted, the count of Perche rallied the remnant of his knights in the open place by the cathedral. Holding the summit of a small mound, he managed to keep his enemies at a distance. Finally William himself led a charge against the count's position. While the regent seized the bridle of his horse, Reginald Croc, a knight of Faulkes' household, ran his lance neatly through the eyehole of his helmet. The count of Perche was mortally wounded, but before he fell he launched three terrific blows at William's helm with such force that they left permanent dents. The loss of their leader discouraged the French. They retreated down the hill into the lower town where they rallied once more and attempted to recapture the Roman city. This effort was a complete failure, and driven back in confusion, the French and rebels were forced to make their escape as best they could through the southern gates of the city.[90]

The battle of Lincoln was a decisive and almost bloodless

[88] The author of the *History* avows his confusion as to the details of the battle of Lincoln (*Hist.*, 16401-16412). Modern historians are equally uncertain. Oman, *The Art of War in the Middle Ages*, I, 412, 418. Norgate, *Minority of Henry III*, pp. 37-45; Tout, The Fair of Lincoln, in the *English Historical Review* (April, 1903). Any consistent account of the battle must be based partially at least on presumptions.

[89] It is not certain that the army attacked the walls at two points. Roger of Wendover describes the assault on the north gate (II, 216). The bishop seems to have led William to an undefended breach in the walls (*Hist.*, 16542-16553). These two accounts may describe the same operation, but this seems improbable.

[90] *Hist.*, 16629-16828. Roger of Wendover, II, 215-216.

victory. The count of Perche, an unknown serjeant, and the English knight Reginald Croc were the only men killed in actual combat, though many of the fleeing infantry were slaughtered by the people of the countryside.[91] Forty-six rebel barons and three hundred knights were captured. Among the prisoners were the earls of Winchester and Hereford, Gilbert de Ghent, Robert fitz Walter, Richard de Muntfichet, William de Mowbrai, and William de Beauchamp.[92] Only two Englishmen of rank made good their escape, William de Mandeville, earl of Essex, and John de Lacy, constable of Chester. Three French barons made their way to London.[93] The whole affair must have been eminently satisfactory to William. The battle itself had been of a kind to gladden his knightly heart. In a day filled with jousts and gallant deeds of prowess few good men had lost their lives. Louis' cause was irreparably injured. God had favored his chosen warriors. But a fair share of the credit must be given to the regent. While his success was primarily due to the mistakes of Louis and the count of Perche, he knew how to make the most of their errors. He had recognized his opportunity, laid his plan, and carried it out with skill and determination. He may not have displayed any signs of military genius, but he completely justified his reputation as a competent commander and a brave knight.

When Louis learned of the defeat of his forces at Lincoln, he raised the siege of Dover and retired to London.[94] William on his side was prompt to follow up his victory. Before he left Lincoln, he ordered his army to reassemble at Chertsey in two weeks time in the hope that a show of force would persuade Louis to come to terms.[95] His hopes were not in vain. The French prince sent the counts of Brittany and Nevers to Chertsey to open negotiations with the regent.[96] On June 12th four members of Louis' council met four members of Henry's be-

[91] Ibid., pp. 215, 219.
[92] Ibid., p. 217. See Norgate, Minority of Henry III, p. 44.
[93] Histoire des ducs, p. 195.   [95] Hist., 17059-17062.
[94] Ibid.   [96] Patent Rolls, I, 68.

tween Brentford and Hounslow.[97] These negotiators succeeded in drawing up a treaty which was satisfactory to everyone except the legate. He was unwilling to allow Louis' ecclesiastical partisans to share the general amnesty provided for by the proposed treaty. As Louis refused to desert his supporters among the English clergy, the negotiations came to nothing.[98] Gualo wished to attack London immediately, but the laymen were unwilling to follow his advice.[99] The city was strong and Louis' troops though few in number were the pick of the chivalry of France. Besides, time was working in favor of the royalists. Discouraged by the battle of Lincoln, the earls of Arundel and Warren, Reginald de Briouse, and over a hundred and fifty other knights and barons returned to King Henry's allegiance during the months of June and July.[100]

Louis' only chance for an eventual victory rested in the arrival of reinforcements from France. Although Philip Augustus had too much respect for the power of Rome to aid his son openly, he allowed his daughter-in-law, the indomitable Blanche of Castille, to raise what forces she could to send to her husband. Blanche finally mustered at Calais a picked body of knights and serjeants which included a prince of Capetian blood, Robert de Courtenay, and the illustrious warrior William des Barres the younger.[101] The authorities differ greatly as to the total strength of Blanche's levy. The estimate of one hundred knights furnished by the *Histoire des Ducs de Normandie* is most acceptable.[102] A hundred noble cavalry with their serjeants would go a long way towards replacing the men lost at Lincoln.[103]

When William learned of the imminent arrival of this new

---

[97] *Ibid.*, p. 69.

[98] Bouquet, *Récueil des historiens des Gaules et de la France*, XIX, 635-637. *Histoire des ducs*, p. 197.   [100] *Rot. Claus.*, I, 310-317b.

[99] *Ibid.*, p. 199.   [101] *Histoire des ducs*, pp. 198, 200-1.

[102] *Ibid.*, p. 198. This is consistent with the same authority's statement that thirty-six knights were in the flag-ship of the fleet, and that there were three other ship-loads of knights (*ibid.*, pp. 200-1).

[103] six ships full of serjeants (*ibid.*).

army, he was profoundly disturbed. His anxiety was increased by the fact that he was probably ignorant of its numbers. One is tempted to believe that Roger of Wendover's estimate of three hundred knights represents the regent's apprehension.[104] If Louis was to be brought to terms, his reinforcements must be intercepted. Three hundred knights might enable him to conquer England—one hundred would allow him to prolong the war indefinitely. On August 24th William mustered his army and fleet at Sandwich.[105] This in itself was a decided triumph, for the mariners of the Cinque Ports had suffered much from John's tyranny and had no great desire to risk their lives and property in the service of his son. Only the regent's assurance that they would be indemnified for their losses persuaded them to answer the summons to the host. The morning was so clear that the English could easily discern the approaching French fleet, led by the flagship under the command of that master pirate, Eustace the Monk.[106] When the mariners, who were at best far from enthusiastic, saw the enemy's formidable array, they fled from their ships in terror, but William finally persuaded them to return.[107] The regent was anxious to take command of the knights and serjeants who were to do the actual fighting once the mariners had brought them alongside the enemy. The other leaders dissuaded him from his purpose—his life was too valuable to risk in so hazardous a combat.[108] Matthew Paris' implication that William stayed ashore because he believed that a ship was no decent place for a knight is almost certainly unjust. Matthew was simply engaged in increasing the fame of Hubert de Burg who was in command of the fleet during the battle.[109] The old earl would naturally scorn a combat at sea because it gave no opportunity for demonstrations of knightly prowess, but his whole record shows that

[104] Roger of Wendover, II, 221.
[105] *Hist.*, 17167-17196; 17262-17280. *Rot. Claus.*, I, 320.
[106] *Hist.*, 17281-17291.
[107] *Ibid.*, 17232-17252. Roger of Wendover, II, 221.
[108] *Hist.*, 17197-17210; 17253-17261.   [109] *Chronica Maiora*, III, 28.

in his opinion any battle was better than none. Standing on the shore, William encouraged the mariners and soldiers in the ships. God had just given them a great victory on land, but He has, on the sea as well as on the land, the power to aid the virtuous. Once more He would assist his own. They would triumph over the enemies of God.[110]

The battle was a decisive victory for the English.[111] All but fifteen of the French vessels were taken or destroyed and thirty-two men of rank were made prisoners. The less important members of the French force were pitilessly slaughtered by the mariners and serjeants.[112] After sending his prisoners to Dover castle, the regent superintended the division of the spoils of battle. A part of the plunder was set aside to endow a hospital dedicated to St. Bartholomew, patron saint of the day of battle, and the remainder was divided among the mariners.[113]

The news of the destruction of his reinforcements reached Louis at London on August 26. As he fully realized that this disaster meant the end of his hopes of conquering England, he sent Count Robert of Dreux to learn if the regent would consider making peace. Holding Robert of Dreux as a hostage, William sent Robert de Courtenay, who had been captured at Sandwich, to bear his answer to Louis. Apparently the reply was favorable, for the French prince promptly requested a personal interview with the regent.[114] There was a difference of opinion in the royal camp as to the best course to pursue. Some were unwilling to negotiate with Louis and wished to lay siege to London in the hope of capturing his entire army. Others urged William to hasten the departure of the French even if he had to resort to bribery.[115] The regent seems to have hesitated between these opposing views. On September 1st he

[110] *Hist.*, 17313-17328.

[111] See H. L. Cannon in *English Historical Review* XXVII (1912), 649-670. Norgate, *Minority of Henry III,* pp. 49-54. Petit-Dutaillis, *Vie de Louis VIII,* pp. 166-168.

[112] *Hist.*, 17573-4. Roger of Wendover, II, 222.

[113] *Hist.*, 17527-17576.

[114] *Histoire de ducs,* p. 202.   [115] *Hist.*, 17635-17670.

ordered the barons of the Cinque Ports to concentrate their ships in the Thames.[116] This manoeuvre may have been intended as a sop to the belligerent party or as a threat to force the enemy to terms. At any rate, William and Hubert de Burg conferred with Louis near London, and the latter expressed his willingness to accept any terms that were consistent with his honor.[117] By Monday, September 11th, the royalist leaders had prepared a draft of the proposed treaty.

The terms offered Louis differed in only one important particular from those which had been agreed upon during the negotiations in June—the French prince's ecclesiastical partisans were excepted from the general amnesty and abandoned to the gentle mercies of the legate.[118] Louis was to release his English supporters from their oaths of allegiance to him. When the rebels had given security in the form of oaths and charters to Henry III for their future behavior, they were to receive their lands as they had held them before the war and were to enjoy all the liberties guaranteed by the charter of 1216. All prisoners taken by either side since Louis' first landing in England were to be freed. Those captured before that date were to be released if three men chosen from Louis' council by the royalist leaders swore that they were in the prince's service when they were made prisoners. The money paid for ransoms was to be retained. If a prisoner had arranged to pay his ransom in installments, he was to make good all arrears, but future payments were cancelled. The debts due to Louis were to be paid. The French prince was to direct his allies, the king of Scotland and the Welsh, to surrender the lands, castles, and prisoners which they had taken in the course of the war. Louis and such of his vassals as Henry's council should designate were to guarantee their observance of the treaty by oaths and charters. Louis

---

[116] *Patent Rolls*, I, 89.

[117] *Histoire des ducs*, pp. 202-3.

[118] There are three slightly different versions of this treaty. *Foedera*, I, I, 148. Martène and Durand, *Thesaurus novus anecdotorum*, I, 857-859. D'Achéry, *Spicilegium*, III, 586-7. See also Norgate, *Minority of Henry III*, pp. 278-280.

would do his best to obtain papal confirmation of the agreement. In short the French would leave England, and conditions there would be restored to the *status quo ante bellum*. The rebel barons who had stood by Louis to the end would be accorded the same treatment as those who had deserted his cause earlier. The treaty was a generous and statesmanlike document.

In addition to the treaty itself there were a number of supplementary agreements. The provision for the release of Louis and his partisans from their sentence of excommunication was a natural part of the peace treaty and probably owed its omission from the official draft solely to the fact that it was considered a private arrangement with the legate.[119] But William apparently hoped to do more than merely liquidate the baronial revolt and the French invasion. He aspired to establish formal peace between the French and English kings by settling the most important point at issue between them. With this end in view he induced Louis to promise that he would do his best to persuade his father to give Henry the lands which he had taken from John.[120] The regent seems to have believed that Philip might actually surrender the continental possessions of the house of Anjou. Soon after the conclusion of peace he showed his own good faith by giving a number of Normans their English fiefs, but within a month he grew discouraged and ordered that no Norman should receive his lands in England until the English obtained theirs in Normandy.[121] Whether or not he ever had any serious intention of fulfilling his promise, Louis recognized it as an integral part of his agreement with the English government. When he ascended the throne of France in 1223, he felt obliged to justify his retention of the Angevin fiefs by claiming that the English had themselves failed to observe the treaty of 1217.[122] Although it was destined to have no effect, the securing of this promise from the French

[119] Roger of Wendover, II, 225. *Hist.*, 17697-17710.
[120] Roger of Wendover, II, 224.   [121] *Rot. Claus.*, I, 329.
[122] Matthew Paris, *Historia Anglorum* (ed. Sir Frederick Madden, *Rolls Series*), II, 256-7.

prince was a decided diplomatic triumph for William. Unfortunately he was forced to buy the concession at a high price. The regency agreed to pay Louis ten thousand marks to indemnify him for the expenses which he had incurred in his invasion of England.[123] A merchant of St. Omer, Florence the Rich, advanced three-fifths of this sum, and William pledged his lands in Normandy as security for the loan.[124] While the paying of an indemnity to a defeated enemy at a time when the financial situation of the government was almost desperate seems of very doubtful wisdom, the regent undoubtedly believed that it was a fair price for Louis' promise in regard to the English lands on the continent. The mistake of the English government lay in the fact that the indemnity was actually paid.[125] William had exchanged hard cash for promises.

The regent had treated the defeated invader with extreme generosity. The next generation was to misinterpret his motives and accuse him of treason. In 1241 Henry III told Walter Marshal that it was known that his father had acted as a traitor in neglecting to capture Louis.[126] Matthew Paris voices the same charge in one of his additions to the chronicle of Roger of Wendover. When Philip Augustus heard of the battle of Lincoln, he asked the messenger, " Does William Marshal still live? " " Yes." " Then I do not fear for my son," replied the king. For this reason, says Matthew, William was thereafter known as a traitor.[127] The *History* gives a far different account of Philip's opinion of the regent. When the French king learned of the battle of Lincoln, he asked if John was dead. " Yes," replied the messenger, " his son is already crowned, and the Marshal is devoted to his defence." " Then we have nothing to gain in England. The land is lost to Louis, and after a while he and his partisans will be driven out since the Marshal

---

[123] *Hist..* 17696-17698. *Histoire des ducs,* p. 204. *Royal and other historical letters illustrative of the reign of Henry III* (ed. W. W. Shirley, *Rolls Series*), no. 7. See also Petit-Dutaillis, *Vie de Louis VIII,* pp. 176-7.

[124] *Patent Rolls,* I, 114-5.

[125] *Ibid.,* p. 168. *Rot. Claus.,* I, 381b, 388b, 415.

[126] Matthew Paris, *Chronica Maiora,* IV, 157.   [127] *Ibid.,* III, 25-6.

has taken the matter in hand." [128] This supposed conversation is evidently misplaced. John died eight months before the battle of Lincoln, and Louis visited France in the interval. The author either knew or chose to invent Philip's comment when he heard of John's death. One cannot but wonder whether he did not place it after the battle of Lincoln in order to combat some-such rumor as the one to which Paris gave credence. The *History* also reports the words of Philip when he heard of the naval battle. " Lords, have I not said that if the Marshal mixed in this affair, Louis and his cause would be ruined." [129] Of course none of these conversations can be taken very seriously by the historian. Matthew Paris, who wrote after 1235, was obviously making use of a current rumor. The author of the *History* might possibly have known what Philip actually said. In 1219 Richard Marshal was at the French court and he may have transmitted to the author the current reports as to Philip's words on these two occasions.[130] Be that as it may, the re-marks of Matthew Paris prove that William's generosity to Louis had left a stain on his reputation.

While this rumor of William's treason was undoubtedly un-true, one can understand how it came into being. As far back as 1205 Hubert Walter had suspected William Marshal of being over friendly to Philip Augustus. This idea had rankled in John's mind for several years and was the basic cause of his quarrel with the earl. When Louis had been bottled up in Lon-don and his reinforcements destroyed, the regent had chosen to negotiate instead of besieging the city and capturing the French prince with all his men. Finally he had given ten thousand marks for a rather chimerical hope of recovering the English fiefs on the continent. But the most that the impartial observer can charge against William is excess of caution and error of judgement. Louis had in London a strong force of picked knights, the flower of the chivalry of France. The citizens were devoted to his cause. A siege would have taken much time and cost many men. Considering the state of England, one can

---

[128] *Hist.*, 17085-17108.   [129] *Ibid.*, 17609-17616.   [130] *Ibid.*, 19120.

easily understand William's decision to make peace at once. Possibly the regent was too ambitious in his scheme to regain Normandy by diplomacy, but if he had succeeded it would have been the fairest star in his crown. On the whole the treaty of 1217 reflects nothing but credit on William's statesmanship.

Louis of France had withdrawn from England, and the rebel barons had submitted to their rightful monarch—the most arduous part of William's task was completed. The decision to issue a charter of liberties and its actual contents showed that the regent possessed definite qualities of statesmanship. The energetic and effective measures by which he raised sufficient money to pay his troops and carry on the war demonstrated his administrative ability. His conduct of the campaign against Louis confirmed his reputation as a brave soldier and a thoroughly competent captain. His generous terms to the defeated rebels displayed his ripe wisdom. But these were merely the outward manifestations of his real achievement. He had secured the co-operation and obedience of haughty and turbulent barons such as Ranulf of Chester and Walter de Lacy, of ambitious officials such as Peter des Roches and Hubert de Burg, and of ruthless mercenary captains like Faulkes de Bréauté and Philip Marc. This triumph of pure force of personality is probably William Marshal's greatest claim to fame.

CHAPTER XI

REGENT OF ENGLAND

Within nineteen months of the signing of the treaty of Kingston William Marshal had relinquished the reins of government and was slowly dying at his manor of Caversham. But despite its brevity, this final phase of William's career was an extremely important one. Having brought the war to a successful conclusion, the regent was faced with the equally arduous task of restoring the country to its normal state. The mere carrying out of the treaty of peace involved the reestablishment of the rebels in their lands, the release of the prisoners taken in the war, and the collection of money to pay the indemnity. It was also necessary to come to an understanding with the French prince's allies—the Welsh and the king of Scotland. The numerous scars of civil war had to be removed by the destruction of adulterine castles, the curbing of lawless royal officials, and the restoration of peace and order. William was to have ample opportunity to demonstrate his abilities as an administrator.

The primary requisite for the successful performance of this gigantic task was the rehabilitation of the royal administration. But the abuses in this administration had been largely responsible for the civil war. Hence one of the first cares of the regent would be to issue a new charter of liberties in order to assure the nation that Henry's government had abjured the errors of John. If the regency was to pay the indemnity to Louis and meet the other obligations of the crown, not only must the regular revenue of the king be secured, but additional funds must be raised by taxation. This required the reorganization of the royal financial system and the taking of an aid from the king's vassals and a tallage from his demesne. If order was to be restored in the realm, the judicial system must be reestablished. This entailed the reorganization of the court of Common

Pleas at Westminster and the inauguration of a general eyre to clear up the judicial business that had accumulated since the time of John. When William resigned the regency in April, 1219, the king's justices were riding their circuits through the counties of England—the reorganization of the royal administration had been completed.

Despite the magnitude of William's achievement during this final period of his public life, few phases of his career are less satisfactory to his biographer. William Marshal is almost completely hidden behind the regent of England. When he emerges it is but to use his power as regent for his own benefit. One cannot even discover to what extent the success of the regency was due to William himself. If one were to declare that Gualo ruled England through William Marshal, the statement could not be disproved. As the orders of the government were issued by William under his own seal, he must bear the credit or discredit for them, but it is like the problem of Louis XIII and Richelieu with less evidence to work with. One can merely say that the regency was successful and that, in the absence of evidence to the contrary, the credit must go to the regent.

The first and most immediate problem was the execution of the terms of the peace. On September 14th the burghers of London were ordered to guard Louis as they would Henry himself while he stayed in England.[1] William de Beaumont, Louis' marshal, was given a safe conduct to allow him to collect the debts owed his master, and the debtors were ordered to pay him promptly.[2] Adam, viscount of Melun, who was ill, received permission to stay in England as long as was necessary.[3] Writs were issued directing the release of all prisoners according to the terms of the treaty.[4] This process alone took a long time. On April 15, 1218, the sheriffs of England were ordered to announce in their respective counties that all prisoners who had complaints to make against their captors in regard to the ransoms demanded were to appear at Westminster three weeks

---

[1] *Patent Rolls*, I, 91.
[2] *Ibid.*, p. 94.
[3] *Ibid.*, p. 93.
[4] *Ibid.*, p. 96.

after Easter to lay them before the council.[5] The reestablishment of the rebels in their lands was an even greater task. During the months of September, October, and November fully a
thousand writs were issued ordering the restoration of confiscated estates.[6] The usual procedure was for each former
partisan of Louis to do homage to Henry III and make a charter
guaranteeing his future loyalty.[7] Then letters close were issued
ordering the royal officers to give him his lands. At times the
lands were restored before the homage was done and the charter
made, but only when some great baron guaranteed that it would
be done in the near future.[8] Apparently, however, many rebels
succeeded in getting possession of their lands without this for-
mality provided for by the treaty. On March 6, 1218 the
sheriffs of Surrey, Hampshire, Kent, and Sussex were directed
to seize the lands of such men until they had done homage and
made the required charters.[9] Thus, William spent the last part
of September and most of October in putting into effect the
treaty of peace with Louis. There seems to be no doubt that he
did this as loyally and honestly as he could.

After spending the first two weeks of October in London,
William retired for a few days to his manor of Caversham
which lay on the left bank of the Thames opposite Reading.[10]
On the 21st he returned to London where a variety of business
awaited him.[11] A number of the former rebels had promised to
be on hand at that time to make their charters of loyalty, there
were some cases summoned to be heard by the regent and council three weeks after Michaelmas, and preparations had to be
made for the great council which was to convene at the end of
the month.[12] There is no way of discovering how many men
formed the council which met on the 21st. to assist the regent
in settling the various matters that came up, but it probably

[5] *Rot. Claus.*, I, 358b.
[6] *Ibid.*, pp. 322-340.   [8] *Rot. Claus.*, I, 322, 332b, 336b.
[7] This was provided for in the treaty.   [9] *Ibid.*, p. 354.
[10] *Patent Rolls*, I, 97-105. *Rot. Claus.*, I, 325-330b.
[11] *Ibid.*, p. 330b.
[12] *Rot. Claus.*, I, 325b; 336b. *Patent Rolls*, I, 99.

was not the full council of the realm. By the end of the month, however, all the magnates of England had gathered together in London to set about the work of reorganizing the kingdom. Henry Plantagenet himself entered his city of London on October 29th amid the acclamations of a populace which had until recently been active supporters of Louis of France.[13] The preliminaries were over, and the stage was set for the rehabilitation of the kingdom.

One of the first cares of this council was to issue a new charter of liberties. The charter of 1216 had been avowedly provisional and had been authorized by only a small minority of the barons of the realm. Then there were a number of important questions that the charters of 1215 and 1216 had left undecided. These included such matters as the administration of the royal forests which had been left unsettled by the Great Charter and such questions as the collection of scutage which had been postponed by the respiting clause of the charter of 1216. A new and final charter, issued with the consent of all the prelates and barons of England, was decidedly necessary. This want was supplied by two documents, the new Charter of Liberties and the Forest Charter, issued on November 6th under the seals of the legate and the regent.[14]

This charter of liberties can, for purposes of discussion, be divided into two distinct parts. The first forty-one articles were, with the exception of the thirty-ninth, simply a reissue of the charter of 1216 with minor changes and additions. The dowry of a widow was definitely set at one third of her husband's estate unless a smaller part had been agreed upon " at the church door." Assizes of *novel disseisin* and *mort d'ancestor* were to be taken by the justices itinerant once a year instead of four times as ordered by the previous charters. All cases of *darrein presentment* were reserved for the central court at Westminster. The earlier charters had provided that if the justices

---

[13] *Chronicle of Merton*, in Petit-Dutaillis, *Vie de Louis VIII*, p. 515. Walter of Coventry, II, 240.

[14] Stubbs, *Select Charters*, pp. 344-351. *Statutes of the Realm*, Charters of Liberties, pp. 17-21. See also McKechnie, *Magna Carta*.

itinerant were unable to finish their business on the court day, the necessary suitors were to stay until the following day so that the cases could be terminated. This charter provided that such unfinished business should be transacted by the justices at some other place on their iter. Difficult cases were to be referred to the court at Westminster. These changes were purely administrative in their nature. The setting of the widow's dowry at one-third of her husband's estate was probably the recognition of established custom.[15] To have the royal justices visit every county of England four times a year would have been far too great a burden on both the administration and the people. Finally the period of civil war was bound to have created many complicated legal questions—these were to be settled by the justices at Westminster under the eyes of the regent and the justiciar. Besides these changes this section of the charter contained two additions. River banks were not to be " prohibited ", that is reserved for the king's hawking, except those which had been subject to such reservation in the reign of Henry II. This clause benefited the nobility who resented being banned from the best hawking grounds because the king desired to use them. The other addition also was for the benefit of the upper classes. The king's officers were forbidden to requisition carts belonging to the demesne manors of ecclesiastical or lay nobles.

The thirty-ninth and the last six articles of the charter of 1217 were new. One of these dealt with county government. It provided that the county court should be held not oftener than once a month and at still longer intervals if such had been the local custom. The sheriff was to make his *tourn* twice a year—at Easter and Michaelmas. The thirty-ninth and forty-third articles were intended to remove abuses which threatened the position of the great feudal landholders—the king and his barons. No man should give away or sell so much of his land that he could not fulfil his feudal obligations to his lord. In short if a vassal sold part of his fief, he was still responsible for the entire service owed the lord of the fee. When a vassal gave

[15] *Le Très Ancien Coutumier de Normandie*, I, i, cap. iii.

land to an ecclesiastical foundation in frankalmoign, the lord lost the service from that land. As he shared in the spiritual benefits, the arrangement was reasonable as long as the transaction was a genuine one, but it was often used merely as a means to avoid paying the lord his dues. Article forty-three forbade a man to give land to an ecclesiastical foundation and then receive it back again as a fief, for thus the lord lost the service due him and the vassal kept the land. If any one attempted to defraud his lord in this manner, the land in question should revert to the latter. Thus William and his fellow barons attempted to strengthen the feudal system. The charter of 1217 dealt with but one of the questions covered by the respiting clause of 1216—that of scutage. Scutage would be collected as it had been in the time of Henry II. The practices of Richard and John to which the barons had so strenuously objected and the restrictions imposed on the king by the Great Charter were alike swept into the discard. The king would take his scutage, but he would not abuse the privilege. The clauses of the Great Charter dealing with the debts to the Jews, the estates of those who died intestate, and the farms of counties were calmly forgotten. The regency had no intention of depriving itself of any sources of revenue. The last clause of this charter dealt with the most serious heritage left by the age of disorder, the castles built during the war between John and his barons. All these were to be destroyed.

The Charter of Liberties of the Forest was apparently intended to cover the questions relating to the royal forests that had been left unsettled by John's charter. There were a number of important provisions besides those dealing with details of forest administration. Any land afforested by Henry II, if it were not part of his demesne, was to be deforested if the owner of the land had been injured by its inclusion in the forest. All lands outside the royal demesne afforested by Richard and John were to be deforested. Any prelate or baron passing through a royal forest could kill one or two wild animals provided he notified the foresters or sounded his horn so that all might know he was acting lawfully. All men outlawed for breaches of the forest laws under Henry II, Richard, and John were pardoned if they found sureties for their future good behavior. In the future no man should lose life or limb for forest offences.

On the whole these charters of 1217 were extremely statesmanlike documents. Ambiguities were removed, some vexed questions were settled, and others discreetly dropped. It is true that many of the clauses added by the council benefitted the feudal nobility, but one must remember that William was a feudal lord and that he had to rely on the co-operation of his fellow barons. The fact that William was able to maintain intact the important rights of the crown even at the cost of minor concessions to the nobility is a great tribute to his force of character. Nor must one neglect to give due credit to his coadjutor, the legate Gualo. One interesting question in relation to this charter remains to be discussed. It purported to be a permanent grant binding on Henry and his heirs for ever. But it bore the seals of the regent and legate, and no permanent grant was valid unless it was authenticated by the Great Seal. Thus, despite its wording, this charter should be considered simply as a temporary grant to be effective until Henry came of age. The declaration issued by the council in November 1218 when the new Great Seal began to run makes it clear that this was apparent to the regent, the legate, and the prelates and barons of the council.[16] The words *in perpetuum* sounded nicely but meant little or nothing.

The most pressing problem which confronted the government in connection with the reorganization of the administrative system was the rehabilitation of the royal finances. The exchequer had not sat to receive the accounts of the sheriffs since Michaelmas 1214.[17] Since the spring of 1215 the entire financial system had been in disorder and, in order to raise the funds needed to carry on the war, the regency had been forced to resort to the various extraordinary measures discussed in a previous

[16] *Patent Rolls*, I, 177.

[17] Turner, *Minority of Henry II*, Part I, *Transactions of the Royal Historical Society*, New Series, XVIII, 284.

chapter. Faced with the necessity of paying the indemnity to Prince Louis, the tribute due to the pope, Queen Berenger's yearly allowance, and the ordinary expenses of administration, the government found itself in serious financial straits. The situation called for a general levy of taxes throughout the realm. In addition the financial system had to be put in order so that the regular revenues of the crown might be secured. These were to be the principal occupations of the regent during the year 1218.

During the period of civil war but one attempt had been made to raise money by taxation. Sometime before April 9, 1217, orders were issued for the collection of a hidage and carucage in all the counties south of the Humber that were not actually in the possession of Louis and his partisans.[13] After the battle of Lincoln the government felt sufficiently optimistic to extend the levy to include Yorkshire and Hampshire.[19] While a writ dated January 9, 1218, referred to this tax as one levied by the council of the realm, no earlier writ mentioned this fact.[20] This single reference may have been due to a confusing of this tax with those authorized by the council of November 1217. The fact that none of the early writs dealing with the hidage of 1217 mentioned the consent of the council, would seem to indicate that while William may have asked the advice of his colleagues, he had ordered the levy without the formal approval of the council.[21] There is no evidence as to how generally this tax was actually collected nor as to the amount of money obtained from it. On April 14th William ordered Faulkes de Bréauté to give five hundred marks of the money raised in the counties under his control to Hubert de

[18] *Rot. Claus.*, I, 335b. This writ shows that the tax was being levied in all the counties below the Humber except Norfolk, Suffolk, Essex, Hertford, Hampshire, Kent, Surrey, and Sussex. For a full discussion of this levy see S. K. Mitchell, *Studies in Taxation under John and Henry*, III, 121-124.

[19] *Rot. Claus.*, I, 318b, 336.

[20] *Ibid.*, p. 348b.

[21] See writs issued for carucage of 1220. (*Rot. Claus.*, I, 437) cited in Mitchell, *Taxation under John and Henry III*, p. 130, note 52.

Burg, but this may have represented merely a fond hope on the part of the regent.[22] Considering the condition of the country, it is doubtful whether the tax could have been collected very effectively before the conclusion of peace. It was still in the process of collection in January 1218.[23]

On October 29th or 30th the great council gave its consent to the levying of a scutage of two marks on every knight's fee.[24] As this tax was for the avowed purpose of "freeing England from the French," that is of paying the indemnity to Louis, rather than in lieu of military service, it might more properly be termed an aid than a scutage.[25] One hundred and seventy tenants-in-chief were given letters authorizing them to collect scutage from their sub-tenants and pay it into the exchequer in two installments—one half on November 30th and the other on January 13th.[26] Letters close were sent to all the sheriffs directing them to assist these tenants-in-chief to collect the scutage from their vassals, and to see that the money was brought to the exchequer on time.[27] Nevertheless the collection was delayed, and on February 22nd the regent ordered the sheriffs to have the scutage money at Westminster on March 25th.[28] They were to compel the attendance of those tenants-in-chief who had letters authorizing them to collect their own scutage, and they were to collect the rest of the money themselves and pay it into the exchequer. According to the account drawn up by Mr. Mitchell the total scutage assessed came to 11,098 marks 11s 5d of which only 4,227 marks 8s 1d was actually collected.[29]

[22] *Patent Rolls,* I, 56.

[23] *Rot. Claus.,* I, 348b.

[24] This scutage is described as *positum per commune consilium regni nostri* (*Rot. Claus.,* I, 371) and *positum de novo per consilium commune comitum et baronum nostrorum Angliae.* (*Patent Rolls,* I, 125).

[25] *de scutagio assiso anno secundo regni regis Henrici III ad Angliam deliberandam de Francis.* (*Pipe Roll 17 John,* Compotus honoris Boloniae, m. 1) cited in Mitchell, *Taxation under John and Henry III,* p. 126, note 26.

[26] *Rot. Claus.,* I, 371-373.

[27] *Ibid.,* p. 371.

[28] *Ibid.,* p. 377b.

[29] Mitchell, *Taxation under John and Henry III,* p. 126.

Not all the revenue produced by the scutage was used to pay the indemnity to Louis. On February 7th Hubert de Burg was given the scutage collected from Kent to maintain Dover Castle, and on April 5th that of Norfolk and Suffolk was added.[30] To levy a general tax on a country impoverished by civil war must have been an extremely difficult task for the regent. His troubles are beautifully illustrated by the attitude of his colleague, Peter des Roches, bishop of Winchester. Bishop Peter objected to paying his scutage and was excused by the barons of the exchequer on the ground that he had not given his assent to the tax.[31] The bishop was too powerful to be coerced and took full advantage of the fact. Faulkes de Bréauté simply neglected to pay and was eventually excused some time after William's death. William was to learn that a regent no matter how capable he might be was not a king.

On November 9th the regent issued writs for the levying of a tallage on the royal demesne.[32] This was to be assessed by the sheriffs in conjunction with special officials sent into the counties for that purpose. In general the tallagers seem to have been royal justices or clerks, but this was not always the case.[33] In November the regent himself sat at Gloucester with William de Chanteloup, Ralph Musard, and Henry fitz Gerold, all barons of some importance, and tallaged some thirteen demesnes including the towns of Gloucester, Bristol, Worcester, and Nottingham.[34] Apparently William was in need of ready cash and, more important yet, of good wine. He collected on the spot a part of the tallage due from Worcester and Gloucester as well as part of the hidage of Worcestershire.[35] The citizens of Bristol were to furnish him with ten *dolia* of wine as part of their tallage, and on December 28th they were

---

[30] *Rot. Claus.,* I, 352, 357b.

[31] Madox, *History of the Exchequer,* I, 675. See Mitchell, *Taxation under John and Henry III,* p. 127 and note 35.

[32] *Patent Rolls,* I, 170.

[33] See Mitchell, *Taxation under John and Henry III,* p. 128 and note 39.

[34] *Rot. Claus.,* I, 375.

[35] *Compotus of William Marshal Senior,* Public Record Office, E 364/1, m 3.

ordered to send it to Gloucester and deliver it to the earl's agents.[86] Thus the regent anticipated the regular tallagers in order to obtain money and wine for immediate use.

Not only was it necessary to raise money by taxation, but steps had to be taken to secure the regular revenues of the crown. During the civil war many of the royal demesnes and escheats had been alienated illegally. On September 29, 1217, William ordered all the sheriffs of England to make inquisition as to what lands pertained to the king's demesne. All such lands were to be seized no matter who might be holding them, and a full list of all the royal demesnes in each county was to be sent to the regent three weeks after Michaelmas.[87] This general seizure was an extremely drastic step, but it was probably necessary under the circumstances. If a tenant had a legal right to a part of the royal demesne, he could appeal to the regent and receive a writ ordering the return of his land. Richard Revel, who was disseised of his land in the royal demesne in Somersetshire, informed the regent that he held it by right of a charter from King Richard. William ordered the sheriff to return the land, to examine the charter, and to communicate its contents to him.[88] Between October 27th and 30th lands seized in this way were returned to some dozen tenants including William of Salisbury, William Brewer, the bishops of Bath and Lincoln, and the chapters of Bath and Welles.[89] This measure assured to the crown the revenues of the royal demesnes which had not been given away. The question of the escheats pertaining to the crown was taken up when the writs were issued for the collection of the tallage. The tallagers in conjunction with the sheriffs were to make inquiry concerning all escheats that should belong to the crown. They were to discover of what the escheats consisted, by whose death they had passed to the crown, how much they were worth in yearly revenue, why they pertained to the king, and how long they had been escheats. These escheats were to be seized, and a full report sent to the

[86] *Rot. Claus.*, I, 375, 348.
[87] *Ibid.*, p. 336b.
[88] *Ibid.*, p. 332b.
[89] *Ibid.*, pp. 333, 338.

regent under the seals of the sheriff and the tallagers.[40] Any injustice done by this general order could be remedied by a special writ. Thus on December 18th the sheriff of Surrey was ordered to give Reginald de Briouse seisin of a manor which had been seized as an escheat.[41] By these decisive if somewhat drastic methods William regained the crown lands which had been alienated during the civil war.

In order to make these various measures effective it was necessary to reestablish the central organ of the financial administration of the realm, the exchequer. Under the terms of the treaty of Kingston Louis had returned the rolls and other documents belonging to the exchequer which had come into his possession when he captured Westminster.[42] William, apparently, planned to hold the first session on November 11th, but he probably postponed it to the 30th.[43] On that day the first installment of the scutage was due, and at least two sheriffs were expected to render their accounts at that time.[44] As a matter of fact some of the sheriffs obtained further postponements. Earl Ranulf of Chester and William de Chanteloup were given until January 13th.[45] The sheriff of Gloucester received a respite to January 30th while Faulkes de Bréauté was allowed to wait until June 11th.[46] The accounts rendered at this time were for the first half of the seventeenth year of John's reign—that is from Michaelmas 1214 to Easter 1215. This completed the exchequer records up to the beginning of the civil war. The fact that arrears which originated in the last year of John's reign or in the first of Henry III's never appeared on subsequent rolls indicates that the sheriffs rendered

[40] *Patent Rolls*, I, 170-1.

[41] *Rot. Claus.*, I, 348.

[42] This clause appears in one version of the Treaty of Kingston. (Martène and Durand, *Thesaurus Novus Anecdotorum*, I, 857-859).

[43] The sheriff of Berkshire was summoned for the feast of St. Martin's but his hearing was postponed for two weeks. *Rot. Claus.*, I, 343.

[44] *Patent Rolls*. I, 171. *Rot. Claus.*, I, 343b, 344.

[45] *Ibid.*, pp. 340b, 343b.

[46] *Ibid.*, pp. 344, 362b.

no accounts for those years.[47] In this long and more or less continuous session from November 30th, 1217, to the summer of
1218 the exchequer showed itself extremely anxious to collect
all revenues due to the crown. For instance John de Cornherd
was summoned to appear two weeks after Easter to explain to
whom he had paid the five marks a year he owed for the manor
of Norton.[48] Apparently John had made no payment since
1204, and the exchequer was trying to collect the arrears.
Again, Robert de Crec was ordered to account for the farm of
a manor in Suffolk which was three years in arrears.[49] The
custodians of the honors in the king's hands were sent lists of
reliefs and other dues owed by their tenants and ordered to collect them.[50] It is evident that the barons of the exchequer made
an extremely careful inspection of the rolls of John's reign to
ascertain what was owed to the crown.

The regent himself took an active part in the rehabilitation
of the king's finances. The detailed reports on the royal
demesnes and on the escheats pertaining to the crown were
sent to him.[51] If anyone claimed part of the king's demesne, he
had to prove his case to William's satisfaction and obtain from
him an order directing the sheriff to return the land. In this
way William made sure that the royal demesne and the king's
escheats were not illegally alienated—at least without his consent. In November 1217 he personally tallaged a number of
royal demesnes.[52] When he ordered the barons of the exchequer to sit on March 25th to receive the scutage payments, he
directed them to keep him informed of the amounts paid in.[53]
As the only connection between England and Ireland rested on
the fact that Henry III was king of England and lord of Ireland,
the collection of revenue from that country depended on the
regent. On November 10, 1217 he ordered the justiciar of Ireland to tallage the king's Irish demesne and to obtain an aid

---

[47] See Turner, *Minority of Henry III,* Part I, pp. 284, 288.
[48] *Rot. Claus.,* I, 358b.   [51] *Rot. Claus.,* I, 336b.
[49] *Ibid.,* p. 347b.   [52] *Ibid.,* p. 375.
[50] *Patent Rolls,* I, 172.   [53] *Ibid.,* p. 377.

from the native kings and the barons and knights of the country.[54] At the same time the tenants-in-chief of the lord of Ireland were requested to grant the aid.[55] In July he sent the justiciar a list of the debts owed the crown by various inhabitants of Ireland and ordered him to enforce payment.[56] In August 1218 he persuaded the merchants of England, Ireland, and Wales to lend the exchequer some five hundred marks to aid in paying the indemnity to Louis.[57] William not only closely supervised the financial administration, but turned his attention to tapping all possible sources of revenue.

The distinction between the regent's private purse and the king's was still extremely vague. William was always in need of money either to meet the current expenses of the government or to pay the debt due to Louis which he had underwritten. On August 30, 1218 he advanced nine hundred marks for the latter purpose.[58] He even added a gold cup of his own and several gold coins to this fund.[59] He showed himself extremely ingenious in devising means of obtaining money immediately without waiting for the comparatively slow action of the regular financial system. From Christmas 1217 to Easter 1219 he held the office of sheriff of Essex and Hertfordshire.[60] The actual duties of this position were performed by his deputies, but he appropriated the revenues, £293 2s 5d, for the immediate needs of the government.[61] Again he never paid into the exchequer any of the scutage he owed on the levy of 1217, but used the money himself for the king's service.[62] At times he would collect a fine on the spot.[63] Throughout his regency, William was continually racking his brains for means of raising money. Wool was seized from merchants at London and Bristol, and they were

[54] Ibid., p. 375.   [56] Rot. Claus., I, 365b.
[55] Patent Rolls, I, 125.   [57] Ibid., p. 369.
[58] Ibid. Compotus of William Marshal Senior, Public Record Office, E 364/1, m 3.   [59] Ibid.
[60] Pipe Roll 2 Henry III, m 1 a, Public Record Office, E 372/62 and Memoranda Roll 2 Henry III.
[61] Ibid. Compotus of William Marshal Senior.   [62] Ibid.   [63] Ibid.

allowed to buy it back at the rate of six marks a sack.[64] As the wool delivered to Florence the Rich was valued at five marks a sack, this was a decided improvement on pure confiscation.[65] Several sums of money obtained in this way at Bristol were turned over to William—at one time fifty marks, at another forty-four pounds.[66] In all the above cases it is clear that William was acting in the king's name and using money that belonged to the crown. A nice question arose over one hundred marks which the bishop of Lincoln gave the regent to persuade him to force Robert de Gaugi to surrender Newark castle. William's executors claimed that this money was given to the earl of Pembroke, while the barons of the exchequer insisted that it was a fine offered the regent of England.[67] The accounts of William's executors make it clear that to all intents and purposes the regent's purse and the king's were identical.

In his handling of the whole financial situation William demonstrated his initiative and sound judgement. Taxes were levied and, in so far as the condition of the country permitted, collected. William did not hesitate to employ drastic measures to check the alienation of the king's demesnes and escheats. His decision to make no attempt to force the sheriffs to account for the years of civil war was an extremely wise one. Above all, the regent showed his ingenuity in raising money to meet current needs. The regular financial system of the country was put in working order, and extraordinary methods were found to raise additional funds. This was one of the most vital of William's tasks, and he performed it extremely well.

Another important activity of the English government which required the attention of the regent was the administration of the royal forests. The Charter of the Forests provided for the deforestation of certain districts and a general reform of the forest administration. To carry this out was a task which required good judgement, ability, and considerable personal prestige. As the regent himself was far too busy to give it his atten-

---

[64] *Rot. Claus.*, I, 351b.

[65] *Patent Rolls*, I, 114.

[66] *Compotus of William Marshal Senior.*

[67] *Ibid. Rot. Claus.*, I, 602.

tion, he entrusted the work to his nephew, John Marshal, who
had proved himself a capable and loyal servant of the crown.
On November 8, 1217, two days after the issuance of the
charter, John Marshal was appointed justiciar of the forests by
letters patent under the regent's seal.[68] This appointment was
not for the period of the king's minority nor during the royal
pleasure, but for " as long as he serves us well." John apparently felt that a grant in such terms under William's seal was
of doubtful legality, for he hastened to obtain a renewal under
the new Great Seal as soon as it was made.[69] The position of
justiciar of the forests was an extremely important one as it
entailed not only the custody of all the royal forests of England
but also of the royal demesnes pertaining to them such as Wood-
stock, Brill, Geddington, Wakefield, Havering, Freemantle, and
Gillingham.[70] In February copies of the Forest Charter were
sent to all the sheriffs of England who were directed to publish it, but John took no steps toward putting it into effect until
mid-summer.[71] On July 24th letters patent were sent to all
sheriffs through whose counties John Marshal was about to go
ordering them to meet him with four legal knights of the
county. These four were to choose twelve others who were to
define the borders of the forests under the justiciar's supervision.[72] A writ of the same date informed John that the men of
Huntingdonshire had made a fine to have the Forest Charter
carried out in their county, and he was directed to proceed there
at once.[73] On August 11th a forester was ordered to maintain
his forest in its present state until John arrived to decide what
should be deforested.[74] By the appointment of John Marshal
to the office of justiciar of the forests William placed that important branch of the government in the charge of a man of
ability on whom he could rely. Despite the fact that it savored
of nepotism, it was a wise measure.

[68] *Patent Rolls*, I, 123.
[69] *Ibid.*, pp. 178-9.
[70] *Ibid.*, pp. 124-5.
[71] *Rot. Claus.*, I, 377-377b.
[72] *Patent Rolls*, I, 162.
[73] *Ibid.*
[74] *Rot. Claus.*, I, 367b.

While the raising of money was necessarily the primary concern of the regent and his colleagues, the administration of justice was an equally important function of a government. During the war the judicial system had fallen into complete confusion, and William had been forced to administer justice as best he could. In March 1217 he ordered Faulkes de Bréauté to bring a number of malefactors before him to answer for their offences.[75] In April a dispute arose between Walter de Beauchamp and the bishop of Worcester. The sheriff of Worcestershire was directed to take six knights or legal men not bound to the bishop and six not bound to Walter who, in conjunction with two knights whom the sheriff of Gloucester would send him, should inquire into the matter. The result of the investigation was to be sent to William under the seals of the twelve knights or legal men, of the two knights from Gloucestershire, and of the sheriff himself.[76] Again in June the sheriff of Warwickshire was told to order the earl of that shire to receive his brother's homage for two manors. If the earl were unwilling to obey, he should appear before the regent to explain his refusal.[77] A few days later a writ informed Philip Marc that one of his men had burned a man's house, abducted his sister, and stolen a horse, nine cows, four pigs, and fifty-two chickens. If the malefactor should refuse to make reparation, he was to be sent to the regent at Oxford.[78] Thus William attempted to administer justice in the absence of the regular royal courts. It is impossible to say how long a time elapsed after the conclusion of peace before the permanent bench at Westminster was reestablished. The regent and council apparently conducted the Michaelmas term of the *curia regis* in October or November 1217, and there is a record of an assize of *mort d'ancestor* taken before this body.[79] Other cases were called before the regent and council during the winter, and there is

[75] *Ibid.*, p. 301.

[76] *Ibid.*, p. 335b.

[77] *Ibid.*, p. 336.

[78] *Ibid.*

[79] *Bracton's Note Book* (ed. Maitland), III, 305, Case no. 1306. See also *Rot. Claus.*, I, 325b; *Patent Rolls*, I, 99.

evidence that the regular court of Common Pleas was func-
tioning.[80]

The charter of liberties had provided that justices itinerant
should visit the counties of England once a year to take assizes
of *mort d'ancestor* and *novel disseisin*, but this provision was
not put into full effect until the following year. Miss Norgate
has taken a passage in the *Annals* of *Dunstaple* as evidence of
a judicial eyre in the autumn of 1217, but this appears to be an
error.[81] It is true that under the year 1217 the *Annals* give an
account of the visit to Dunstaple of six justices headed by the
abbot of Ramsey and Stephen de Segrave, but a close study of
this chronicle reveals that its chronology for the years 1217
and 1218 is extremely confused.[82] It also records under 1217
the making of the new Great Seal—an event known to belong
in November 1218.[83] Again the first entry under 1218 describes
the replacement of the legate, Gualo, by Pandulf. Gualo was
still in office in November of that year.[84] While on page fifty-
three the *Annals* speak of the justices under the year 1217, on
page fifty-five they refer to the "above justices" under the
heading 1219.[85] Finally, the *patent rolls* show that the abbot
of Ramsey, Stephen de Segrave, and four associates visited
Dunstaple toward the end of November 1218.[86] There
seems no reasonable doubt that the visit described by the
Annals was that of November 1218, and that the heading 1217
is an error. Discarding then the testimony of the *Annals* of
Dunstaple, there is no evidence of an eyre before the autumn of
1218. A few parties of justices, however, were sent out with
special commissions. In April 1218 Matthew fitz Herbert and
three associates were sent into Hampshire to inquire into crimes

[80] *Rot. Claus.*, I, 347, 377-8.

[81] Norgate, *Minority of Henry III*, pp. 86-7.

[82] *Annales de Dunstaplia, Annales Monastici*, III, 53.

[83] *Patent Rolls*, I, 177. *Rot. Claus.*, I, 381b.

[84] *Patent Rolls*, I, 177. He apparently sailed late in November. *Rot. Claus.*,
I, 384.

[85] *Annales de Dunstaplia, Annales Monastici*, III, 54-5.

[86] *Patent Rolls*, I, 207.

committed since the peace with Louis and to judge the malefactors according to the laws and customs of England.[87] On
February 13, 1218, four men, who apparently were not regular
royal justices, were commissioned by letters patent to take an assize of *novel disseisin* in Cornwall.[88] In August a similar group
were ordered to take an assize in Yorkshire.[89] On August 11th
two royal justices, Martin de Pattishall and Ralph Harang, and
an unidentifiable colleague were commissioned to take an assize
of *novel disseisin* in Buckinghamshire.[90] While a general judicial visitation of the counties of England was postponed until
the autumn of 1218, some cases, probably the most pressing,
were heard by special commissions.

Besides the restoration of the administrative system a number
of other problems were involved in bringing the country to a
peaceful state. No sooner had peace been made with Louis
than the restless English knights were for holding a tournament
at Blyth. No one loved a tournament more than William or believed in them more thoroughly as a training school for young
knights, but he had to recognize that they were a danger to the
peace of the realm. He felt obliged to forbid the meeting, but
he carefully pointed out that he did this only because he feared
that it would create disturbance.[91] In August 1218 he was
forced to order William of Salisbury and others who were planning a tourney to put it off until the realm should be completely
at peace.[92] It must have been a sad blow to the gay young
knights of England to find the flower of English chivalry so un-
reasonable. The knight-errant had been overweighed by the
cares of state. Another necessary step to keep the peace was the
reduction of the adulterine castles built during the war. When
the sheriffs were ordered to publish the Charter of Liberties and
the Forest Charter their attention was particularly called to the
clauses dealing with illegal castles.[93] Still it was necessary to
issue writs ordering the destruction of specific strongholds.[94]

[87] *Ibid.*, p. 147.
[88] *Ibid.*, p. 173.
[89] *Ibid.*, pp. 174-5.
[90] *Ibid.*, p. 165.
[91] *Ibid.*, p. 116.
[92] *Ibid.*, p. 174.
[93] *Rot. Claus.*, I, 377.
[94] *Ibid.*, p. 380.

Finally, there was the very real problem of forcing the royal officers to obey the orders of the government. The one who gave most trouble was Robert de Gaugi, the constable of Newark castle. At the beginning of the war between king and barons the bishop of Lincoln had turned over his castles to John who had made Robert constable of Newark. The latter swore that if John died he would surrender the castle to no one but the bishop.[95] On June 10, 1217 the regent directed Robert to deliver the fortress to the bishop.[96] As Hugh of Lincoln could not at the moment be spared from the business of the kingdom, one of his knights, armed with his letters patent, was sent to receive Newark in his name. Apparently William suspected that Robert might use his oath to John as an excuse for refusing to give the castle to the bishop's deputy, and to avoid this the knight bore letters patent of the legate which certified that he had detained Hugh on the king's business. Robert refused to obey this mandate on the ground that the government owed him money. On June 23rd the regent promised to see that he was paid if he turned over the castle to the bishop's agent.[97] This had no effect, and two more mandates addressed to him were equally unavailing.[98] Finally, on October 26th Robert went to London and solemnly surrendered Newark to the king. He promised to evacuate it within forty days and turn it over to the bishop or his deputy bearing his letters. In the meantime he promised not to harm the bishop or his men. William, with excellent reason, did not trust him and ordered the constables of Lincoln and Nottingham to force him to keep his word.[99] Robert returned to Newark to go cheerfully on his way completely oblivious of his promise. In January the government decided to resort to strategy. The see of Lincoln, probably with the consent of the bishop, was seized into the king's hands, and Robert was directed to surrender Newark to the royal custodians.[100] This order was ignored as coolly as the previous ones. There was nothing left but force, and on March 14th the sheriff

---

[95] *Rot. Pat.*, p. 193b. [97] *Patent Rolls*, I, 71. [99] *Ibid.*, p. 121.
[96] *Patent Rolls*, I, 68. [98] *Ibid.*, pp. 81, 85. [100] *Ibid.*, pp. 134-5.

of Nottingham was ordered to collect all the forces at his command to assist the bishop to expel Robert.[101] As Newark was a great fortress garrisoned by seasoned troops, the chances of its being reduced by such means were slight. It was a bluff, and Robert knew it. By that time bishop Hugh was growing discouraged and, it may be, doubtful of the regent's desire to enforce his orders. He finally decided to offer William a hundred marks if he would come to his assistance in person.[102] This materially increased the regent's indignation against Robert, and he prepared to subdue him. On July 4th he directed Ralph Musard to send thirty miners to Stamford where he had ordered his forces to muster.[103] Roger of Wendover speaks of the collecting of a great army, but as a matter of fact it was not very large.[104] The close roll gives a list of twenty-four knights who took part in the expedition, but some of them were great barons such as John Marshal and Reginald de Briouse who would probably have their own followers.[105] They were reinforced by the bishop's knights, one of whom was slain in the attack on Newark.[106] William left London on July 8th and reached Newark on the 19th.[107] From there he ordered the mayor of Lincoln to send him the materials needed for the siege.[108] The regent himself stayed on the scene for four days during which a sally from the castle was repulsed and the siege engines put in position. Then he retired to Nottingham leaving bishop Hugh in command of the operations.[109] A few days later Robert came to terms with the bishop, evacuated the castle, and hastened to Wallingford to make a formal surrender of his charge to the king and regent. Newark was turned over to Peter des Roches who was ordered to give it to its rightful owner.[110] The whole story shows very clearly how difficult it was to enforce the obedience of the king's officers. Nor was Robert the only offender.

[101] *Rot. Claus.*, I, 378.
[102] *Ibid.*, p. 602.
[103] *Ibid.*, p. 365.
[104] Roger of Wendover, II, 227-8.
[105] *Rot. Claus.*, I, 379b.
[106] Roger of Wendover, II, 227-8.
[107] *Patent Rolls*, I, 160-1.
[108] *Rot. Claus.*, I, 365b.
[109] Roger of Wendover, II, 227. *Patent Rolls*, I, 161-2.
[110] *Ibid.*, p. 164.

On May 6, 1218 William ordered Hugh de Vivonne to surrender certain lands to Gilbert de Clare, earl of Gloucester.[111] In January 1219 he repeated this order.[112] On March 7th he informed Hugh that if he did not obey at once, his lands would be seized.[113] In September 1220, over a year after William's death, Hugh had not yet complied with the government's demand.[114] Apparently the king's agents were not always responsible for the ineffectiveness of the regent's orders. In the spring of 1219, soon after William had ceased all active participation in the government, the sheriff of Sussex wrote a most plaintive letter to Peter des Roches and Hubert de Burg.[115] He quoted three mandates addressed to him by William, dated April 14, June 18, and June 29, 1218, ordering him to give certain lands to Robert Marmion Junior and one of Peter des Roches dated March 24, 1219 of the same nature.[116] The sheriff assured his superiors that he had obeyed these orders and given Robert Marmion full seisin of all the lands his father had held in Sussex. But Robert de Mortimer and Ralph Tirel, constable of Pevensey castle, refused to permit Robert Marmion to retain the lands. In this and other matters they had prevented the sheriff from obeying the orders of the government.

These cases of disobedience to his commands should not be taken as evidence that William was an ineffective ruler. The marvel is not that he was obeyed so poorly but rather that he was obeyed at all. It was sufficiently difficult for a king with all his royal authority to enforce his will. For a regent who had taken over the government in the midst of anarchy it was an almost impossible task which was made more difficult by his disinclination to remove any officer appointed by the late king. This evidence of the insubordination of the royal officers and the turbulence of the baronage is introduced to show under

---

[111] *Rot. Claus.*, I, 360b.

[112] *Ibid.*, p. 387.

[113] *Ibid.*, p. 405b.

[114] *Ibid.*, p. 429b.

[115] Shirley, *Royal Letters*, I, 13-15.

[116] Mr. Shirley has misdated these writs. The correct dates can be established by comparing with the rolls. See *Rot. Claus.*, I, 358b, 363b; *Patent Rolls*, I, 159.

what tremendous difficulties William labored. That he accomplished as much as he did is almost incredible.

The problems that faced the regency during this period were by no means confined to England. It was necessary to reach an understanding with the Scots and the Welsh who had been Louis' allies in the war. Acting in accordance with the terms of the treaty of peace, Louis had directed his former allies to surrender the lands, castles, and prisoners which they had taken during the war. On September 23, 1217 William requested Alexander of Scotland to obey Louis' orders and to deliver the castle of Carlisle and all the lands and prisoners he had taken to Robert de Vieuxpont, who was on the same day appointed sheriff of Cumberland.[117] As William had some doubts of the efficacy of these letters, he ordered the great men of the north —the archbishop of York, the bishop of Durham, the earls of Chester and Ferrars, the count of Aumale, the constable of Chester, and several others—to assist Robert in taking Carlisle by force if such measures should prove necessary.[118] Alexander, however, showed no disposition to resist the execution of the treaty. He apparently surrendered the lands, castles, and prisoners without protest and requested letters of conduct to allow him to do homage to Henry for his English fiefs. These were issued on November 3rd, and three days later William instructed the constable of Chester to meet Alexander at Berwick to conduct him to the king.[119] On December 19th the regent notified the sheriffs of the counties in which the honor of Huntingdon lay that Alexander had performed his devoir to Henry III and had been given his English lands.[120]

Llywelyn and his fellow princes presented a far more serious problem than the king of Scotland. Although the great frontier fortresses had protected the western counties of England from Welsh inroads during the war with Louis, the marcher barons had suffered heavily from their ancient enemies. We have already seen the difficulties which William and other barons

---

[117] *Ibid.*, pp. 93-4.
[118] *Ibid.*

[119] *Ibid.*, pp. 119, 122.
[120] *Rot. Claus.*, I, 348.

of the region had had with the Welsh in 1215 and 1216. Reginald de Briouse, who had become head of his family at the death of his brother Giles in 1215, had married one of Llywelyn's daughters and formed a close alliance with him against John and his supporters.[121] This formidable coalition was a very serious menace to the lands of all the marcher barons who had remained loyal to John. William with his vast lands in the marches and in south Wales was particularly involved. On the day of Henry III's accession to the throne when everyone was about to sit down to the coronation banquet, a messenger informed William that the constable of his castle of Goodrich, which commanded the valley of the Wye between Hereford and Monmouth, was hard pressed and in need of instant succor. The earl promptly despatched an adequate force of knights, serjeants, and cross-bowmen to the relief of his castle, but many believed that this stroke of misfortune on the very day of Henry's coronation was a bad omen.[122] William, as we have seen, soon entered into negotiations with Reginald de Briouse in the hope of weaning him from his Welsh allies, but he was unsuccessful until his prestige was increased by the victory of Lincoln. No sooner had Reginald made his submission to Henry than his enraged father-in-law invaded his lands.[123] It was probably this situation which brought William into the marches to his castle of Striguil early in July.[124] Reginald, however, was forced to conclude a private peace with his formidable antagonist. This merely released Llywelyn and his army for attacks on other marcher lords. During the latter part of July and all of August William was occupied with preparations to cut off the reinforcements which Blanche was sending to Louis. Llywelyn considered this a splendid opportunity to attack the county of Pembroke. He and young Rees, a powerful prince of south Wales, concentrated their armies on William's town of Haverford, but before they had made any attack upon it, the bishop of St. Davids appeared to offer

[121] *Brut y Tywysogion*, p. 287. [123] *Brut y Tywysogion*, pp. 299-301.
[122] *Hist.*, 15349-15372. [124] *Patent Rolls*, I, 79. *Rot. Claus.*, I, 314.

terms of peace in the name of the earl's vassals. They were
to give Llywelyn twenty hostages from the noblest families of
the region as a guarantee that they would either pay him a
thousand marks by the following Michaelmas or become his
subjects for ever.[125]

When peace was concluded with Louis, the latter ordered
Llywelyn to surrender the lands, castles, and prisoners he had
taken. This command alone would probably have had no effect
on that prince, but he was unwilling to face the combined forces
of all England and decided to make peace. Still he was in no
hurry, and it was not until the middle of the following March
that he did homage to Henry at Worcester.[126] In the meantime,
however, he ceased his depredations and ordered his fellow
princes to do likewise. With the exception of Morgan, lord of
Caerleon, they seem to have obeyed this mandate.[127] Caerleon
lay on the river Usk on the boundary of the lordship of Striguil, and the lands of its lords had been greatly diminished by
previous lords of Striguil and by William himself. Morgan had
taken advantage of the general war to attack his powerful
neighbor, and he obstinately refused to make peace while William held a foot of his inheritance.[128] He had no intention of
permitting a treaty between Henry III and the French prince
to interfere with his private war on a grasping marcher baron
even if the latter happened to be regent of England. Early in
October William's baillif of Striguil collected his vassals and
allies to put an end to Morgan's activities. He laid siege to
Caerleon and captured it, thus adding a very important fortress to the defences of his master's domains in Netherwent.[120]

[125] *Brut y Tywysogion*, pp. 301-303.   [127] *Hist.*, 17747-17749.
[126] *Patent Rolls*, I, 142. *Rot. Claus.*, I, 379.   [128] *Ibid.*, 17757-17762.
[129] *Ibid.*, 17780-17784. The baillif may have been John d'Erley who was William's deputy in Striguil in 1219. (*Ibid.*, 18173). The date of the capture of
Caerleon is uncertain. According to *Brut y Tywysogion* it took place immediately after Louis' departure. The *History* after mentioning Morgan's refusal to
accept the general peace says that Caerleon was taken *l'autre an, apres la seint
Michel*. This would place it in October 1218. It is, however, clear from the
History that this was followed by a great council at Worcester at which the

Toward the middle of March 1218 William and his young master held court at Worcester in the hope of settling the troubles in Wales. There Llywelyn demanded that William return to Morgan the lands he had taken from him on the ground that the peace treaty provided for the return of all captured territories. From this it would appear that the lands in question had been conquered by William or his deputies during the last war. It was not a question of lands taken from the lords of Caerleon by earlier lords of Striguil. William was disposed to give up his conquests, but his vassals vehemently opposed such a course. One of them undertook to argue the question before the assembled prelates, earls, and barons. He pointed out to them that Morgan had continued the war after the peace with Louis. Refusing to be included in the general peace, he had slain a number of William's knights, burned twenty-two churches, and ravaged his lands. Morgan ought to suffer the consequences of his acts. The assembly agreed with this point of view, and William retained the castle of Caerleon and the territory dependent on it.[130] In 1220 Morgan appealed to Henry III to reinstate him in his lands, and in 1222 the council of the realm ordered that Caerleon be seized into the king's hands, but it eventually remained in the Marshal family.[131] Llywelyn was appeased by being given the custody of the castles of Cardigan and Carmarthen during the king's minority.[132] As these fortresses were the keys to Pembrokeshire, this was a considerable sacrifice on William's part even though they were not his own castles. Thus bribed, Llywelyn soon persuaded his fellow princes to do homage to Henry, and the Welsh question was settled—for about a year.

In the light of the rumors current in later years to the effect

legate Gualo and William were present. As William's last visit to Worcester or its neighborhood was in April 1217, the date given in *Brut y Tywysogion* must be correct. This agrees with the *apres la seint Michel* of the *History*.

[130] *Hist.*, 17788-17872.

[131] *Rot. Claus.*, I, 436b. *Patent Rolls*, I, 352. *Calendar of Patent Rolls* 1364-7, pp. 266 et seq.

[132] *Rot. Claus.*, I, 379. *Patent Rolls*, I, 143.

that William had been over generous to Louis in 1217, his subsequent relations with the French king and his subjects are of particular interest. Of course, as the courteous and wary victor should, he had in person conducted Louis to the sea-coast.[133] He had shown his kindly disposition to his late foes by allowing the invalid viscount of Melun to remain in England until he had recuperated.[134] There were two French barons with whom he was in particularly close friendship—two brothers of the house of Dreux. William had known the family for some time. Their father, Robert II, count of Dreux, had been a member of the young king's household at Lagni in 1180 and had been with Philip Augustus at Gisors in 1188. It would not be surprising if William had at some time or other met that harrier of the Norman marches—Philip of Dreux, bishop of Beauvais, brother of Robert II. Then in 1214 Robert III had been captured by the English in a skirmish outside the walls of Nantes and had spent some time as a prisoner in England. His brother, Peter, called Mauclerk, had in 1212 become count of Brittany by his marriage to Alis who was the eldest daughter of the widow of Geoffrey Plantagenet by Guy de Thouars and hence a half-sister of the murdered Arthur. Peter and Robert came to England with Louis in April 1217, the former in the hope of regaining the honor of Richmond, the English fief of the counts of Brittany.[135] Both the brothers seem to have become friendly with William very quickly. Peter was one of the chief French delegates to the abortive peace conferences in June 1217, and it was Robert whom Louis sent to William to ask for an interview after the naval battle.[136] Both these barons served as guarantors of the loan made to the regent by Florence of St. Omer and his son.[137] On October 2nd Peter of Dreux was given the manor of Cheshunt in Hertfordshire which he claimed by right of his

[133] Roger of Wendover, II, 225. *Patent Rolls*, I, 95-6. *Rot. Claus.*, I, 324b-325.   [134] *Patent Rolls*, I, 93.
[135] *Histoire des ducs*, p. 188.
[136] *Patent Rolls*, I, 68. *Histoire des ducs*, p. 202.
[137] *Patent Rolls*, I, 114.

wife.[138] On October 31st Robert was given the manor of Shrivenham in Berkshire and Brill with its forest as well as a hundred marks a year.[139] On May 6, 1218 Peter was granted the honor of Richmond with the exception of a few fees, and Henry fitz Gerold was ordered to make an investigation to discover just what pertained to the honor.[140] Finally on January 16, 1219 the sheriffs of Lincolnshire, Cambridgeshire, Norfolk and Suffolk, Nottingham, and Hertford were notified that all the honor with the exception of thirty fees reserved by the king had been given to Peter.[141] As these lands had been in the custody of the earl of Chester, this was a tremendous concession to the French baron. Considering the part Peter played in the relations between France and England after 1230, one may wonder if William was hopeful of his assistance in recovering Normandy. William's relations with Philip Augustus seem to have been almost as cordial as with the house of Dreux. In February 1218 Philip returned some land in Normandy to its former lord " at the request of our most dear and faithful William Marshal." [142] The regent's second son, Richard, was actually at Philip's court when his father died.[143] William may be said to have had a decided affection for the French and their king.

As the pope was the recognized suzerain of England and his power the principal bulwark of the royal cause, the relations between the regency and the Holy See are of particular importance. Innocent III had died some months before his vassal, John, but his successor Honorius III continued his policy. By December 3, 1216 the new pope had learned of John's death, but his general information as to the conditions in England

---

[138] *Ibid.*, p. 97. *Rot. Claus.*, I, 325b.

[139] *Patent Rolls*, I, 117. *Rot. Claus.*, I, 339. He could not have held Brill long as it was given in custody to John Marshal on November 8th (*Patent Rolls*, I, 124).

[140] *Ibid.*, p. 174. *Rot. Claus.*, I, 360-360b.

[141] *Ibid.*, p. 385b.

[142] *Cartulaire Normande* (ed. L. Delisle, *Société de l'histoire de Normandie*), p. 39, no. 254.   [143] *Hist.*, 19120-1.

seems to have been limited. He immediately sent a letter to Gualo extending his condolences for the king's death and committing young Henry to the legate's care. The barons of England were to take an oath against Louis, and those who supported the invader were denounced. Similar letters were addressed to Peter des Roches, to the bishops of Worcester and Exeter, to the archbishop of Dublin, to the barons of England in general, to the archbishop of Bordeaux, and to the barons of Poitou and Gascony.[144] To support these missives he wrote letters to a number of laymen whom he believed to be the most loyal supporters of the royal cause. The first was addressed to " the noble man William, earl of Pembroke, marshal of England." He was congratulated on his fidelity to the royal party and urged to persevere in his faithful service. Similar letters were sent to Savaric de Mauleon, the earls of Arundel and Warren, and Hubert de Burg.[145] As the earls of Arundel and Warren were both partisans of Louis, Honorius' information seems rather imperfect. He probably had received from the legate a meagre announcement of John's death and had addressed his letters to any laymen he could think of who might be on the right side. By January 17, however, he had received fuller advices. He wrote to the king of Scotland, Robert de Ros, Llywelyn, the barons of the Cinque Ports, the earls of Warren, Arundel, Clare, and Norfolk commanding them to cease conspiring against England and to return to their fidelity despite the oaths they had taken to Louis.[146] The pope did not seem to realize that William the Lion had been succeeded by Alexander II as king of Scotland, but otherwise his information was accurate. Two days later he addressed a letter to " the noble man William, earl of Pembroke, justiciar of England." [147] He condoled with him about John's death and urged him to remain faithful to Henry III whom Gualo had crowned. Similar letters were sent to the " castellan of Cornwall," [148] Robert

---

[144] *Regesta Honorii Papae III* (ed. Petrus Pressutti, Rome, 1888, Vatican Press), no. 142.

[145] *Ibid.*, no. 143.

[146] *Ibid.*, no. 245.

[147] *Ibid.*, no. 262.

[148] Possibly Henry fitz Count.

de Vieuxpont, the earls of Chester and Ferrars, Geoffrey de Neville, the castellan of Dover,[149] the barons of the Cinque Ports, the castellan of Nottingham,[150] all other faithful constables, the archbishops of York and Rouen, Faulkes de Bréauté, and Richard Marsh, the chancellor. From the fact that William is addressed as justiciar it is obvious that the letter to which Honorius was replying must have been sent shortly after Henry's coronation. It is also clear that the pope regarded Gualo as the ruler of England—William was a great layman who could give him effective aid. The papal identification of individuals in England was still somewhat hazy, and the messenger might well have had difficulty in locating the " castellan of Cornwall." A papal letter of July 8th, probably written after the pope had learned of the battle of Lincoln, shows clearly the position which he conceived William to hold. Gualo was directed to confer with the bishops of England as to what should be done in the present circumstances. He left it to him whether or not to accept William, the king's marshal, as his associate.[151] This letter indicates that the pope did not consider William as regent of England, but merely as the most prominent layman of the realm. On November 6, 1217 the regent wrote in the king's name to the pope to report on the condition of the kingdom, to express his gratitude for the papal support, and to explain why the thousand marks of yearly tribute owed to Rome could not be paid at once.[152] In January Honorius confirmed the treaty of peace between Henry and Louis and revoked the papal denunciations of the latter and his allies provided they faithfully observed the treaty.[153]

In May 1218 the regency seems to have felt obliged to make a special effort to conciliate the Holy See—probably because there was no immediate prospect of being able to pay the tribute promised by John. Master Philip of Hadham was sent to

[149] Did Honorius realize that this was Hubert de Burg?
[150] Philip Marc?
[151] Pressutti, no. 653.
[152] Shirley, *Royal Letters,* I, no. VII.
[153] *Layettes du Trésor des Chartés,* I, no. 1273-4.

Rome bearing gifts for the pope and five of his cardinals.[154] William apparently shared his biographer's opinion of the means necessary to gain a favorable hearing in the Eternal City. When Philip Augustus desired papal aid in his effort to persuade Richard to make peace in 1198, the *History* says " he called one of his clerks and gave him the relics without which one cannot succeed at Rome, for it is always necessary to oil palms at the court of Rome. There is no need of chanting other psalms. The relics of St. Rufin and St. Albin have there great power. Otherwise, whatever one may say, laws or lawyers are not worth an apple. Such is their custom, and he who is not supplied with that sort of relic can scarcely pass their door." [155] Whether or not this pious view reflected William's opinions, he acted on that principle. In accounting for his use of the rings from the royal treasury at Devizes he stated that five rings with emeralds had been sent to five cardinals by Master Philip and a ring with a large ruby of high quality to the pope himself.[156] On the back of the membrane of the close roll of May 1218 there is a list of the cardinals of the Roman curia.[157] Opposite five of the names are crosses which seem to indicate the ones worthy of being bribed—or at least complimented with gifts. William had every intention of keeping his own voice close to the papal ear, for in December his favorite clerk, Michael, was appointed England's procurator in Rome.[158] All these efforts had their due effect. By March 1219 William was referred to as *rectori regis* in the papal missives, but Honorius still considered the legate ruler of England.[159] On April 23rd he wrote a personal letter of appreciation to William— which must have reached England a month or so after the latter's death.[160] Honorius realized and appreciated his faith and devotion to Henry in his time of tribulation. Henry's tranquillity was regarded by the pope as dearly as his own. In

---

[154] *Rot. Claus.*, I, 467, 602.
[155] *Hist.*, 11355-11372.
[156] *Rot. Claus.*, I, 602.
[157] *Ibid.*, p. 379.

[158] *Patent Rolls*, I, 183.
[159] Presutti, no. 1973.
[160] *Ibid.*, no. 2021.

recognition of his services he granted that William should not answer for any land he held in fee except before the lord of the fief in question. It is not quite clear why William had wanted this privilege—for he must have suggested it to the pope. It might be connected with his difficulties with the bishop of Ferns in Ireland which will be discussed later. He also may have preferred not to have to answer for his actions before the council as in the case of Morgan of Caerleon. As Henry was the lord of most of his fees, this made him practically independent until the young king came of age. Unfortunately he never enjoyed the privileges so generously granted. On the whole the regent seems to have been on excellent terms with the Holy See despite the fact that the pope considered him as simply a useful chief of police for the legate. In view of the extremely hazy idea of conditions in England shown by Honorious, this evidence cannot be taken very seriously in discussing the relative importance of legate and regent in the realm.

As the second year of the reign of Henry III drew to its close, William might well feel proud of the accomplishments of his regency. Faced with an empty treasury, a rebellious baronage, and a foreign invader, he had raised money, won over many of the rebels, and defeated the invader. He had sought to lay a sure foundation for the future on the basis of generosity to the repentant rebels and a guarantee to all men of their rightful liberties. He had restored order in the land, rehabilitated the administrative system, brought the king of Scotland back to his fealty, and made the Welsh marches as peaceful as they could be. His prestige in the country seems to have been tremendous. Imagine Ranulf, earl of Chester, disgorging without a protest the rich honor of Richmond to which he had a claim. Could there be a better proof of William's position? All through those two strenuous years his colleagues and subordinates had cooperated faithfully and had with some few exceptions obeyed his orders. Peter de Maulay and William of Salisbury might quarrel so fiercely that the latter had to seek the regent's writ to admit him to see his

nephew in the castle of Corfe.[161] The young Marshal and
Faulkes de Bréauté might almost come to open war over the
honor of Huntingdon.[162] The earl of Pembroke ruled serenely
over all. Jealousy there must have been. Peter des Roches and
Hubert de Burg were not men to see another in the supreme
position with any lightness of heart, but while William sat in
the saddle they obeyed his orders. There were none of those
fierce dissensions in the government that were to harass the
kingdom so soon after his death. England was at peace because
it was ruled by a great personality. Unfortunately two years
under the burden of government had sapped the strength of
the old earl. He felt his powers failing and saw no one to take
his place—all he could do was to try to make it possible for
England to exist without a regent until its king could really
grasp the reins of government. It was not his fault that the
grasp was destined to be a feeble one.

In September 1218 William paid his last visit to his lordship
of Striguil.[163] There in his castle towering over the Wye, the
chief seat of all his vast lands, he stayed a week or so until
the affairs of state recalled him to London. On October 2nd
he stopped at his manor of Crendon, the *caput* of the honor of
Giffard, and on the 9th he reached Westminster.[164] Toward
the end of the month the prelates, earls, and barons of England gathered about him to consult on the affairs of the kingdom. There was the legate Gualo who had aided William so
faithfully and who was within the month to leave for Rome.
Stephen Langton, archbishop of Canterbury, who had returned
from Rome in May, was once again in his place as primate of
all England. Fourteen bishops, nine abbots, eight earls, and
fifteen great barons are known to have been present besides
William himself, the legate, the two archbishops, and the justiciar.[165] It was before this assembly that William took the

---

[161] *Patent Rolls*, I, 79.
[162] Shirley, *Royal Letters*, I, no. V.
[163] *Rot. Claus.*, I, 370.
[164] *Patent Rolls*, I, 169. *Rot. Claus.*, I, 370.
[165] *Patent Rolls*, I, 177.

important step of putting into currency the new Great Seal that he had had made.

The first document issued under the new seal is of particular interest. It declared that by order of the common council of the realm no letters patent of confirmation, alienation, sale, gift or any grant in perpetuity and no charters whatever were to be issued under the Great Seal until the king should come of age. If by chance any charter or other grant in perpetuity should be issued contrary to this decree, it should be considered as invalid. These letters were attested by Gualo, the archbishops of Canterbury and York, William Marshal, and Hubert de Burg in the presence of the whole council or at least a considerable part of it.[166] The necessity for this pronouncement is obvious. In general William had made no perpetual grants in the king's name, but even if he did they would not bind Henry as they merely bore the regent's seal. Now the situation was different. There was a Great Seal, the symbol of the authority of England's king, and that king was still too young to rule. His government must be limited in its use of the royal power. It is somewhat hard to understand why William should have had a Great Seal made while the king was still a minor, but there are a number of plausible explanations. In the first place he probably wanted to restore everything to normal, and a Great Seal was a part of a normal government. Then too it would relieve the regent of some of the cares of state. He could still issue writs in the king's name, but so could Peter des Roches or Hubert de Burg. The government of England would follow its king—not an ageing earl. Finally he may well have realized that his end was near. He had ruled England because he was William Marshal whom all men admired and trusted, and his seal could run as his own. Did he feel that his successors would be simply the king's ministers hiding their personalities behind the Great Seal? Whatever his reasons, it was a definite step in preparation for his retirement from office.

[166] *Ibid.*

This change seems to have had an immediate effect in relieving William of some of the details of government. For the first two years he had attested practically every writ issued in the king's name. After the introduction of the new seal, Peter des Roches attested fully as many as the earl, and many lesser men such as the treasurer, Eustace de Faulkenburg, did likewise.[167] When William was sick, Peter des Roches issued the king's letters. The death of the earl brought no change in the rolls other than the disappearance of his name as a witness. Thus William paved the way for an easy transition from his rule to that of his successors. It is a remarkable tribute to his ability that at his death things could go on as they had without confusion.

William's last important administrative activity was the inauguration of the first general eyre of Henry III's reign. This was the final step in his rehabilitation of the English administration. A general judicial visitation was needed to finish the process of restoring order in the various counties and to remove the last scars left by the civil war. In addition, as the proceeds of justice formed an important part of the royal revenue, it was a valuable financial measure. On November 4, 1218, letters close were despatched to all the sheriffs, except those of seven western counties, ordering them to prepare for the visits of the king's justices.[168] They were to summon all archbishops, bishops, abbots, earls, barons, knights, and free tenants in the county, four legal men from each *ville,* the mayor and twelve legal burghers from each borough, and anyone else who should by custom appear before the justices. All these were to be at the place appointed for the first session on the fifteenth day after the feast of St. Martin, that is on November 25th. All pleas of the crown which had accumulated since the last eyre, all assizes and pleas which had been set for hearing at the first visit of the justices, and all pleas and assizes which had been

---

[167] *Rot. Claus.,* I, 383-4. *Patent Rolls,* I, 179-190.

[168] The counties omitted were Gloucestershire, Worcestershire, Herefordshire, Staffordshire, Shropshire, Warwickshire, and Leicestershire. (*Rot. Claus.,* I, 403b.)

before the bench at Westminster but had not been terminated there were to be brought before the justices itinerant. Every one who had held the office of sheriff since the last visit of the king's justices was to appear with the judicial writs which he had received while in office. The same day letters patent were issued which were addressed to the various sheriffs and contained the names of the justices who had been commissioned for their respective counties.[169] These letters patent together with the *capitulis* or instructions to the justices and the form of oath they were to exact from the assembled counties were turned over to one of the justices for each circuit.[170] Eight groups of justices were to cover all England with the exception of the seven western counties mentioned above.[171] These men were not all professional jurists. In most cases the group was headed by a prelate and a baron. For instance in Yorkshire and Northumberland there were the bishop of Durham and Robert de Vieuxpont with Martin de Pattishal and two other professional justices. Other groups were headed by such men as the abbot of Reading and William de Chanteloup, the bishop of Salisbury and Mathew fitz Herbert, and Geoffrey de Bocland, dean of St. Martins, and Faulkes de Bréauté. Thus each group combined the authority and prestige of a high ecclesiastic and a baron with the legal experience of professional jurists.

The supervision of the eyre required the continual attention of the regent. He had to facilitate the work of the justices and answer their questions and complaints. For instance Jacob de Poterna had been sent by King John to head a group of justices in Cornwall, Devon, Somerset, and Dorset, but the outbreak of the civil war had prevented them from actually making the eyre. The extracts from the rolls and the writs which had been given to these justices were needed by the group which William was sending into the same counties. The regent ordered Jacob to turn over these records to William de Hussburn, who was bearing to the bishop of Bath the commissions for the justices

---

[169] *Patent Rolls*, I, 206-208. Each justice received letters close notifying him of his appointment. *Rot. Claus.*, I, 403b.   [170] *Ibid.*   [171] *Ibid.*

in those counties.[172] In December William despatched a letter
to the justices itinerant in Kent—apparently in answer to a request from them for fresh instructions. They were to hear all
cases and amerce all who deserved it except earls and barons
who could only be amerced by their peers of the council. If any
great lord, such as the archbishop of Canterbury or the earl de
Clare, claimed special privileges, he was to be ordered to appear
before the council at Westminster fifteen days after St. Hilary's.
The same disposition was to be made of any case which was too
difficult for the justices to settle.[173] In January William informed the justices in Sussex that Richard de Pagenham claimed
that in the time of John he had obtained a writ of *mort d'ancestor* against the archbishop of Canterbury. The jurors had
been chosen and had made their views, but the outbreak of
the war had prevented the taking of the assize. Now the writ
was lost. William ordered the justices to investigate, and if
they found that Richard's statement was true, to take the assize
despite the absence of the writ.[174] In February the regent was
obliged to remind the justices in Lincolnshire that they had no
authority to amerce earls or barons—the Charter of Liberties
reserved that for the council.[175]

Two letters published by Shirley show with unusual clarity
the part played by William in the supervision of this eyre and
the difficulties with which he had to contend. The first was
addressed to " their reverend lord, Lord William Marshal, earl
of Pembroke" by Geoffrey de Bocland and his associates " justices itinerant of the lord king in the county of Norfolk." [176]
Geoffrey and his associates explained at great length the details
of a particularly intricate case which had come before them.
The last sentence shows plainly William's position as the foun-
tain of justice. " These things we have told you at the request
of the above mentioned Roger and Sarah, so that you may
know the truth of the matter and may do what pleases you

[172] *Rot. Claus*, I, 382b.
[173] *Ibid.*, p. 383b.
[174] *Rot. Claus.*, I, 404b.
[175] *Ibid.*, p. 387b.
[176] Shirley, *Royal Letters*, I, no. XIV.

and what seems to you to be just." The other letter is of a different tenor. It was addressed to "their lords and dear friends" Peter des Roches, William Marshal, and Hubert de Burg, by Hugh, bishop of Lincoln, John Marshal, and their associates, justices itinerant in Lincolnshire.[177] The justices were exceedingly annoyed. Apparently they had taken an assize of *novel disseisin* between Gilbert de Ghent and William, count of Aumale, and had later received a writ removing the case from their jurisdiction. The bishop and his associates "marvelled, if it was permitted to them to marvel, at the commands of so many lords." It would appear that contradictory orders had been issued in the king's name by two different persons, and the justices were annoyed because of the false position in which they were placed. They suspected that the government had been listening to men who slandered them. The king's ministers had chosen them as their justices, and it was their duty to support them. The justices were sending their clerk to lay the whole matter before the government. He would await their answer. This illustrates the difficulties of William's task.

The duties of these justices itinerant were by no means purely judicial. One of their most important functions was to administer an oath to all the knights and free tenants of the counties. The *Annals of Dunstaple* give the contents of this oath.[178] The freemen swore "to observe firmly and faithfully the peaces of Holy Church, the king, and the realm and to maintain and defend, in good faith, all who observed it. They would obey all reasonable commands of the king and guard his regal rights.[179] They would adhere to and guard the good laws and customs of the English realm. If indeed anyone should presume to go against these laws and customs, at the command of the king and council, they would come together in force and if they could, compel him to make amends. They swore not to

---

[177] *Ibid.*, no. XVI.
[178] *Annales de Dunstaplia, Annales Monastici*, III, 53.
[179] *iura regis*.

fail to observe this oath for hate, favor, or fear. They would do justice and receive it according to the reasonable customs and laws of England. They swore to observe these things despite any other oath which they had taken or should take in the future. Thus they aided the Marshal." One can easily see the value of such an oath, provided it were observed, in the process of restoring order. Then various special tasks were entrusted to the justices. On December 8, 1218 William informed the justices in Lincolnshire that a castle which had been burned in John's reign was still standing. They were to see to its complete destruction before they left the county.[180] The same group of justices was directed by the regent to make a survey of all fees in Lincolnshire, Nottinghamshire, and Derbyshire which were held in chief from the honor of Brittany. They were to choose thirty of these to be kept by the crown while the others were to go to Peter of Dreux, count of Brittany. When the justices were unable to find thirty suitable fees in those counties, one of their number, John Marshal, told them to take them from any county below the Humber. They sent William a full list of the thirty fees reserved to the crown.[181] Apparently the justices were used for any work the government might wish to have done in their respective counties.

The inauguration of this eyre was William's final administrative achievement. He died before the justices itinerant had completed their circuits through the counties of England. Hence the recital of his public activities as regent, which has been the theme of the last two chapters, must come to an end. But before leaving William Marshal, regent of England, to stand by the bed-side of the dying earl of Pembroke, one other phase of his public career must be examined. Few public men have been entirely uninfluenced by personal considerations. Few regents have administered their trusts in a purely disinterested manner. To obtain an adequate picture of William Marshal as regent one must attempt to discover to what extent he allowed his private interests to influence his conduct of the

---

[180] *Patent Rolls,* I, 182.   [181] *Rot. Claus.,* I, 404b.

affairs of the realm. While the question is of considerable interest to the general historian, it is of vital importance to the biographer of William Marshal. He was given a glorious opportunity to use his official position for the benefit of himself, his family, and his friends. To know to what extent he succumbed to this temptation is necessary if one is to form a true estimate of his character.

For the last thirty months of his life William Marshal was in reality two distinct persons. Any letter patent or close of the period before Henry's seal began to run will illustrate this. The letters were issued under the seal of Earl William Marshal, governor of the king and the kingdom, but they were attested by Earl William Marshal, a great baron of England. As regent William was, except for some few limitations largely self imposed, king of England. He did not, however, cease to be earl of Pembroke and lord of Leinster, one of the most powerful feudal lords of the realm. It is extremely interesting to see how William Marshal, regent of England, treated William Marshal, earl of Pembroke. One is inclined to believe that William saw this distinction very clearly. When Llywelyn appealed to the king and council of England against the depredations committed by the earl of Pembroke in the lands of Morgan of Caerleon, one of the earl's vassals presented his side of the case. The same man could hardly act as regent and earl at the same moment. Again his executors claimed that it was the earl of Pembroke who had accepted a hundred marks from the bishop of Lincoln to aid him in driving Robert de Gaugi from Newark. Hence they need not account for that sum to the exchequer as they would if it had been the regent.[182] At any rate whether William and his contemporaries realized it or not, the distinction was certainly there.

Sometime before John's death William had gotten into difficulties with the bishop of Ferns in Ireland over some land. The earl, apparently, seized it despite the protests of the bishop who promptly appealed to Rome. In due time Felix, archbishop

[182] *Ibid.*, p. 602.

of Tuam, and Henry, archbishop of Dublin, informed William
that his lands in Ireland were under interdict because he was
unlawfully detaining property of the see of Ferns. The bishops
of England had been ordered to excommunicate him and all
his accomplices. He was warned to make prompt restoration.[183]
The affair disappeared from the records for a year or so, but
early in 1218 the bishop of Ferns, on the authority of papal letters, brought the case before an ecclesiastical court presided over
by the archbishops of Dublin and Tuam. On April 18, 1218 the
king wrote to these two prelates on the subject—in fact despatched a writ of prohibition to them. The king's dear and
faithful William Marshal, earl of Pembroke, had shown him
that Albinus, bishop of Ferns, acting on the authority of papal
letters, had brought suit against him in an ecclesiastical court
for a lay fee which he claimed to hold of the king. He called
the king to warrant him as he should, but the king was a minor.
Therefore the prelates were forbidden to hold the plea until
Henry should be of age and could warrant his vassal. Other
letters forbade the bishop of Ferns to prosecute his case and
directed the justiciar to see that the judges did not hear it.
These letters were attested by Peter des Roches and bear no
mention of William's seal.[184] The regent, however, wished to
be sure that the earl of Pembroke was properly treated. Two
days later other letters patent were addressed to Geoffrey Marsh,
justiciar of Ireland. If the two archbishops disobeyed the royal
prohibition and heard the case, he was to take security from
them that they would appear before the king to answer for
their offence in holding a plea regarding a lay fee in an ecclesiastical court against the king's prohibition. The bishop of Ferns
was to likewise give pledges that he would explain why he
prosecuted his plea. These letters in favor of William Marshal
were attested by himself.[185] The earl, apparently, sent his own
version of the matter to Rome, for on June 25th the pope
ordered the judges to compromise the case if possible and re-

[183] *Royal Society of Antiquaries of Ireland*, Series II, V, 138.
[184] *Patent Rolls*, I, 148-9.   [185] *Ibid.*, pp. 173-4.

quested the bishop of Ferns and William to come to some agreement.[186] Thus the regent, acting in the king's name, prohibited the holding of a plea against the earl of Pembroke. According to the law of England his position was perfectly sound. It was not an abuse of authority, but merely an interesting example of the working of a double identity.

Before his death John had returned to William his castle of Dunamase which he had taken in 1210 as a pledge for his future loyalty, but he had kept the homage and service of Meiler fitz Henry. It is true that he had provided that if Meiler should die or become a monk, William should receive his lands, but as long as Meiler held his fees, he held them from John. It is possible that John, realizing that Meiler had incurred William's enmity while carrying out his orders, wished to protect his old servant from the righteous wrath of the lord of Leinster. At any rate he kept Meiler's fees in his own hands although they were an integral part of Leinster. This situation gave rise to a most fascinating letter, issued under the seals of the legate and Peter des Roches at Bristol on December 2, 1216. It ordered the justiciar of Ireland to return to William the service of Meiler. John had taken it in his hands as security for the earl's faithful service. While John lived, William had always been faithful to him as he was now to Henry, and the king greatly commended his fidelity. The justiciar was to allow ships to come and go freely to William's port of New Ross.[187] The sentence on the earl's faithfulness to John is delightful. The king had taken Meiler's service as security—but let not anyone think for a moment that it was necessary. A letter sent to Meiler at the same time is equally interesting. He was ordered to answer to William for the fief he held of him and render him due service, for " this William was always faithful and devoted to our father while he lived and now he adheres steadfastly to us, and we have greatly commended his humility before all the magnates of our realm; he has proved himself in this time of need to be like gold tested in a furnace." [188] William

---

[186] Pressutti, no. 1468-1471.   [187] *Patent Rolls*, I, 9.   [188] *Ibid.*, p. 10.

had probably asked the legate to order the justiciar to return him Meiler's fee, but he could hardly have dictated the compliments. William was by that letter reinstated in all his possessions in Ireland.

William had always shown himself a friend of commerce or at least a believer in the prosperity it brought. He had founded the port of New Ross and a number of chartered towns in his lands in Ireland and had granted charters to the burghers of Haverford and Pembroke. As regent he made sure that ships were not hindered in coming to New Ross and that his English lands were well supplied with fairs and markets. On March 3, 1218 he granted himself an annual fair at his manor of Sturminster in Dorsetshire to be held on Tuesday, Wednesday, and Thursday of Pentecost week.[189] Three days later he established a weekly market at his manor of Speen in Berkshire.[190] On June 3rd he ordered the sheriff of Buckinghamshire to allow William Marshal to hold a market every Thursday on his manor of Crendon.[191] In August he granted a fair every year and a market every Thursday on his manor of Toddington in Bedfordshire.[192] In September he established a weekly market at Bosham in Sussex.[193] By this means he not only encouraged trade, but materially increased the revenue of the earl of Pembroke.

In addition to establishing fairs and markets on his manors, William made use of his position as regent to extend his possessions in lands and castles. After Marlborough was taken from the French in the spring of 1217, William retained the custody of that stronghold and drew thirty-two pounds a year from the revenues of Wiltshire for its maintenance.[194] To repair this castle at the end of the war he appropriated the hidage of the manor of Wantage.[195] He also took possession of a mill near one of the gates of the town of Marlborough.[196] This castle and the lands pertaining to it were held by the Marshal family until 1222.[197] In February 1219 William

[189] Rot. Claus., I, 353.   [192] Ibid., p. 368.   [195] Ibid., p. 574b.
[190] Ibid., p. 354.   [193] Ibid., p. 370.   [196] Ibid., p. 466.
[191] Ibid., 363b.   [194] Ibid., p. 521.   [197] Ibid., p. 521.

granted himself the custody of Gloucester castle with a manor to provide for its maintenance.[198] Thus he used his power as regent to obtain the custody of two important fortresses. On the other hand in order to bring peace to the marches he had willingly given Llywelyn the custody of Cardigan and Carmarthen, both fortresses of vital importance to the safety of Pembrokeshire. William also took the custody of a few fiefs which were in the hands of the crown, but they were all comparatively small and unimportant.[199]

The most questionable act of William as regent was his acquisition of a share of the honor of Perche. When the count of Perche was slain in the battle of Lincoln in May 1217, his uncle, the bishop of Châlons, fell heir to his lands. As the bishop was a Frenchman, the honor would naturally remain in the king's hands until the conclusion of peace. In June the regent gave the custody of it to the king's uncle, William Longsword, earl of Salisbury.[200] But when peace had been made with Louis, the government could not ignore the claims of the bishop of Châlons. On December 2nd the regent issued letters of safe conduct to permit that prelate to journey to England to present his claims to his family estates.[201] There is no contemporary evidence as to what transpired, but according to testimony given in the inquest of 1242, the bishop sold his rights in the honor of Perche to the regent and William Longsword.[202] William Marshal's share included the demesne manors of Newbury and Toddington, with the exception of land worth one hundred shillings a year in each, and half of the manor of Shrivenham.[203] In all probability he also obtained half the knight's fees held of the honor. As the regent established a market on his manor of Toddington in August 1218, this division of the honor of Perche must have taken place before that time.[204] These lands were still in the possession of

---

[198] *Ibid.*, pp. 388, 399.
[199] *Patent Rolls*, I, 117, 168. *Rot. Claus.*, I, 361, 367b, 368b.
[200] *Ibid.*, p. 311b.
[201] *Patent Rolls*, I, 129. [203] *Ibid.*, pp. 748, 864, 866.
[202] *Book of Fees*, p. 1154. [204] *Rot. Claus.*, I, 368.

the Marshal family in 1245.[205] It is impossible to justify William's part in this transaction. The honor of Perche belonged either to the bishop of Châlons or to the king as an escheat. The two earls had no legal right to purchase it from the bishop without the king's assent. Apparently the whole affair was conducted in secret. There is no mention of it on the contemporary patent or close rolls and neither of the earls appear to have answered for these lands in the aid of 1217-1218. William had used his power as regent to extend his own possessions, and he undoubtedly realized the impropriety of the proceeding.

Nepotism has always been common among public men, and William's record as regent was not absolutely clear in this respect. He showered favors upon his eldest son. During the war he had given him the custody of lands of eight rebel barons including the earls of Winchester and Huntingdon and of Gilbert de Ghent.[206] Most of these fiefs were returned to their owners after the conclusion of peace, but thirty fees belonging to Gilbert de Ghent remained in the possession of the young marshal.[207] In addition to these William the younger had in 1218 the custody of some forty-six fees in Buckinghamshire and Bedfordshire.[208] In February 1218 he was granted the proceeds from the money exchanges, which were royal monopolies, in the cities of London, Winchester, Durham, York, and Canterbury.[209] In short, during his father's regency he was one of the most favored barons of the kingdom. John Marshal, the regent's nephew, also prospered during this period. To the office of justiciar of the forests, which entailed the custody of all the royal manors pertaining to the forests, was added the custody of a score of fees in Dorset and Somerset.[210]

[205] *Calendar of Patent Rolls* 1364-7, p. 267.
[206] *Rot. Claus.,* I, 299b, 305b, 309b, 310, 311. *Patent Rolls,* I, 45.
[207] *Pipe Roll 3 Henry III,* Public Record Office.
[208] *Pipe Roll 2 Henry III,* Public Record Office.
[209] *Patent Rolls,* I, 138.
[210] *Ibid.,* pp. 123-4. *Pipe Roll 3 Henry III,* Public Record Office.

William did not confine his generosity entirely to his relatives. His faithful knight, John d'Erley received the custody of an heir with his lands.[211] Henry fitz Gerold had been in the rebel camp at the time of John's death, but he returned to his allegiance soon after William took over the government.[212] During August and September 1218 he was granted markets on three of his manors.[213] Jordan de Sackville received his lands in Ulster which he had lost when John crushed Hugh de Lacy in 1210.[214] He was appointed a justice itinerant in the autumn of 1218.[215] Thus three of the most distinguished of William's knights profited from their master's position.

The importance of this discussion of the extent to which William used his position as regent for the benefit of himself, his family, and his men must not be overemphasized. One must be careful not to project into the thirteenth century the ethical ideals of the twentieth. There is no evidence that any of William's contemporaries criticized him on this ground. The *History* does not assert that he used his power as regent to enrich his faithful vassals, but it is fairly clear that the author would have approved of such a proceeding. When the barons asked William to accept the regency, he asked counsel of three of his men, John d'Erley, John Marshal, and Ralph Musard. Ralph gave this reason for urging him to accept—" it seems to me very good and proper that you should be able to enrich your men and others and us who are here." [216] In short, according to Ralph, William should accept this office because of the benefits it would enable him to heap on his faithful servants. The sole action of William's as regent that may reasonably trouble his admirers is the acquisition of his share of the honor of Perche. But this was only one incident and should not be taken too seriously. In no case that is known did William allow his personal interests actually to interfere with those of

[211] *Rot. Claus.*, I, 344.   [212] *Ibid.*, p. 295b.
[213] *Ibid.*, pp. 368, 369b, 370.
[214] *Calendar of Documents relating to Ireland*, no. 775.
[215] *Patent Rolls*, I, 208.   [216] *Hist.*, 15439-15442.

the realm. On the contrary, he gave up to Llywelyn the custody of Cardigan and Carmarthen and offered to return Caerleon to Morgan in the hope of establishing peace in the marches. The fact that William drew some profit from his occupancy of the high office of regent does not prove that he was not a disinterested ruler. The strict moralist may, if he chooses, point to a blemish in William's record—it can easily bear it.

To estimate accurately the part played by William in the rehabilitation of the realm is utterly impossible. Peter des Roches and Hubert de Burg were perfectly capable of performing the mechanical features of this task. The wisdom and energy shown by the government may have been due to the legate, Gualo. William may have been merely an old man who served as a figure-head for his colleagues. But this does not ring quite true. The William Marshal who charged headlong through the breach at Lincoln was no senile old man to be ruled by two priests and a jurist. Behind the treaty of Kingston, the Charter of Liberties, and the multiple activities of the government one cannot but see a capable and energetic statesman. Whether or not he furnished the ideas, William issued the orders of the government. One cannot say with certainty that he possessed administrative ability—that may have been supplied by his colleagues. But it is a reasonable supposition that it was his personality that kept those colleagues to their task. His wisdom was needed to determine the general policies of the government and his force of character to insure their execution. The turbulent barons and headstrong royal officials obeyed him—after a fashion. Hubert de Burg and Peter des Roches, who would quarrel fiercely soon after his death, co-operated with him loyally. William's great quality was that most intangible one—character.

CHAPTER XII

THE DEATH OF A BARON

By March 1219 William Marshal knew that death was close at hand. The time had come to resign the reins of government and to devote his rapidly ebbing strength to settling his personal affairs and assuring the salvation of his soul. The fourth son of a minor baron, William had attained the highest dignity in England short of the crown itself. Now he was to step down from his exalted office to die as earl of Pembroke. He had lived by the sword, but he was to die peacefully at his favorite manor surrounded by his family, friends, and vassals. The *History's* account of William's last days is of particular interest because of the light it casts on his private life. Throughout the poem the author depicts the knight and great baron and recounts his mighty deeds, but here one sees the kindly and thoughtful lord and the affectionate husband and father. There could be no stronger defence or fairer picture of feudal society than these last scenes of the life of William Marshal.

Early in January 1219 the earl paid his last visit to his native county, Wiltshire, and spent a week at Marlborough, his father's stronghold during the reign of Stephen and probably his own birthplace.[1] By January 16th he was back at Westminster.[2] Although he fell sick early in February, his administrative activities did not diminish until the end of the month.[3] During the first week of March, Peter des Roches attested the royal letters at Rochester while the regent lay sick in London.[4] Toward the 7th of March William, despite his malady, mounted his horse and rode from Westminster to the Tower of London.[5] There,

[1] *Patent Rolls,* I, 184. *Rot. Claus.,* I, 385.
[2] *Ibid.*
[3] *Hist.,* 17881-17883. *Rot. Claus.,* I, 387b-388b. *Patent Rolls,* I, 188.
[4] *Rot. Claus.,* I, 388b, 389, 405.
[5] *Hist.,* 17885-6. *Rot. Claus.,* I, 389.

attended by his countess, he waited to see if his condition would improve. Despite the efforts of his physicians he grew worse steadily and realized that he had little chance of recovery.[6]

As soon as William felt certain that death was approaching, he summoned his eldest son and his favorite knights to join him at the Tower. As he lay in that grim fortress by the Thames, his thoughts wandered to his manor of Caversham in the pleasant county of Oxford. If he were to die, he wished to do so on his own lands with his own vassals about him. The country air might even add a few months to his life. Calling his son and Henry fitz Gerold, he ordered them to make preparations for carrying him up the Thames to Caversham. About March 16th they placed him in a boat which bore him up the river to his manor while the countess followed him in another vessel.[7] Thus from the Tower, the seat of the English kings, he moved to Caversham, the seat of the earls Giffard. Symbolically it was the resignation of the regency and the return to the status of a private individual—the next step was the actual renunciation of his high office.

With this in view the regent summoned to him the prelates and barons of the realm. As Caversham could house no more than William and his suite, the young king, the legate, the justiciar, Peter des Roches, and the other great men of the kingdom took up their quarters across the river in Reading.[8] There in the early days of April assembled the great council of England to witness William's resignation of the cares of government. On April 8th or 9th the regent requested the king, the legate, the justiciar, the bishop of Winchester, and the earls to attend him at Caversham.[9] After greeting them and seating them about his bed-side, William addressed his young master.

[6] *Hist.*, 17887-17896.

[7] *Ibid.*, 17897-17936. *Patent Rolls*, I, 189.

[8] *Hist.*, 17943-17948.

[9] The last royal letters attested by William were dated at Caversham on April 9th (*Rot. Claus.*, I, 390). Letters were attested at Reading by Peter des Roches on the 10th, 11th, and 12th (*ibid.*) This indicates that William resigned his office on the 9th.

" Good sweet lord, I wish to speak to you before these barons. When death came upon your father, the legate Gualo and the men of rank who were loyal to you met at Gloucester, and there, by God's will, you were crowned. They entrusted you to me. Defending your land at a time when the task was most difficult, I have served you faithfully, and I would continue to do so if it pleased God to give me strength. But he wills that I remain no longer in this world. Therefore your barons must choose someone to care for you and your realm to the satisfaction of God and man. May He give you a guardian who will do you honor." [10] Thus the old earl resigned his office into the hands of his young master and the barons who had actually given it to him.

The regent's statement aroused the ire of the bishop of Winchester, Peter des Roches. He had co-operated loyally with William Marshal, but he had no desire to see the power transferred intact to a new regent—unless he himself were that regent. Peter therefore insisted that while William had undoubtedly been chosen as the guardian of the kingdom, he, Peter had been entrusted with the king's person. The earl denied this and pointed out that he himself had asked the bishop to care for the king who was too young to follow the army about the country. Whatever authority Peter had had was simply delegated to him by the regent. William himself was governor of the king and kingdom.[11] One can easily see the bishop's purpose in advancing this question. There was to be a redistribution of the power, and if he could show that he already had the guardianship of the king, he could use that dignity as a lever to improve his position. William Marshal had been a real regent. Peter aspired to be his successor, but if that was impossible, he hoped at least to control the king's person.

Bishop Peter's attitude showed clearly how difficult it would be to find a satisfactory successor to William. Peter des Roches was one of the ablest men in the kingdom and had been William's foremost assistant in the administration. But the justiciar,

[10] *Hist.,* 17949-17992.   [11] *Hist.,* 17893-18018.

Hubert de Burg, was equally able and no less ambitious. Neither of these men could be expected to submit to the authority of the other. The obvious solution was to choose some great baron who could continue William's policy of keeping the balance between these two men and using them both for the good of the realm. One can imagine William running his eye over the earls as they sat about his bed and deciding that no one of them was capable of carrying on his work. The ablest and most powerful of the English barons, Earl Ranulf of Chester, was in distant Palestine, and there was no one to take his place. England did not lack able men, but no one of them was so outstanding that all men would recognize his peculiar worth. Some such thoughts as these passed through William's mind as the bishop spoke. When Peter had finished, the earl asked the legate to take the king back to Reading and to return the next day. He wanted time to think the problem through, and his suffering was sapping his strength.[12]

Early in the morning William summoned to him his wife, his son, his nephew, John Marshal, and those of his knights in whom he had the greatest confidence. He told them that he had changed his mind about the advisability of choosing a new regent. If one man were chosen all the others would be jealous. He had decided to entrust young Henry and his realm to the pope in the person of the legate, Pandulf.[13] When the council had assembled once more, William addressed the legate "Sire, I have thought at length over what we talked of yesterday. I wish to entrust my lord the king to God, to the pope, and to you his representative." Then turning to the king he said " Sire, I pray God that if ever I have done anything pleasing to him, he will give you the grace to be a gentleman. If it should happen that you follow the example of some evil ancestor, I pray Him not to grant you a long life." [14]

William's formal resignation had of necessity taken place before the small group of men who had gathered about his bed, but he wished to have it repeated before all the assembled

---

[12] Ibid., 18019-18030.　　　[13] Ibid., 18031-18062.　　　[14] Ibid., 18063-18087.

barons. As he could not do this himself, he sent his son as his deputy to hand over the king to the legate before the whole council of the realm. Taking the king by the hand, the young marshal presented him to the legate in the presence of all the barons, despite an attempt by Peter des Roches to prevent the ceremony.[15] Thus William retired from his arduous position. This whole transaction is extremely interesting.[16] What William had really done was to prevent the election of a new regent and turn the young king over to the direct control of the overlord of England, the pope. He had been chosen regent by the barons of the realm with the approval of the legate. By entrusting the king to the legate in the presence of the barons, he obtained at least their tacit consent to the transaction. William had no possible legal right to appoint his successor, but he could surrender his charge into the hands of the overlord of England. The earl's foresight showed him what lay in store for the country because of the jealousy of her rulers, and he did his best to avert the approaching calamity. As he saw no one who could fill his position, he abolished it with the approval of those who had created it. This, William's last public act, was one of his most statesmanlike.

William Marshal, regent of England, had passed into history, and William Marshal, earl of Pembroke, lay dying at his fair manor on the Thames surrounded by his family, his household, and his vassals. The Countess Isabel had been with him from the very beginning of his illness.[17] His eldest son, William, his nephew, John, and his five daughters had hastened to his side when they learned of his sickness.[18] Richard, his second son, was in France at the court of Philip Augustus.[19] The three younger sons, Gilbert, Walter, and Anselm, were probably at Caversham though the *History* does not actually mention their presence. John d'Erley, who had been in charge of the lordship of Striguil,

---

[15] *Ibid.*, 18092-18118.

[16] For a secondary account of these proceedings see Norgate, *Minority of Henry III*, pp. 104-106.

[17] *Hist.*, 17896.

[18] *Ibid.*, 17898, 18034, 18503-18519.

[19] *Ibid.*, 19120-1.

had joined his lord at Caversham.[20] Of the other knights who were there only Henry fitz Gerold and Thomas Basset are known by name, but it is clear that a number of others were present.[21] Then the *History* mentions a Templar, brother Geoffrey the earl's almoner, and his clerk Philip.[22] No more are named, but the *History* makes clear that the dying earl was attended by a considerable suite of knights, squires, and servants.[23]

The day after his resignation of the regency, William summoned his people to his bedside. "Lords," he said, "I thank God that now whether I am to live or die, I can boast that I am free of a heavy burden. It would be well if I should complete my will and take care for my soul, for my body is the prey of fortune. This is the time to free myself from all earthly cares and turn my thoughts to things celestial." [24] The phrase " complete my will " must be taken literally. William had made a will as early as the year 1200, and he had probably added to it from time to time.[25] Now he would make sure that everything was covered and dictate the final document. The *History's* account of this proceeding is peculiarly intriguing. Sitting on his bed surrounded by his household, the aged earl reviewed in his mind the several members of his family and examined the provision which he had made for the future of each one. The Countess Isabel would hold for her life time her own vast inheritance—Striguil, Pembroke, Leinster, and the honor of Giffard.[26] William need not worry about her. William, his eldest son, would immediately fall heir to the Marshal lands and those acquired by his father, and after his mother's death, he would inherit all her fiefs. Hence William's will need only provide for the younger sons and the daughters. Richard Marshal received Longueville and at least part of the Giffard lands in Bucking-

[20] *Ibid.*, 18149, 18172-18174.
[21] *Ibid.*, 18204, 18308-18310.
[22] *Ibid.*, 18318-18320, 18685.
[23] *Ibid.*, 18263-18266.
[24] *Ibid.*, 18124-18135.
[25] Dugdale *Monasticon*, VII, 1136.
[26] *Rot. Claus.*, I, 392b. *Patent Rolls*, I, 195. *Layettes du Trésor des Chartes*, I, no. 1354.

hamshire—both part of his mother's inheritance.[27] Gilbert's share is unknown, but the *History* makes it clear that he received some land.[28] Walter was given Sturminster which William had acquired from the count of Meulan.[29] When he reached this point the earl turned to his knights, " Lords, one of my sons, Anselm, has received nothing even though he is very dear to me. If he lives to become a knight and shows merit, he will find, even though he has no land, someone who will love and honor him above all other men. May God give him prowess and skill." [30] Thus spoke the self-made man who had by his own efforts won his way from the bottom to the top of feudal society. Four of his sons were to have the advantages which the possession of land gave, but, almost wistfully, he hoped that the youngest might follow his father's footsteps and win his way by sheer merit. But John d'Erley objected to having Anselm placed under such a handicap. " Ah! Lord, do not do that. Give him at least enough money to buy shoes for his horses! " The old earl gave way and granted Anselm lands worth one hundred and forty pounds a year.[31] His sons provided for, William's thoughts turned to his five daughters. The four eldest were married, and their marriage portions took the place of any other legacy. William might well feel proud of the distinguished marriages which he had arranged for them. The eldest, Matilda, was the wife of Hugh Bigod, son and heir of Roger Bigod earl of Norfolk.[32] Isabel had married one of the most powerful barons of England, Gilbert de Clare, earl of Gloucester and Hertford.[33] Lady Sibile was wedded to William de Ferrars who was destined in due time to succeed his father as earl of Derby.[34] The fourth daughter, Eve, had married William de Briouse, who in 1221 succeeded his father, Reginald, as the head of that

[27] *Ibid.*, no. 1397. *Rot. Claus.*, II, 98b. *Calendar of Charter Rolls 1226-1257*, p. 142.

[28] *Hist.*, 18140. Gilbert was a priest (*ibid.*, 14890). In 1225 he received two benefices which were in the gift of the crown. (*Patent Rolls*, I, 531-540.)

[29] *Bracton's Note Book*, no. 71.　　　[32] *Ibid.*, 14917-14928.

[30] *Hist.*, 18139-18148.　　　[33] *Ibid.*, 14933-14936.

[31] *Ibid.*, 18149-18157.　　　[34] *Ibid.*, 14937-14940.

great marcher house.[35] Once more William addressed his
knights, " I am disturbed about my daughter, Jeanne. If while
I lived I had married her well, I would be more at ease. I wish
her to have land worth thirty pounds a year and two hundred
marks in cash to keep her until God takes care of her." [36]

In making his testament no good Christian should forget the
claims of Holy Church. As early as the year 1200 William's
will had provided for a legacy of thirty carucates of land to the
abbey of Tintern Minor which he had established in Leinster.[37]
At some time he added the bequest of his Herefordshire manor
of Upleden to the Templars.[38] Now he bequeathed fifty marks
to the abbey of Nutley and a similar sum to each abbey in his
lands beyond the sea.[39] This probably refers to the various
foundations which lay in the lordship of Leinster.[40] To each
chapter in those same lands he left ten marks. If this means
cathedral chapters, Leinster was undoubtedly referred to. Thus
William's testament fulfilled its double purpose—to care for
the future of his family and of his own soul.

Some days later the earl's almoner, brother Geoffrey of the
Temple, drew up his testament in its final form.[41] To this document were attached the seals of William, his wife, and their
eldest son.[42] Then the will was sent to the legate, the primate,
and the bishops of Winchester and Salisbury. They were asked
to confirm it with their seals and become William's executors.[43]

---

[35] *Ibid.*, 14941-14943.

[36] *Ibid.*, 18158-18168.

[37] Dugdale, *Monasticon*, VII, 1136.

[38] *Hist.*, 18239. Upleden was part of Bosbury, Herefordshire.

[39] *Ibid.*, 18653-18665.

[40] *utre la mer* could refer to William's Irish or Norman lands, but the text
adds *que je poi saveir et nomer* which could not refer to the foundations of
Longueville which William must have known very well. In fact I know of no
abbeie in Longueville.

[41] *Hist.*, 18319-18322.

[42] *Ibid.*, 18328-18332.

[43] *Ibid.*, 18334-18342; *mestre executor* must mean honorary executor. The
abbot of St. Augustine, Bristol, Henry fitz Gerold, and John d'Erley were the
actual executors, *executores testamenti* (*Compotus of William Marshal Senior*).

While the church had nothing to do with the disposal William made of his lands, the division of his movable property came under its jurisdiction.[44] The prelates confirmed the testament and solemnly excommunicated anyone who should violate its provisions. The necessary formalities completed, the document was returned to William.[45] His mind was relieved of another burden.

When he had finished his testament, only one worldly thought weighed on William's mind. He had heard that his old enemy, Llywelyn, was mustering his forces for a raid on the English lands in south Wales. The old earl turned to John d'Erley "John, do not tarry. Go to your bailiwick. I am disturbed about my men in Netherwent and especially about your son who if he should be foolishly advised, might make some expedition in which our men would suffer." [46] Suddenly William's thoughts shifted from his Welsh lands to his own imminent death. " By the faith which you owe me, do not delay. My illness grows much worse. When you return, bring me the two silken cloths which I left with Stephen d'Evreux. Above all, hasten to come back." [47] William Marshal lay helpless at his manor of Caversham, yet the prestige of his name saved his lands from a Welsh incursion. Llywelyn turned back for, as the *Annales Cambriae* explain, he feared William.[48] Once he was certain that the great earl was dead, his forces swept over the frontier into Pembroke. Such was William's reputation in the marches.

When John d'Erley returned to Caversham, he reported that all was well in the marches and gave William the silken cloths.[49] The earl took them in his hands and showed them to Henry fitz Gerold. "Henry, look at these beautiful cloths." "I see them, Sire, but they seem a little worn if I see them well." William was troubled. " Spread them out so that we shall see them better." When the cloths were fully displayed, they ap-

---

[44] See Beaumanoir (ed. Salmon), I, 157. Properly speaking the testament dealt only with movables. Bequests of land were simply death-bed gifts. See Glanville, VII, I, pp. 96-101.　　[47] *Ibid.*, 18180-18188.
[45] *Hist.*, 18343-18350.　　[48] *Annales Cambriae*, p. 74.
[46] *Ibid.*, 18171-18178.　　[49] *Hist.*, 18196-18202.

peared very beautiful. The earl summoned his son and his knights. "Lords, look here. I have had these cloths for thirty years. I bore them with me when I returned from the Holy Land so that they might be laid over my body when it is buried." "Sire," said the young marshal, "we do not know where you wish to be buried." "Good son, I shall tell you. When I was in the Holy Land, I gave my body to the Temple in order that I might be buried there. I shall give the Templars my fair manor of Upleden. I wish to be buried in the Temple, for so I have sworn."[50] Then William gave specific directions for his funeral. John d'Erley was to take the cloths and cover him with them when he died. If the weather should be bad when he was borne to his grave, John was to protect the silks with a covering. After the funeral, the cloths were to be given to the Templars to use as they saw fit.[51] The young marshal was instructed to give food, drink, clothes, and shoes to a hundred poor on the day of his father's funeral.[52]

On the day that he sealed his testament William sent a messenger to Aimery de St. Maur, master of the Temple in England, to ask him to come to him.[53] When he arrived, William summoned the countess and his vassals. "Lords, attend my words. It was some time ago that I gave myself to the Temple. Now I wish actually to join the order, for I can wait no longer."[54] He then sent his almoner for his Templar's mantle which he had had made secretly a year before. William addressed his countess. "*Belle amie,* you are going to kiss me, but it will be for the last time." As she embraced him, they both wept. The Templar's mantle was spread before the earl, and the countess left the room with her daughters.[55] The master addressed the new brother—"Marshal, attend. It pleases me that you give yourself to God. He has granted you a great favor—that you will never be separated from him. He has shown you this in your life, and He will do the same after your death. In the world you have had more honor than any other

[50] *Ibid.,* 18203-18242. [52] *Ibid.,* 18605-18608. [54] *Ibid.,* 18351-18358.
[51] *Ibid.,* 18243-18260. [53] *Ibid.,* 18324-18326. [55] *Ibid.,* 18359-18387.

knight for prowess, wisdom, and loyalty. When God granted you his grace to this extent, you may be sure that he wished to have you at the end. You depart from the age with honor. You have been a gentleman, and you die one.[56] I am going to London to see to our affairs." [57] This is a truly delightful passage. The aged earl kisses his wife for the last time and takes the mantle of the Temple. He will die in that great order devoted to God's service. Brother Aimery welcomes William into the order. God would never have allowed William to become the foremost knight of the age if He had not intended to receive him into Heaven. The identification of the virtues pleasing to God with the chivalric ones of prowess, wisdom, and loyalty is complete. God grants a man the power to be a perfect knight and then at his death receives him into Heaven. Could there be a more illuminating glimpse into the mind of the chivalric age?

Little remains to be told of the life of William Marshal—nothing in fact but a few scenes at his bedside. Vividly portrayed by the author of the *History*, these scenes shed much light on the man and his times. Day and night the earl's son and his faithful vassals watched over him. At night the young marshal, John d'Erley, and Thomas Basset stood guard, while the other knights shared the day watches. Never were there less than three knights at his side.[58] One day as William was sitting on his bed supported by Henry fitz Gerold, the latter asked his lord to answer a question that was troubling him. The clergy taught that no man would be saved who had not returned everything that he had taken from anyone.[59] William had taken armor, horses, and ransoms from many knights. How could he hope to get to Heaven unless he returned them? This question may well have troubled many a knight—Henry wanted the opinion of the flower of chivalry. " Henry," replied the earl, " listen to me a while. The clerks are too hard on us. They shave us

---

[56] The text reads *Buens fustes, buens vos en partez.* The word " good " would obviously fail to convey the meaning of *buens.* I believe that " gentleman " does.
[57] *Hist.,* 18389-18406.   [58] *Ibid.,* 18299-18314.   [59] *Ibid.,* 18476-18478.

too closely. I have captured five hundred knights and have appropriated their arms, horses, and their entire equipment. If for this reason the kingdom of God is closed to me, I can do nothing about it, for I cannot return my booty. I can do no more for God than to give myself to him, repenting all my sins. Unless the clergy desire my damnation, they must ask no more. But their teaching is false—else no one could be saved." "Sire," said John d'Erley, "that is true. And you have hardly a neighbor who can at his death say as much." [60] William would give the church her due, but he refused to repent of his knightly deeds. The clergy must not ask too much of mortal man.

One day William's five daughters came in to see him. The earl was surrounded by his knights while his son sat by his bedside. William called John d'Erley to him—"I am going to tell you an extraordinary thing. I do not know why it is, but it has been three years or more since I have had as great a desire to sing as I have had for the last three days." John advised him to sing if he could—it might bring back his appetite. "Be silent," replied the earl, "It would not do me any good, and everyone would believe me to be crazy." Henry fitz Gerold solved the difficulty. "Sire, for the sake of God, the glorious, call your daughters so that they may sing and comfort you." At her father's request, Lady Matilda sang a verse of a song in a simple, sweet voice. When Jeanne's turn came, she sang a verse of a refrain, but she did it very timidly. William gently reproved her. "Do not have a shamefaced air when you sing; that is not the way to become a good singer." Then he showed her how it should be done. When the girls had finished singing, their father dismissed them. "Daughters, go to Jesus Christ. I pray Him to guard you." [61]

Some days later the abbot of Nutley, a house which the earls Giffard had established on their manor of Crendon, came to pay his respects to his patron.[62] He had just returned from the

---

[60] *Ibid.*, 18480-18502.
[61] *Hist.*, 18503-18584.
[62] John gave William the *regalia* of this abbey in 1200. *Rot. Chart.*, p. 74b.

chapter general of his order, that of Arrouaise.[63] The good prelate had informed the " sovereign abbot ", John II abbot of Arrouaise, of William's illness and had requested him to admit the earl to the " benefits " of the order and to command the various chapters to pray for his soul. Abbot John had replied that he knew William to be a gentleman of great worth. Most willingly would he grant the earl a share in the good works performed by the order, and prayers for the salvation of his soul would rise from every house that recognized the rule of Arrouaise. Letters to this effect, duly sealed by the head of the order, had been entrusted to the abbot of Nutley. William thanked the prelate for his thoughtfulness and told him of the legacies he had left to the various monastic foundations in his lands. Tears came to the abbot's eyes as he replied, " Sire, you have been very generous, and God, I am sure, will repay you with interest in the glory of Paradise." [64] If the prayers and pious works of monks are pleasing to God, William's salvation was certain. From the far flung houses of the order of Arrouaise, from the Cluniac priory of Longueville, from the seats of the black canons at Bradenstoke and Cartmel, from Cistercian Tintern by the Wye, and from the numerous monasteries of the lordship of Leinster a vast cloud of prayers rose to Heaven for the soul of William Marshal.

On May 13th, the day before the earl died, John d'Erley asked him what he wished done with the rich robes which lay in his wardrobe. William did not hear the question, but his clerk, Philip, loudly volunteered his advice. " Sire, you have there many beautiful robes of scarlet and of vair, all entirely new, and at least eighty adorned with precious furs. As the furs are beautiful and unworn, you could obtain much money for them which you could use to secure your salvation." " Be silent, mischievous man! " replied the earl. " You have not the heart of a gentleman, and I have had too much of your advice. Pentecost is at hand, and my knights ought to have their new

---

[63] He had started to the meeting in August. *Rot. Claus.*, I, 378b.

[64] *Hist.*, 18610-18672.

robes. This will be the last time that I will supply them, yet you seek to prevent me from doing it." William ordered John d'Erley to distribute the rich garments to the knights of the household. If there were not enough, he was to send to London for more. When the robes had been given out, each knight had one, and some were left to give to the poor. Having made his last gifts to his faithful vassals, the earl's thoughts turned to those who were not at Caversham. He begged his son to take leave of them for him. God as well as he would thank them for their loyalty.[65] William was more than a perfect knight—he was a feudal lord of the highest type.

All that night the young marshal watched at his father's bedside. At dawn he was relieved, but he returned to the earl's chamber toward noon. Seeing that his father was turned toward the wall and resting quietly, he ordered the knights with him to be silent. But William heard them. " Who is that?" he asked. "It is I, John d'Erley." The earl tried to turn over, but the pangs of death seized him. "John," he said, "hasten to open the doors and windows. Summon the countess and the knights, for I am dying. I can wait no longer, and I wish to take leave of them." John obeyed and then returned to his master who had fainted. When he regained consciousness, William asked John to sprinkle his face with rose water to revive him until he had spoken to his men. As his wife, his son, and the knights approached the bed, he said, " I am dying. I commend you to God. I can no longer be with you. I cannot defend myself from death." The abbot of Nutley entered with some of his monks, but the earl did not notice them. Just then a servant informed John d'Erley that the abbot of Reading was outside, but John, occupied with his master, paid no attention. The earl, however, had heard the message and ordered them to admit the prelate. Approaching the bed the abbot addressed William. " Sire, the legate salutes you. He sends you word by me that last night at Cirencester he had a vision about you. God has given to St. Peter and his successors, the popes, the

[65] *Hist.*, 18679-18735.

power to bind and unbind all sinners. By virtue of this power, delegated to him by the pope, the legate absolves you from all the sins you have committed since your birth which you have duly confessed." The earl turned toward the abbot, joined his hands in prayer, and bowed his head. He had received the supreme gift of the church militant—the plenary indulgence of the Apostolic Vicar. The abbots of Reading and Nutley then heard William's last confession and absolved him. The earl died with his eyes fixed on the cross.[66] He had met an enemy whom he could not defeat.

William's body was carried to the abbey of Reading and placed in a rich chapel which he had founded. When mass had been said, the corpse was borne to Staines. There William de Warren, earl of Surrey, William de Mandeville, earl of Essex, Robert de Vere, earl of Oxford, Gilbert de Clare, earl of Gloucester and Hertford, and many great barons and prelates joined the cortege. From there the bier was borne in due state to Westminster Abbey where another mass was celebrated. The next day the earl was buried in the Temple church beside his old friend, Aimery de St. Maur, who had died some days before him.[67] Stephen Langton, archbishop of Canterbury, and William de St. Mère Église, bishop of London, officiated at the burial. Standing beside the grave the primate pronounced William's eulogy. "Lords, you see what the life of the world is worth. When one is dead, one is no longer more than a bit of earth. Behold all that remains of the best knight who ever lived. You will all come to this. Each man dies on his day. We have here our mirror, you and I. Let each man say his paternoster that God may receive this christian into His Glory and place him among His faithful vassals, as he so well deserves." [68]

[66] *Ibid.*, 18788-18976.
[67] *Ibid.*, 18986-19046. William of Newburgh, p. 526.
[68] *Hist.*, 19047-19084.

INDEX

MEDIEVAL ACADEMY REPRINTS FOR TEACHING